Hiking
Indiana

Phil Bloom

FALCON®

HELENA, MONTANA

Falcon® Publishing is continually expanding its list of recreational guidebooks. All books include detailed descriptions, accurate maps, and all information necessary for enjoyable trips. You can order extra copies of this book and get information and prices for other Falcon® books by writing Falcon, P.O. Box 1718, Helena, MT 59624, or by calling toll-free 1-800-582-2665. Also, please ask for a copy of our current catalog. Visit our website at www.Falcon.com or contact us by e-mail at falcon@falcon.com.

Cover photo by Daniel Dempster.

All black-and-white photos by the author unless otherwise noted.

Project Editor: Molly Jay
Maps by Jodie Peters
Page compositor: DD Dowden
Book design by Falcon® Publishing, Inc.

CAUTION

Outdoor recreational activities are by their very nature potentially hazardous. All participants in such activities must assume responsibility for their own actions and safety. The information contained in this guidebook cannot replace sound judgment and good decision-making skills, which help reduce exposure, nor does the scope of this book allow for the disclosure of all the potential hazards and risks involved in such activities.

Learn as much as possible about the outdoor recreational activities in which you participate, prepare for the unexpected, and be cautious. The reward will be a safer and more enjoyable experience.

♻ Text pages printed on recycled paper.

Contents

Acknowledgments

Hiking can be a solitary endeavor. Sometimes it's the best way to enjoy nature.

Researching and writing a hiking guidebook, however, requires considerable help, and there are several people to whom I am grateful.

To begin with, my parents, Mike and Joanne Bloom, deserve credit for giving me my first taste of the outdoors. I'm sure my brothers and sisters remember the times when Mom and Dad would take us for hikes along the banks of the Salamonie River or some other state park.

It was Bill McArdle, scoutmaster of Boy Scout Troop 20, who taught me and hundreds of other boys the basic hiking skills that helped make those 20-milers endurable.

Years later, I met Judy Esterline, who with her colleague Judy Deimling showed me a new way to hike—by going slower and with eyes wide open to what was at your feet. They made the woods come alive with their knowledge of wildflowers and native plants.

A special thanks to Kay Ellerhoff, formerly of Falcon Publishing, who helped make the professional connection that allowed those past influences to be transformed into this work.

This project took time. So much, in fact, that it outlasted two hiking editors at Falcon—Randall Green and David Lee. Molly Jay is the third. Thanks to each for their patience.

A long-distance acknowledgment goes out to Tracy Salcedo in California, whose attention to detail in the editing process was remarkable. Through phone calls and e-mails, she helped keep me on the right path.

Thanks also to the supportive editors at my newspaper, the Fort Wayne Journal Gazette,—editor in chief Craig Klugman, managing editor Sherry Skufca, former sports editor Justice B. Hill, and my current boss, Jim Touvell, who allowed me the time away from the office to complete this project.

Thanks to the many coworkers, friends, and family whose interest in how "the book" was progressing contributed regular reminders that I needed to stick with it or let them all down.

Several people at the Indiana Department of Natural Resources merit acknowledgment for their assistance and support, beginning with Becky Weber at the Division of State Parks and Reservoirs.

Also, thanks to all of the state park naturalists who offered insight on the special places at their properties, particularly Jim Eagleman at Brown County, Barbara Mummey at Turkey Run, Amelia Stoltz at Harmonie, and Fred Wooley at Pokagon.

Thanks as well to Carolyn McNagny at ACRES Land Trust.

It can get lonely out there on the trail, so I particularly enjoyed the time shared with special people. Thanks to my brother-in-law, Dr. John Herber, with whom I spent a splendid day on the Lakeview and Boundary Trails, the last hike taken in this marathon.

Thanks to my children—Jacob and Jennifer. I hope you always remember our time on the trails in the same special way that I have remembered those spent with my parents, brothers, and sisters.

The person who deserves the most praise is Jessie, my wife. Without her, this book would not exist. Her encouragement was constant. Her personal sacrifices many. Her love sustaining. She is the best hiking partner I've ever had.

Jessie, I'll go hiking with you . . . anywhere, anytime. Always.

Map Legend

Interstate	(00)	Marsh	
US Highway	(00)	Campground	▲
State or Other Principal Road	(00) (000)	Cabins/Buildings	▪
Interstate Highway	⟹	Peak	9,782 ft.
Paved Road	⟹	Hill	
Gravel Road	⟹	Elevation	9,782 ft. ✕
Unimproved Road	===⟹	Gate	•—•
Trailhead	◯	Overlook/Point of Interest	◘
Main Trail(s)/Route(s)	▬ ▬ ▬	National Forest/Park Boundary	
Alternate/Secondary Trail(s)/Route(s)	– – – –	Map Orientation	N
City	◯		
Parking Area	(P)	Scale	0 0.5 Miles
River/Creek	∿	Boardwalk	ⅢⅢⅢⅢⅢ
Intermittent Stream	–·–·–	Signpost	Ⓐ
Spring	✎	Gatehouse	▮
One Way Road	One Way	Visitor Center	⚑
Railroad Tracks	┼┼┼┼┼┼	Airport	✕
Powerline	•—•—•	Cemetery	†
Meadow		Falls	
Picnic Area	⊼	Beach/Dunes	
Bridge	⌣		

Overview Map

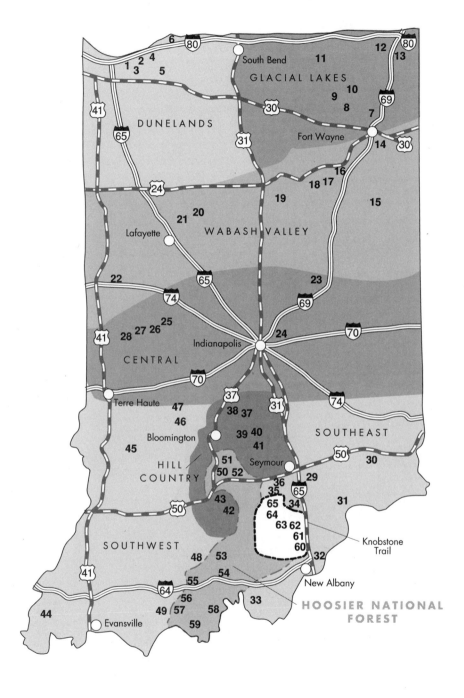

Introduction

God crowned her hills with beauty,
Gave her lakes and winding streams,
Then He edged them all with woodlands
As the settings for our dreams.

—From the official state poem, "Indiana,"
by Arthur Mapes

This is a hiking guide to Indiana. Why Indiana? Why not?

After all, it was from here that renowned hiker and conservationist John Muir began his exploration of nature and wilderness. Following his recovery from a work accident, Muir walked 1,000 miles from Indianapolis to the Gulf of Mexico. He later went west to California, founded the Sierra Club, and was instrumental in establishing several national parks.

It is only by coincidence that Muir is connected to Indiana, but within the state boundaries are the kinds of natural wonders that he might have appreciated had he stuck around.

The Hoosier State is far more than steel mills, the Indianapolis 500, the largest high school basketball gymnasiums in the world, and flat fields of corn and soybeans. Yet Indiana's natural treasures are seemingly unknown or unappreciated by many people, including a lot of Hoosiers.

Indiana has a richly diverse offering of these natural treasures, from the Indiana Dunes National Lakeshore on Lake Michigan to the rolling hills of Brown County State Park, from the banks of the Wabash River to the Charles C. Deam Wilderness in the Hoosier National Forest.

Indiana's mix of wild places and civilization may be exemplified best by the outline of the state. Except for a dip in the northwest corner where Lake Michigan intrudes, much of the western, northern, and eastern state boundaries are as straight as a surveyor's ruler. By contrast, the hand of nature carved out the rest, as shown in the twisting course of the Ohio River to the south, and the Wabash River along the lower third of the west boundary.

Publicly held land—where most hiking trails are located—accounts for less than 5 percent of Indiana's 36,185 square miles. Large cities dominate the state—Indianapolis with more than one million residents; Fort Wayne, Gary, South Bend, and Evansville all with more than 100,000 residents.

The result is a significant strain on the natural resources of Indiana, which the state Department of Natural Resources (DNR) has attempted to address through recent land acquisitions. Since 1995, the DNR has opened three state parks—Falls of the Ohio, Fort Benjamin Harrison, and Charlestown. The newest state park, Prophetstown, is being developed near Lafayette.

Other projects aimed at placing more land into the public trust include

Trail sign.

development of the Patoka River National Wildlife Refuge; proposed restoration of the Grand Kankakee Marsh; and conversion of the Jefferson Proving Ground, a former military post, to the U.S. Fish and Wildlife Service.

In addition, private groups such as The Nature Conservancy and ACRES Land Trust, which began life as Allen County Reserves and has grown to include out-of-county acquisition efforts, are involved actively in preserving natural places. The Indiana Heritage Trust has provided a funding mechanism for land acquisition since 1992 through the sale of environmental license plates.

The DNR manages 23 state parks, nine reservoirs, 17 fish and wildlife areas, 11 state forests, and more than 150 nature preserves. Hiking opportunities exist at nearly every location—from routes of 0.25 mile or less to the 58-mile Knobstone Trail, Indiana's scaled-down version of the Appalachian Trail.

Some trails have historic significance, like the Wabash Heritage Trail. Others have geologic significance, like the Knobstone. Most are just fun to hike.

Yet it is sometimes hard to escape the rush of the modern world, even on a trail. Consider, for example, a spot on the Wabash Heritage Trail. At this point, alongside Burnett's Creek, the dirt path converges upon a paved county road, a railroad track, and a four-lane interstate highway that passes overhead. There may not be another location in the state where as many avenues of transportation intersect.

The DNR completed an inventory of hiking opportunities in 1996 for its Indiana Trails 2000 Initiative, a project intended to promote and enhance hiking opportunities across the state. The inventory charted 392 trails, covering 950 total miles, that are designated specifically for hikers. Other trails cater to mountain bikes and horseback riders, but also can be used by hikers. Obviously, the 65 hikes included in this book offer only a sample of all that Indiana has to offer.

ECOLOGY

Before European settlers arrived in Indiana, the state wore a blanket of trees—huge trees.

More than 85 percent of Indiana, about 20 million acres, was forested, primarily with hardwood species such as beech, hickory, maple, oak, sycamore, tulip poplar, and walnut trees. The trees of this dense forest towered 150 to 200 feet high and measured as much as 9 or 10 feet in diameter. Settlers managed to cut down almost all of these trees as they cleared the way for farming. The work proceeded at such a pace that Indiana led the nation in lumber production in 1899.

Ironically, much of the rocky soil in southern Indiana proved unsuitable as cropland. As agriculture gave way to industry, many farms were abandoned, paving the way for establishment of the Hoosier National Forest, a patchwork covering almost 200,000 acres in southern Indiana.

What wasn't forest in presettlement Indiana was either prairie land and/or wetland, and both suffered a fate similar to the woodland.

Before the Kankakee River was reduced to a drainage ditch, the Grand Kankakee Marsh was to the Midwest what the Everglades is to southern Florida. Including the Kankakee Marsh, nearly 2 million acres of wetlands dotted the state, but only a fraction remains. The marshes, along with the prairie lands that were home to bison, were plowed under for farmers and industry.

But Indiana is not a wasteland. Despite such runaway efforts to subdue the land, pockets of natural splendor remain due to steadfast efforts to safeguard or restore their integrity.

Examples of rare or endangered flora in Indiana include Canada blueberry and Forbe's saxifrage at Portland Arch; yellowwood trees at Brown County State Park and Yellowwood State Forest; Deam's foxglove on the Knobstone Trail; black cohosh at Harmonie State Park; and eastern hemlock at Turkey Run State Park, and, obviously, at Hemlock Bluff Nature Preserve and Hemlock Cliffs in the Hoosier National Forest.

The fauna of Indiana includes thousands of species, from the smallest insects to white-tailed deer. Aquatic insects, freshwater mussels, Karner blue butterflies, spiders, ticks, crawfish, salamanders, bluebirds, bald eagles, bobcats, coyotes, wild turkeys, river otters, ruffed grouse, largemouth bass, and catfish are just a few of the species that inhabit the state. But there are other species that no longer exist in Indiana. Among those that have been lost are elk, bison, wolves, mountain lions, and black bears.

GEOLOGY

Like giant bulldozers, ancient glaciers shaped nearly the entire Indiana landscape, which was part of a giant sea in the Paleozoic Age, about 250 to 570 million years ago.

The Pleistocene ice age began almost two million years ago and ended about 10,000 years ago. The glacial advance scraped southward across Indiana but never reached the Ohio River.

As a consequence, southern Indiana is distinguished from the rest of the state by hilly terrain with deep ravines, lowland areas, and underground streams that have carved out caves in the limestone bedrock. The cave system is known as karst topography.

The most recent glacial advance—the Wisconsin lobe—moved no more than one-third of the way through the northern part of the state. As it retreated about 10,000 years ago, its meltwaters created rolling hills, rivers and streams, and hundreds of small lakes. Another glacial feature of the northern lakes region is the deposit of gravel, sand, and soil known as moraine. A morainal deposit appearing as a long, narrow ridge is referred to as an esker.

Between the northern lakes region and the southern hills and lowland region is a relatively flat expanse known as the Central Till Plain, which draws its name from its mixture of glacial deposits. It is the largest geographic region in the state, bounded by the Wabash River to the north and the farthest advance of the Wisconsin glacier to the south. Despite its flat appearance, the highest point in the state—1,257 feet above sea level near Richmond in Wayne County—is in this region.

Two minerals have played important roles in Indiana industry—limestone and bituminous coal. Limestone cut from central Indiana was used in the construction of several famous buildings, including the Empire State Building and the Rockefeller Center in New York City, and the National Cathedral and the Pentagon in Washington, D.C.

Two of the most recognizable water features of Indiana lie at its borders—a sliver of Lake Michigan in the northwest corner, and the Ohio River, which forms the entire southern boundary of the state.

Numerous rivers crisscross the state, but none has greater influence than the Wabash River, which is appropriately designated as the official state river. From its headwaters just across the Ohio River border, the Wabash cuts across the northern half of Indiana and meanders 475 miles south to Evansville, where it joins the Ohio River. The Wabash watershed drains two-thirds of the state.

Other major rivers include the St. Joseph and St. Marys rivers, which meet in Fort Wayne to form the Maumee River, which flows eastward into Lake Erie. The White River system drains much of southern Indiana.

HUMAN HISTORY

Indiana's name means "Land of Indians" and while there is evidence of prehistoric inhabitants from 160 B.C., the greatest influence of Native American culture came less than 200 years ago.

Nomadic cultures from the Paleo Indian and Achaic eras may have roamed parts of Indiana as far back as 10,000 B.C., but the earliest significant influence of Native Americans came during the Early, Middle, and Late Woodland periods, which extended from about 500 B.C. to 1000 A.D. The mound-

4

building Adena (Early Woodland) and Hopewell (Middle Woodland) cultures gave way to Late Woodland era–peoples, and eventually to the Mississipian culture, which lasted from 1000 to 1450 A.D.

Native populations probably peaked during the early 1700s. Numerous tribes inhabited the state at that time, the largest being three northern tribes—the Miami, the Potawatomi, and the Delaware. Members of all three tribes were descendants of the Early Woodland peoples. At one time or another, the area was also home to such tribes as the Chickasaw, Huron, Kickapoo, Menominee, Mohican, Piankashaw, Shawnee, and Wea.

French explorer Robert Cavalier was the first known white man to enter Indiana, coming through in 1679 in search of a passage to the Pacific Ocean. French fur traders soon followed, setting up trading posts near present-day Fort Wayne, Lafayette, and Vincennes. The first permanent white settlement was established at Vincennes in 1731.

Competition between the expansion-minded French and British over fur trade with Native Americans was a factor leading to war between the two countries over the rights to American soil. The British won, and France surrendered its claim to Indiana in 1763.

The British began military occupation of Indiana during the Revolutionary War. Fort Sackville at Vincennes became a focal point in the conflict, but George Rogers Clark and his Virginia troops seized it from the British for good in 1779. Eleven years later, Congress established the Indiana Territory, which included present-day Indiana, Illinois, Wisconsin, and parts of Michigan and Minnesota.

As settlers gained greater control of the territory, Native American resistance increased. Tecumseh, a Shawnee leader, was attempting to build a confederacy of 14 tribes, but those forces were defeated at the Battle of Tippecanoe in 1811 by troops under the command of General William Henry Harrison, who was later elected U.S. president. Tecumseh, meanwhile, sided with the British in the War of 1812.

Indiana became the 19th state on December 11, 1816. Its population at the time was about 64,000.

In 1838, nearly 700 members of the Potawatomi tribe were forced out of the state at gunpoint and marched hundreds of miles to a reservation in Kansas.

Lavish road and canal construction projects drove the state to bankruptcy by 1840, but railroads brought economic improvement prior to the Civil War. However, it was not until the 1880s that the discovery of natural gas and the development of the automobile produced an industrial boom.

By 1900, the population reached 2.5 million. Today, it is more than 5.5 million.

Some other noteworthy historical dates and events:

1816 to 1830: Abraham Lincoln spends his boyhood and young adult years on an Indiana farm.

1824: Indianapolis is established as state capital.

1841: William Henry Harrison, winner of the battle of Tippecanoe, dies after only 30 days in office as U.S. president.

1867: John Muir leaves Indiana to become one of the country's leading conservationists and founder of the Sierra Club.

1889: Benjamin Harrison, son of William Henry Harrison, is elected U.S. president.

1906: U.S. Steel builds a factory in Gary.

1909: Gene Stratton-Porter's novel *Girl of the Limberlost* is published.

1911: The first Indianapolis 500 auto race takes place.

1916: McCormick's Creek is established as the first state park.

1935: Hoosier National Forest is created.

1966: Indiana Dunes is designated as a national lakeshore, and land acquisition for Muscatatuck National Wildlife Refuge begins.

1982: Congress establishes the Charles C. Deam Wilderness in the Hoosier National Forest.

FUNDAMENTALS

Hiking is a simple activity, which perhaps explains its popularity. In most instances, hiking does not require specialized gear, although all sorts of gadgets are available. Hiking does not require special training. Nevertheless, there are some basic guidelines that all hikers should follow.

First, you must choose the right hike. Figure out what you want to accomplish with a hike. Do you want to discover new places? Explore nature? Simply get some exercise? Next, understand your limitations and do not overdo it. Figure out how physically fit you are and what you can handle before charging off on longer, more demanding hikes.

Take a map whenever possible, even if it is only the brochure available at the park gate or nature preserve registration box. For longer hikes, or hikes in remote areas like the Hoosier National Forest, obtain a compass and U.S. Geological Survey topographic maps and learn how to use them.

Stay on designated trails. Taking shortcuts, especially on switchbacks, only contributes to erosion and may disturb or damage sensitive areas.

Pack water, even for short hikes. Water is essential to keeping the body hydrated. A rule of thumb is to drink 16 ounces before embarking on a hike, then pause every half hour for another 4 to 6 ounces. If water must be drawn from a lake or stream, be sure to purify it, either with a filter, iodine tablets, or by boiling it.

Avoid crowds by planning your hike for midweek. State parks draw their biggest crowds during the summer months, especially on weekends.

Some trails, particularly those through the ravines of southern Indiana, cross streams that can be hazardous during periods of heavy rain. Do not attempt to cross a stream unless you are sure you can make it safely across.

Finally, practice the leave-no-trace outdoor ethic—pack it in, pack it out. This is a mandatory policy in the Charles C. Deam Wilderness, but it is a good approach to adopt for all situations. Pack out everything—gum wrappers, cigarette butts, and twisty ties. Avoid building campfires unless absolutely necessary. Leave the place you have visited looking as if you were never there.

Also, avoid needless noise. Nothing disturbs the solitude of nature more

Smoky the Bear offers a safety reminder.

than hearing boisterous people tromping down the trail.

But most of all, enjoy.

CLOTHING

Seasons and weather conditions usually dictate proper attire on the trail, but so will the length and difficulty of each hike.

Begin at the bottom by properly outfitting your feet. Most trails can be hiked in tennis or gym shoes, but longer hikes and hikes in rugged terrain require a good pair of hiking boots—and do not forget socks. I prefer to start with a thin pair of socks, over which I wear heavier wool socks. For me, this combination helps prevent blisters. Pack an extra pair of socks for longer hikes; changing them along the way can be refreshing.

Pack rain gear. Weather changes can occur rapidly in Indiana, so it is best to be prepared. A light jacket will suffice on short hikes, but a full outfit of water-repellent, breathable outerwear is a must for longer trips.

The rest is personal preference, but make sure the clothing is appropriate for the season. Some people wear long pants and long-sleeved shirts even in warm weather, while others choose shorts and T-shirts. Be assured, the latter will be uncomfortable even on the hottest of days if the trail leads through heavy brush or areas with mosquitoes.

In cool or cold weather, dress in layers. It is easier to remove a layer if you get too hot than it is to add something you do not have.

WEATHER AND SEASONS

Indiana has a varied climate, but it can usually be described as humid in summer and cold in winter. Temperatures in winter can dip well below zero, and summer days can be unbearably hot and humid. Weather conditions can be unpredictable, especially in early summer when powerful storms can pop up on short notice. Average June temperatures range from a low of 60 degrees F to the mid-80s for central Indiana, with variances to the north and south. Average January temperatures range from the low 20s to the upper 30s. Annual rainfall averages about 38 to 40 inches, with additional precipitation coming from snow that varies from 10 inches in the south to around 40 inches in the north.

Certain areas of the state have become synonymous with certain seasons—Brown County State Park for fall foliage; Pokagon State Park for cross-country skiing and the toboggan run that carries sledders downhill at speeds reaching 50 miles per hour; and Indiana Dunes State Park for summer fun. But the attraction of these locales is not limited to one season. Brown County is just as beautiful in spring for wildflowers, as is Pokagon, Olin Lake Nature Preserve, and a host of other areas.

Spring: If you like wildflowers, consider a hike at this time of year. It is easy to find woodlands carpeted with a variety of Virginia bluebells, large-flowered trillium, columbine, Jack-in-the-pulpit, Dutchman's breeches, and Solomon's seal. Spring is also a good time for watching

8

wildlife, especially migrating birds like Canada geese, ducks, sandhill cranes, and certain songbirds.

Indiana springs are known for erratic weather patterns and are prone to violent storms that can spawn tornadoes. It is also a good idea, when hiking at this time of year to pack along rain gear and perhaps a sweater or fleece jacket to ward off sudden temperature changes. Some trails may be messy because of spring thaw, or even impassable due to rain or flooding.

Summer: June, July, and August can be among the toughest months to hike in Indiana. Not only can the weather be stifling, but it is also a time when trails, campgrounds, and parks are frequently packed with vacationers. Although the weather can reach extremes, it is also more stable than in other seasons, allowing for extended periods of good hiking. Be alert for quickly developing thunderstorms with dangerous lightning. Summer is also the season for bugs—mosquitoes, bees, wasps, hornets, flies, and gnats.

Fall: If there is a better time of year to hike in Indiana than spring, it is during the fall. Temperatures begin to drop in September and October, especially at night, when it can get quite chilly. Daytime temperatures often are still warm enough for shirt sleeves, or even shorts. With schools back in session after the Labor Day weekend, trail traffic diminishes and campsites are more available. But the real beauty of autumn is the rich display of color presented by the hardwood forests and woodlands across the state. Oak, maple, tulip, hickory, and other trees switch color schemes from uniform green to orange, red, and yellow. Since hunting seasons begin in autumn, it is a good idea to make yourself more visible by wearing one or more pieces of blaze orange clothing.

Winter: If solitude is your desire, this may be the time to consider a hike, especially in the southern half of the state where snow is a less frequent obstacle. Daytime temperatures can be almost mild, and traffic along the trails is definitely at its low point. Even in the deepest woods, it is often easier to see wildlife because of the absence of leafy vegetation. If there is snow on the ground, wildlife tracks can be easily spotted. Trails can be slippery, though, either because of precipitation or from being frozen.

ANIMALS

You don't have to worry about bears or wolves in Indiana, although both used to roam the state years ago. The largest mammal in the state today is the white-tailed deer, which is abundant in most parts of Indiana. Canada geese are almost as plentiful as deer, especially in the northeastern lakes region. Other common animals are squirrels, rabbits, raccoons, and turkeys, as well as foxes, coyotes, and opossums.

Bobcats and badgers are also present, although both species are on the state's endangered species list, which includes more than 80 species.

There are poisonous snakes in Indiana, the copperhead being the most common. It is usually found in southern Indiana, where timber rattlesnakes and cottonmouths are also found, but only rarely. The eastern Massassauga rattler is found in swampy areas of northern Indiana, but its numbers are so few that it is considered endangered by the state.

Snakebites are rare, and almost always nonfatal, but play it safe by steering clear of snakes. Timber rattlesnakes live in high, rocky terrain and are found on rock ledges. A timber rattler will usually, but not always, send a warning by raising and rattling its tail. Copperheads frequent the same habitat as timber rattlers, but they are not as easy to detect. The copper red head and brown bands allow the snake to blend into fallen leaves. Copperheads offer no warning before striking. Be careful walking over fallen logs. Cottonmouths have an especially aggressive nature, but this aquatic species is the least common of the state's poisonous snakes. The simplest way to avoid poisonous snakes and their dangerous bites is to be alert and watch your step.

Indiana has played an active role in restoration efforts involving federally endangered species like the bald eagle and peregrine falcon, and has also made a concerted effort to establish a self-sustaining population of river otters.

BUGS

Hikers in Indiana need to be aware of only a couple of pesky insects. The most serious concerns have to do with ticks and stinging insects such as bees, hornets, and wasps.

Ticks carry diseases that can cause serious problems for humans. More than a dozen species of ticks have been found in the state, but the two of particular concern are wood ticks, which carry Rocky Mountain spotted fever, and deer ticks, which carry Lyme disease. Consequently, hikers should check themselves for ticks, particularly after a hike in brushy and grassy areas where ticks reside.

Mosquitoes and gnats are a nuisance, especially during warm, wet seasons. They generally can be dealt with by using insect repellents. Two spiders—the black widow and brown recluse—have bites that can be life-threatening, but such occurrences are not common.

HOW TO USE THIS GUIDEBOOK

The chapters in *Hiking Indiana* are organized largely by geographic regions, beginning in the northwest corner of the state with the Dunelands and working southward to finish with the Knobstone Trail.

Within each chapter, the hikes are presented in sequence, which changes from area to area. For instance, hikes in the Dunelands are presented from west to east, beginning with the Beach Trail near Gary and working east toward Michigan City, while hikes in the Hill Country head north from Bloomington in a clockwise sweep.

If you are familiar with other Falcon guidebooks, you may notice the absence of elevation charts in *Hiking Indiana*. That is because very few of the hikes have significant elevation changes, and those that do rarely change by more than 250 feet. However, some of these hikes, particularly those in southern Indiana, can provide the most avid hiker with a pretty good workout.

Dunelands

One word defines the Dunelands of northwest Indiana—conflict.

Whether it has been by the natural forces that originally shaped the area or the social forces of modern times, conflict has been at the heart of the Dunelands story.

Lake Michigan—the first of the Great Lakes—was formed by glacier movement more than 14,000 years ago. Left behind when the glacier receded was the residue that makes up the dunes, which in some instances are still being formed today. Mount Baldy at the east end of the Indiana Dunes National Lakeshore and Smoking Dune at the West Beaches are "living" dunes—in other words, they continue to grow and move as they are reshaped by the wind that created them.

Mount Baldy—nearly devoid of plant life—creeps inland at the rate of 4.5 feet per year, gobbling up trees in its path. At Smoking Dune, a boardwalk has been rerouted over a section now buried in sand.

As magnificent as the Dunelands are—including bogs, marshes, ponds, and varied forests—the area remains in conflict because of competing forces. The Indiana Dunes National Lakeshore, established by Congress in 1966, is fragmented by private residences and the smokestack industry over its 23-mile stretch. The older Indiana Dunes State Park, which lies almost in the center of the national lakeshore, is less affected by the same forces but has its own problem—overuse. Most of the annual 850,000 visitors congregate at the beach or explore the nearby dunes.

Although most of the hikes in this section are in close proximity to the dunes, some are not. One of the more remote hikes is the Heron Rookery Trail, located about 10 miles southeast of Chesterton but still a part of the national lakeshore complex supervised by the National Park Service. Another is the Bailly Homestead and Chellberg Farm site near the Little Calumet River.

The dunes have long been an area of discovery. In fact, they are the birthplace of the science known as ecology—the study of how living things relate to each other and their environment.

Henry Cowles, father of the science of ecology, was intrigued by the mystery of the dune environment, first as a graduate student and later as head of the botany department at the University of Chicago in the early 1900s. Cowles was puzzled by the coexistence of plant species usually found in different environments—arctic bearberry and prickly pear cactus, northern jack pine and dogwood. The more important discovery was the progression of plant life from the beaches to inland areas—sand stabilized by grasses, followed by shrubs, and then trees.

Because of organizations like Save the Dunes Council, the mysteries that Cowles and his students unlocked are preserved at the Indiana Dunes National Lakeshore and the Indiana Dunes State Park.

Trails in this section are presented starting in Gary to the west, and moving east to Michigan City.

1 Dune Succession Trail

Type of hike:	Day hike, loop.
General description:	An intrepretive hike that highlights the stages of dune development through plant succession.
General location:	Near Chesterton in northwest Indiana.
Total distance:	1 mile.
Difficulty:	Moderate.
Elevation gain:	100 feet.
Jurisdiction:	Indiana Dunes National Lakeshore.
Special attractions:	The intradunal pond, the dunes, and the viewing platform.
Maps:	Portage USGS quad; National Park Service brochure.
Permits/fees:	There is a $3 parking fee for West Beaches Recreation Area from May 1 to October 1.
Camping:	None at West Beaches, but Indiana Dunes State Park has 286 sites, modern to primitive, and Indiana Dunes National Lakeshore Dunewood Campground has 79 sites open seasonally. Both are located east of the West Beaches Recreation Area.
Trailhead facilities:	There is a visitor center and a beach house with restrooms at the trailhead. There are drinking fountains at the beach house.

Finding the trailhead: From Indiana 49, go west 9 miles on U.S. Highway 12 to a four-way stop. Turn right on Lake and Porter County Line Road, cross the railroad tracks, and go to the West Beaches sign. Turn right (east) to enter. From the gatehouse, drive east for 0.8 mile to the visitor center parking lot. To begin the hike, walk from the parking lot to the beach house and on through to the beach.

Key points:
0.0   Trailhead.
0.2   Reach the beach.
0.3   Arrive at the viewing platform near the intradunal pond.
0.5   Follow the boardwalk.
0.6   Climb the staircase to the inner dune and tree graveyard.
0.7   Reach the viewing platform atop the highest inner dune.
1.0   Return to the parking lot.

The hike: From the parking lot, follow the paved road for 0.25 mile to the beach house and beach, which can be a very busy area on hot summer days. Walk through the beach house and turn right (east) to pick up the trail by finding the marked posts that correspond to the intrepretive brochure. Along the trail, you will discover how dunes are built by elements of nature—wind, sand, and vegetation. Part of the hike is on loose sand, the rest on boardwalks and staircases that are designed to reduce dune erosion.

Pause for a moment on the wood deck at 0.3 mile to view the intradunal

The staircase on the south side of the dune on the Dune Succession Trail.

pond, created when strong winds blasted through an opening in the dune and scooped out sand to beneath the water table. Plants found here—horned bladderwort and Kalm's lobelia—differ from plants along the nearby dunes.

These are fairly new dunes, perhaps formed in the past 5,000 years. Marram grass is one of the first "dune-builders," and is evident along the beach and on the beginning section of the hike. Marram grass stabilizes the sand through an underground network of roots and rhizomes. Another important

Dune Succession Trail

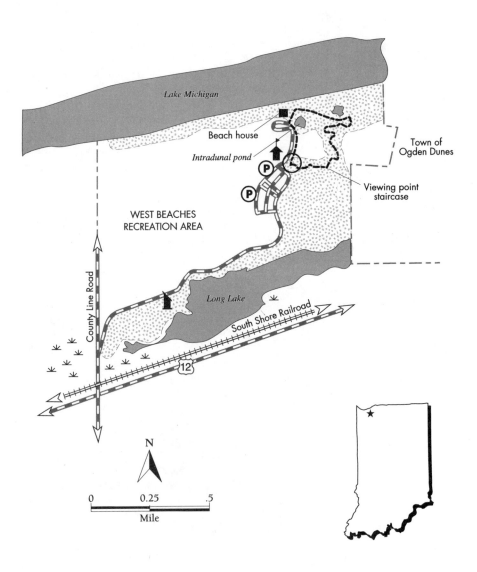

plant is the cottonwood, which appears on the leeward side of the first dune. Although these cottonwoods appear short, they are just the tips of much taller trees buried in the sand. Protected from the wind, the leeward area is host to little bluestem grass, sand cherries, hop trees, and more wildflowers, such as puccoon and sand cress.

At the midway point of the hike there is a stand of jack pines, which provides shelter for arctic bearberry. Both are northern plant species uncommon this far south, but carried here by ice age glaciers.

Jump on to a boardwalk at 0.5 mile to continue the hike, which heads through a steep-sided valley created by a blowout that occurred when strong winds carved out an opening in the dune. A portion of the old boardwalk has been buried, evidence of how the dune continues to wander under the force of wind. The extensive boardwalk and staircase system leads uphill on a wooded dune featuring black oak, hickory, basswood, dogwood, and sassafras trees. Such trees indicate how protected this area is from the wind and storms coming off Lake Michigan. The staircase system helps reduce erosion, as well as make the climb easier. Atop the hill at 0.7 mile is an overlook, followed by a 169-step stairway to the bottom of the dune and a soft, sandy hike back to the parking lot at the 1-mile mark.

Options: There are two additional inland hiking options—the 1.2-mile West Beach Trail and the 1.5-mile Long Lake Trail. Both are loop trails.

2   Cowles Bog

Type of hike:	Day hike, loop.
General description:	A loop hike around a bog, through wooded dunes, past marshes, and along the Lake Michigan shoreline.
General location:	Twelve miles east of Gary in the northwest part of the state.
Total distance:	5 miles.
Difficulty:	Easy to moderate, except for strenuous dune climbs near the beach.
Elevation gain:	100-foot dune climbs near beach.
Jurisdiction:	Indiana Dunes National Lakeshore.
Special attractions:	Cowles Bog and the Lake Michigan shoreline.
Maps:	Dune Acres USGS quad; Dunes National Lakeshore map.
Permits/fees:	None required.
Camping:	None at Cowles Bog, but Indiana Dunes State Park (1.5 miles east) has 286 sites, modern to primitive, and Indiana Dunes National Lakeshore Dunewood Campground (6 miles east) has 79 sites.
Trailhead facilities:	There is a small parking area and a portable toilet at the trailhead. No water is available.

Finding the trailhead: From Chesterton, drive 2 miles north to U.S. Highway 12, turn left (west). Drive 1.4 miles to Mineral Springs Road, and turn right (north). Cross the tracks of the Chicago South Shore Railroad, drive 0.6 mile, and turn right (east) on a dirt road just short of the security post for Dune Acres. Drive 0.1 mile on the dirt road to a parking lot, then walk back down the dirt road to the Cowles Bog Trailhead on the west side of Mineral Springs Road.

Cowles Bog

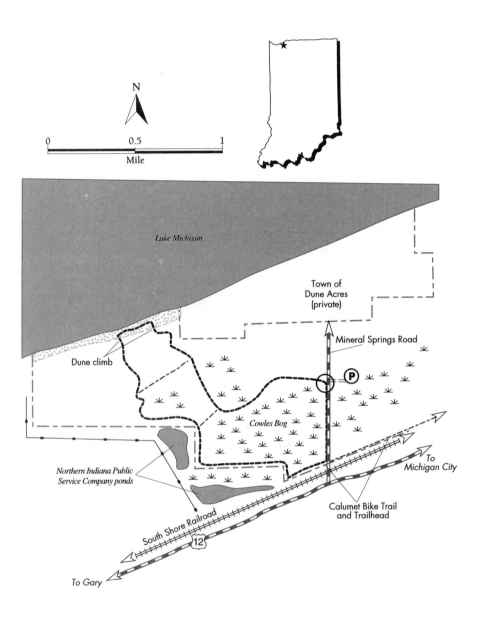

N

0   0.5   1
Mile

Lake Michigan

Town of
Dune Acres
(private)

Mineral Springs Road

P

Dune climb

Cowles Bog

Northern Indiana Public
Service Company ponds

To
Michigan City

Calumet Bike Trail
and Trailhead

South Shore Railroad

12

To Gary

Key points:
- 0.0 Trailhead.
- 0.1 Pass Cowles Bog.
- 2.0 Reach Bailly Beach and Lake Michigan; turn left.
- 2.2 At a trail marker that may be buried by sand, turn left.
- 2.3 Climb the dune.
- 3.6 Reach the Northern Indiana Public Service Company (NIPSCO) pond.
- 4.5 Reach the Calumet Bike Trail Trailhead and Mineral Springs Road.

The hike: Cowles Bog is a historically significant site. It was here in the early 1900s that Dr. Henry Cowles, a professor at the University of Chicago, did much of his scientific research on plant ecology. The area was designated a national natural landmark in 1965. Access to the bog is restricted, but it can be seen from a distance while hiking the trail. The trail is well-defined, with marked intersections, although wind-blown sand can obscure the marker along the beach.

This is an easy stroll at the start, as you walk back along the parking lot entry road before crossing to the west side of Mineral Springs Road to the actual trailhead. The trail begins fairly straight and level. A boardwalk splits a marshy area on the north side of the bog. Sprays of ferns coupled with duck weed and skunk cabbage provide a rich, green backdrop, and wildflowers give the area a sweet aroma. Dune ridges rise and fall along the right side of the trail.

At 0.9 mile, you will reach a juncture with a shortcut trail that goes left (south) around the bog. Turn right (north) instead. Climb a sandy hill and begin a meandering stroll over humps and ridges of the wooded inner dunes that are dotted with occasional ponds.

At 1.5 miles, there is another shortcut trail. Again, stay right (north). Near the 2-mile mark, climb a steep crest of the outer dune, which provides a clear view of downtown Chicago to the west. Immediately to the west is a coal-fired power plant, an ironic contrast to the serenity of the Cowles Bog area. Descend the dune to the beach and turn left (west), walking about a quarter of a mile before turning inland. The trail marker for this turn can be difficult to find and sometimes is nearly buried by blowing sand. If the marker is not distinguishable, head southeast toward the dune, and the path up the dune will become visible.

It is another steep climb on a soft, sandy trail to the top of the dune, which drops off sharply to the right. Walk 30 to 40 yards on a level grade before heading downhill. With each stride it will seem as if you slide an extra foot in the loose sand.

Cross several dips and rises over sand hills that form the inner dunes of the property. Keep to the right (south) as you pass both of the connecting shortcut paths from the outbound trek. Before reaching the second connecting path, you will pass a small pond at the edge of the NIPSCO power company property that forms the southern boundary of Cowles Bog.

Just beyond the 3.6-mile mark, reach a service road with the bog on the north side, and large NIPSCO ponds on the south. The road is arrow-straight to the east for 0.75 mile, then it bends right for 100 yards, and connects to a crushed stone roadway. Walk 0.25 mile to a parking lot that serves as the starting point of the Calumet Bike Trail. Turn left out of the parking lot at 4.5 miles, and walk 0.5 mile north along Mineral Springs Road to the trailhead and parking area. Although the trail concludes along this paved stretch of roadway, you will still get a good look at the bog on both sides.

3   Little Calumet River Trail, Bailly Homestead, and Chellberg Farm

Type of hike:	Day hike, loop.
General description:	This loop hike begins near the historic Bailly Homestead, continues along the Little Calumet River through marsh and meadow, and concludes at the Chellberg Farm.
General location:	Four miles west of Chesterton in northwest Indiana.
Total distance:	3.1 miles.
Difficulty:	Moderate.
Elevation gain:	Minimal.
Jurisdiction:	Indiana Dunes National Lakeshore.
Special attractions:	The Bailly Homestead, Little Calumet River, and Chellberg Farm.
Maps:	Chesterton and Dune Acres USGS quads; Dunes National Lakeshore brochure.
Permits/fees:	None required.
Camping:	None is allowed on site, but nearby Indiana Dunes State Park has 286 sites, modern to primitive, and Indiana Dunes National Lakeshore Dunewood Campground has 79 sites. Both are located east of the homestead.
Trailhead facilities:	A small visitor center and gift shop, and a restroom building are located just off the parking lot. Water is available in the restrooms.

Finding the trailhead: From the Interstate 94/Indiana 49 intersection in Chesterton, go 1.6 miles north on Indiana 49 to U.S. Highway 12. Go west 1.4 miles on US 12, following brown National Park Service signs to Mineral Springs Road and turn left (south). Go 0.5 mile on Mineral Springs Road to a four-way stop. Pass through the intersection, and continue another 0.3 mile on Mineral Springs Road to a right turn into the Bailly and Chellberg parking lot.

Key points:
- 0.0   Trailhead.
- 0.3   Reach the Bailly Homestead.
- 0.4   Cross Howe Road to the Little Calumet River.

1.3	Arrive at the bridge over the Little Calumet River.
2.3	Cross Howe Road.
2.5	Reach the junction with a side trail to the Bailly family cemetery.
2.8	Drop into the ravine below the Chellberg Farm.
2.9	Reach the Chellberg Farm.

The hike: In 1822, Honore Gratien Joseph Bailly de Messein, a French-Canadian, chose this site for a trading post because the Little Calumet River offered a canoe route that intersected with two major land routes used by Native Americans. Bailly gained wealth by selling furs for as much as $5 apiece to the American Fur Company, which was owned by Jacob Astor. When beaver hats became unfashionable in Europe, Bailly switched to the tavern business. A devout Catholic, Bailly often entertained visiting priests who held mass at the family home. Bailly's death in 1835 ended his plans to develop a town on what is now the site of Bethlehem Steel.

Almost four decades later, in 1872, Swedish immigrants Anders and Johanna Kjellberg purchased 40 acres from their former employer, Joseph Bailly's son-in-law. They took up farming, and later changed the spelling of their name to Chellberg.

These days the Bailly site, which is designated a national historic landmark, includes the main house, kitchen/chapel, a two-story cabin, a brick house, and a fur-trading cabin. Volunteers bring to life the turn-of-the-century Chellberg Farm by dressing in period clothing and tending to the daily chores of planting, harvesting, cooking, and caring for the livestock.

Although the area carries the Bailly and Chellberg names, they were not the first inhabitants. There is evidence that prehistoric people lived and

Hikers cross the bridge over the Little Calumet River at Indiana Dunes National Lakeshore.

Little Calumet River Trail, Bailly Homestead, and Chellberg Farm

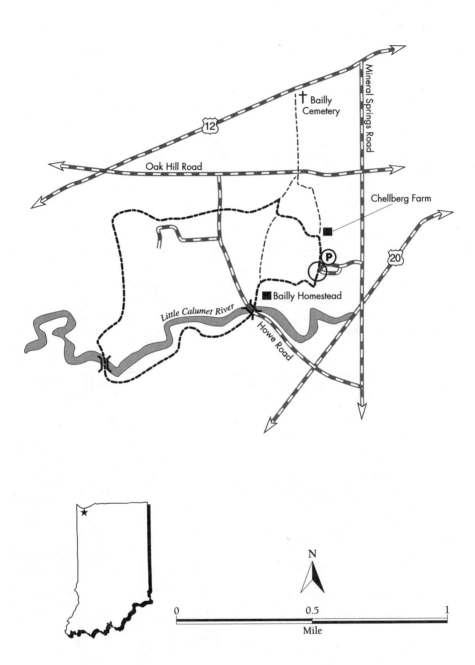

A hiker enters the meadow on the Little Calumet River Trail part of the Indiana Dunes National Lakeshore.

hunted along the Little Calumet River as far back as 200 B.C.

The areas around the Bailly Homestead and Chellberg Farm are heavily used, with the back part of the trail along the Little Calumet River more remote and scenic. The hike begins at a visitor center near the parking lot and follows a well-manicured trail of wood chips as it descends into a ravine, crosses a footbridge, and climbs the other side of the ravine into a clearing at the site of the Bailly Homestead at 0.3 mile.

Continue the hike by going west from the Bailly Homestead, crossing Howe Road at 0.4 mile, to a portion of the trail that follows the Little Calumet River for about 1 mile. The trail is a well-worn dirt path. Plastic trail signs with red arrows point the way.

The trail passes through gullies and over three footbridges as it meanders southwest along the river. At 1.3 miles, you will reach a bridge that crosses back over the Little Calumet. On the other side of the river, the trail follows a boardwalk through a swampy edge of the river bottom that in spring and summer puts on a flowery show. Off the boardwalk, the trail heads north, ascending the left (west) side of a gully before crossing a footbridge to the right (east) side.

At 1.8 miles, the trail enters a meadow, and alternates between woods and meadows as it heads north and then east to cross Howe Road again at 2.3 miles. At 2.5 miles, the trail splits; you can go left (northeast) to the Bailly family cemetery or right (south) to the Chellberg Farm. Go right for 0.1 mile to another split in the trail and turn left (east) to reach the farm. The trail descends into a ravine at 2.8 miles, and crosses a footbridge at the bottom. Climb the other side of the ravine to reach the farm.

After visiting the Chellberg Farm, complete the hike by picking up the trail on the south side of the farmhouse, passing the maple sugar house, and walking 0.2 mile back to the parking lot.

---

4 Beach Trail

Type of hike:	Day hike, loop.
General description:	A loop trail through woods and along Lake Michigan, concluding with a climb through dunes.
General location:	3 miles north of Chesterton in the northwest part of the state.
Total distance:	7 miles.
Difficulty:	Strenuous.
Elevation gain:	About 200 feet from the Lake Michigan shore to Mount Tom.
Jurisdiction:	The Indiana Department of Natural Resources, Division of State Parks & Reservoirs.
Special attractions:	The Lake Michigan shoreline and the three tallest

dunes in the area—Mount Tom, Mount Holder, and Mount Jackson.

Maps: Dune Acres USGS quad; Indiana Dunes State Park brochure.

Permits/fees: There is a $2 park entry fee for vehicles with Indiana license plates; $5 for out-of-state vehicles. Season passes are available.

Camping: Indiana Dunes State Park has 286 drive-in campsites, from modern to primitive, plus a youth tent area. The Indiana Dunes National Lakeshore Dunewood Campground has 79 drive-in or walk-in sites open seasonally.

Trailhead facilities: There is a large parking lot and a nature center at the trailhead. Water is available at the nature center and at other locations throughout the park.

Finding the trailhead: From Chesterton, drive 3 miles north on Indiana 49 to the park gatehouse. From the gatehouse, drive 0.1 mile to the first road on the right (east). Turn right and drive 0.6 mile to the nature center parking lot. The trailhead for Trails 8, 9, and 10 is clearly marked at the south side of the nature center.

Key points:
0.0 Trailhead.
0.1 At the junction with Trails 8 and 10, go right (northeast) on Trail 10.
0.9 Arrive at the junction with side trail to bird observation tower at marsh.
1.3 Reach the junction with Trail 2, go straight.
3.0 At the beach, go left.
5.5 Reach the junction with Trail 8 and go left.
6.8 Arrive at the crossroads with Trails 8 and 9, go right to nature center parking lot.

The hike: Established in 1925, Indiana Dunes State Park is one of the oldest parks in the state park system. The park features a combination of sand dunes, woods, and marshes nestled within the boundaries of the Indiana Dunes National Lakeshore. The dunes are home to a diverse blend of plant species.

The park has a network of eight trails that can be hiked separately or in combination. The best way to get a good feel for the park and the dune environment is to take a hike that includes all or part of Trails 8, 9, and 10. This hike is best taken in the morning for two reasons: (1) white-tailed deer and other wildlife are more visible just after sunrise, and (2) on hot summer days the sand has not yet been toasted by the sun.

The route can be walked in either a clockwise or counterclockwise direction, but I prefer the latter. Hitting the high, sandy dunes right off might discourage you from completing the rest of the hike, which is worth the effort. On the leeward side of the dunes, the trail is easy to follow. So is the beach portion, but hikers along the beach must watch for markers to connect with Trail 8 near the swimming beach. The trails in the park are busiest on weekends and holidays.

Beach Trail

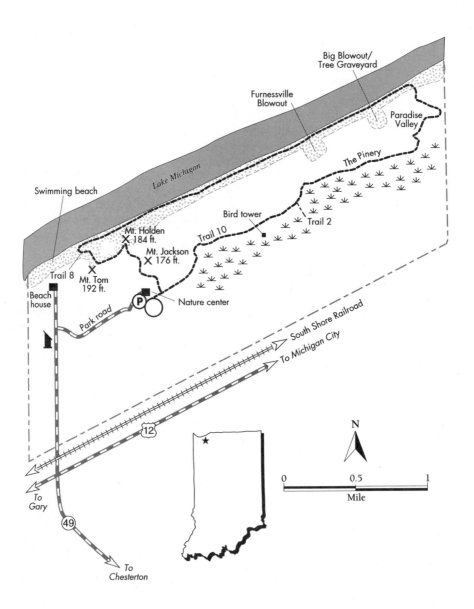

Begin the hike at the nature center. There is a slightly tricky maneuver at the outset when the path from the nature center reaches a crossroads with Trails 8 and 9. Go straight about 10 yards, and the trail splits. Take the right (northeast) fork to get on Trail 10. It is a gentle stroll between heavily wooded older dunes on the left and an extensive marsh on the right. Unlike the much younger dunes toward the lakeshore, these back dunes contain an established forest of oak, hickory, sassafras, and maple trees, along with an abundance of ferns and wildflowers.

Just before the 1-mile mark, there is a short spur trail on the right (south)

The tree graveyard along Lake Michigan shoreline at Indiana Dunes State Park.

to a bird observation tower that overlooks an extensive marsh stretching for a couple of miles through the heart of the park.

At 1.3 miles, things begin to change. Pass a junction with Trail 2, which comes in from the right. Go straight (east) and within 0.25 mile you will reach an area called The Pinery—the last stand of virgin white pine trees in the area.

Just beyond the 2-mile mark, cross a boardwalk and enter Paradise Valley, a flat expanse that swings through a splash of wildflowers and ferns. This is the turning point of the hike, as the trail curves to the northwest over a small dune to reach the shore of Lake Michigan. On most days, you can see the Chicago skyline from here. Take note of the zipping sound as your feet sweep through the loose sand. Quartz crystals combine with moisture, pressure, and friction to create "singing sand." Few beaches in the world have this type of sand. If it is too difficult to walk through the loose sand, slip down to the shoreline where pounding waves have packed the sand tighter.

While hiking the lakeshore, be alert for tall signposts on the sandy ridges that identify the Big Blowout/Tree Graveyard, the Furnessville Blowout, and the Beach House Blowout. Blowouts occur when strong winds carve out large chunks of established dunes, sometimes exposing graveyards of dead trees previously buried in sand.

Plants are plentiful along the shoreline side of the dunes—Kalm's Saint Johnswort, spiderwort, marram grass, and little bluestem are common. Also watch for places where swallows build nests into the compacted sand.

Nearing the supervised beach at the west end of the park at 5.5 miles, look for the signpost for Trail 8, and take a left turn to begin climbing Mount Tom. It will not be easy, so pause atop Mount Tom for a couple of reasons—to catch your breath and to take in the view.

A wooden staircase descends Mount Tom to the left (east) as the trail crosses a saddle to Mount Holden (184 feet above Lake Michigan). The trail turns south as it descends from Mount Holden before beginning a more gradual climb of Mount Jackson. Go down the wide, sandy swath off the southwest side of Mount Jackson, pick up the trail, and follow its lengthy downhill path to the crossroads where Trail 8 meets up again with Trails 9 and 10. Turn right (west) and return 100 yards to the nature center parking lot.

5 Heron Rookery Trail

Type of hike::	Day hike, out-and-back.
General description:	A linear trail along the Little Calumet River with a stop at a heron rookery site.
General location:	Southeast of Chesterton.
Total distance:	2.4 miles.
Difficulty:	Easy.
Elevation gain:	Minimal.

Heron Rookery Trail

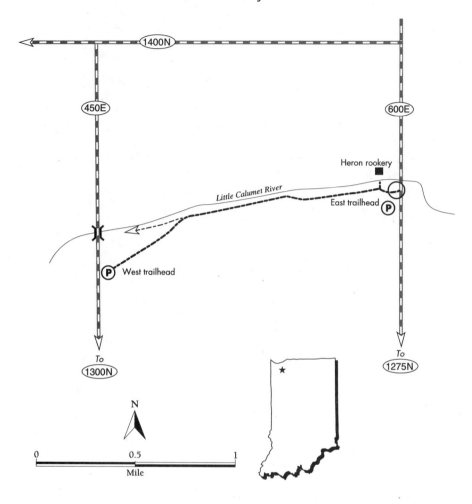

Jurisdiction: Indiana Dunes National Lakeshore or National Park Service.

Special attraction: Heron rookery.

Maps: Michigan City West and Westville USGS quads; Dunes National Lakeshore brochure.

Permits/fees: None required.

Camping: None allowed on site, but Indiana Dunes State Park (1.5 miles west) has 286 sites, modern to primitive, and Indiana Dunes National Lakeshore Dunewood Campground (6 miles west) has 79 sites.

Trailhead facilities: There is a porta potty, but nothing else at the trailhead. No potable water is available.

The parking lot sign at Heron Rookery Trail, part of the Indiana Dunes National Lakeshore.

Finding the trailhead: Go 2 miles west on U.S. Highway 20 from its intersection with U.S. Highway 421 on the south side of Michigan City. Turn left (south) on LaPorte/Porter County Line Road and go 2 miles to Porter County 1500 North. Turn right (west) and go 1 mile to Porter County 600 East. Turn left (south) and go 0.7 mile to the Heron Rookery Trail parking lot on the right.

Key points:
- 0.0   Trailhead.
- 0.0   Start at the heron rookery viewing site.
- 0.4   Cross the first small footbridge.
- 1.0   Reach the junction with the trail to the west-end parking lot.
- 1.2   Arrive at the west-end parking lot.

The hike: From the northwest corner of the east-end parking lot, walk about 15 yards to a fork in the trail. The right (north) turn leads to a spot on the south bank of the Little Calumet River from which you can see the heron rookery—a protected area on the north bank where great blue herons annually return to a colony of nests high in the treetops.

Herons are storklike wading birds with long legs and pointed bills. There are about 50 species of herons worldwide, and the great blue heron is the largest American variety. An adult great blue heron stands 4 feet tall and has a 7 foot wingspan.

Back at the trail juncture, a left (west) turn leads to a peaceful walk along the Little Calumet River, a small but vital river both for Native Americans and early pioneer settlers. The trail is very narrow, and on wet days can be a sloppy, slippery hike. The footing can be a little tricky at times where the river washes out the bank. This portion of the hike begins in a meadow, then reaches a fence and a short set of steps down to the river. The trail hugs the riverbank more closely beyond this point. At times it is right at the water level, and at other times 10 to 15 feet above the water. The area is rich in wildflowers.

Three small footbridges along the trail cross over feeder streams at 0.4, 0.8, and 0.9 miles. After the third bridge, the trail widens a bit. Look for a bridge over the Little Calumet, a sign that you are nearing the trail's end. The trail splits at 1 mile, with the left fork leading to the west-end parking lot and the right fork hugging the riverbank to the bridge on Porter County 450 East. If you stay to the right, turn left (south) once you reach the road. It is about 0.1 mile to the west-end parking lot.

Retrace your steps to return to the main lot at the east end.

6 Mount Baldy Trail

Type of hike::	Day hike, loop.
General description:	A steep climb up a "living" sand dune to a scenic view of Lake Michigan.
General location:	On the west edge of Michigan City in northwest Indiana.
Total distance:	Less than 1 mile to the top of the dune and back.
Difficulty:	Strenuous.
Elevation gain:	100 feet.
Jurisdiction:	Indiana Dunes National Lakeshore.
Special attractions:	Sunset on Lake Michigan with the Chicago skyline as a backdrop.
Maps:	Michigan City West USGS quad; Dunes National Lakeshore brochure.
Permits/fees:	None required.
Camping:	None is available on site, but nearby Indiana Dunes State Park has 286 sites, modern to primitive, and Indiana Dunes National Lakeshore Dunewood Campground has 79 sites. Both are located to the west of this site.
Trailhead facilities:	There are restrooms and picnic tables, but the small parking lot will handle only 10 to 15 vehicles. There is water available in the restrooms.

Finding the trailhead: From the intersection of Indiana 35 and U.S. Highway 12 in downtown Michigan City, go 2 miles west on US 12 to the Mount Baldy entrance of the Indiana Dunes National Lakeshore. Turn right off US 12 and follow the entry road 0.1 mile to the parking lot. The trailhead is at the north end of the lot near a kiosk.

Mount Baldy Trail

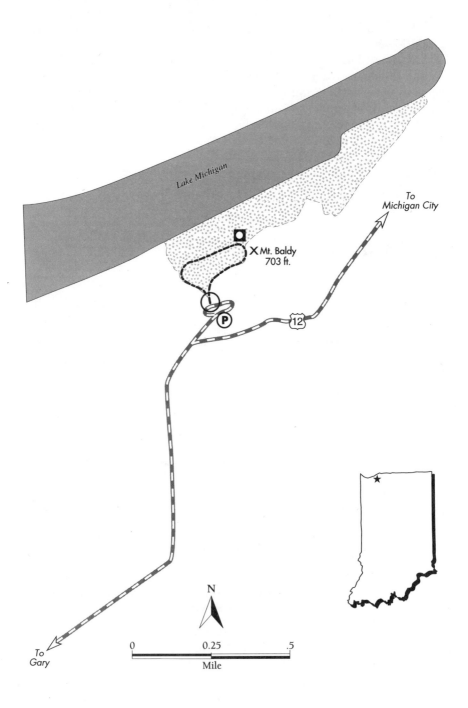

Lake Michigan

To
Michigan City

X Mt. Baldy
703 ft.

P

12

To Gary

N

0   0.25   .5
Mile

Hikers enjoy the view from Mount Baldy.

Key points:

   0.0   Trailhead.

   0.1   Reach the trail junction; go left to the beach and right to Mount Baldy.

   0.4   Arrive at the top of Mount Baldy.

The hike: Even though this is a short trail, it is not easy. Hiking in sand is almost a break-even proposition—for every stride taken, about half is lost sliding in the loose stuff. But the effort here is well worth it because of the spectacular view from Mount Baldy and the opportunity to witness a "living" dune in action.

It is less than 1 mile to climb to the top of the dune and back, but it can seem longer. The distance also can change depending on how many trips are made running down the lake side of the dune and trudging back to the top. A tip for climbing the sandy slope—try walking in the indentations left by others. The depressed sand offers a little more solid footing. Avoid walking on the sides of the trail because that will only destroy vegetation and make the dune susceptible to erosion.

The trailhead is at the north end of the parking lot near a kiosk that displays information about dune development. A short stretch of wooden steps makes the early portion of the trail a bit easier to walk, plus reduces erosion.

At 0.1 mile, the trail splits—the left branch offering a shortcut to the beach and the right branch leading to the top of Mount Baldy. Continue right along the sandy slope to the top of Mount Baldy, where the sights include a converted nuclear power facility and Michigan City to the east, the Indiana Dunes National Lakeshore below and west, and, far in the distance to the west, the skyline of Chicago. This is also a splendid place to watch a sunrise or sunset.

Scores of people frolic on Mount Baldy, running up and down its sandy face. The top of the dune is massive, and its leeward side is testimony to the force of nature. Pushed by wind off Lake Michigan, the dune advances inland a few feet each year, swallowing up trees in its path. The steady progression defines the term "living" dune. The leeward side also provides an alternative return route to the parking lot (or a challenging ascent of Mount Baldy), but it is much steeper than the designated trail.

Glacial Lakes

People who move to northeast Indiana frequently are confused when they hear locals talk about going to "the lake" on summer weekends. They begin to think they may have moved closer to one of the Great Lakes than first imagined. True, Lake Michigan and Lake Erie are at most a few hours away from most of northern Indiana. But in reality, what the locals call "the lake" actually is a generic reference to any body of water where they, a relative, or close friend have a cottage. There are more than 100 natural lakes in Steuben County, and a few hundred more form a beltway connecting LaGrange, Noble, and Kosciusko counties.

Some are small ponds only a few acres in size. Others represent the largest natural lakes in the state, including the 3,000-acre Lake Wawasee in Kosciusko County, the 1,900-acre Lake Maxinkuckee in Marshall County, and the 1,000-acre Lake James in Steuben County.

Regardless of size, nearly all of the lakes that grace this area of the state were created by glaciers that last passed through Indiana about 10,000 years ago.

But the ten largest lakes pooled together pale in comparison to long-lost Beaver Lake, which was situated in northwest Indiana. At 28,500 acres, it was the largest lake in the state until drainage of the nearby Kankakee River eventually dried up the shallow water.

When ancient glaciers bulldozed across the state, they pushed along tons of debris in the form of rocks, mud, and sand. As the glaciers retreated, blocks of ice were left behind in pockets and depressions. As the ice blocks melted, lakes were formed. A common type of lake in northeast Indiana is the kettle lake—deep water-filled holes with steeply contoured shorelines. A prime example is Lake Lonidaw at Pokagon State Park. The lake is only a few acres in size, but it is more than 40 feet deep.

Lake Lonidaw is protected as part of a state nature preserve, but nearly every other lake in northern Indiana is highly developed—ringed by cottages, trailer courts, campgrounds, marinas, or golf courses. The "lake" season typically runs from Memorial Day weekend through Labor Day weekend, a time during which the nearby small towns experience population explosions with the influx of vacationers.

Nevertheless, it is possible to find pockets of nature that provide an escape from the hubbub. Olin Lake Nature Preserve and Crooked Lake Nature Preserve are two such sites. Olin Lake is the largest undeveloped lake in the state, and, at more than 100 feet, Crooked Lake is the deepest.

Hikers can get to the scenic shorelines of both lakes, as well as other glacial lakes, by hiking along the trails in the locations listed in this chapter. Trails are presented in a clockwise direction from the north at the Eagle Trail in Bicentennial Woods toward Angola.

7 Eagle Trail in Bicentennial Woods

Type of hike:	Day hike, loop.
General description:	A short loop along a wooded trail by a quiet creek, with a side trek to a secluded marsh.
General location:	North of Fort Wayne.
Total distance:	1.5 miles.
Difficulty:	Easy.
Elevation gain:	Minimal.
Jurisdiction:	ACRES, Inc.
Special attractions:	Several gigantic oak, maple, and sycamore trees, some estimated to be 200 to 250 years old.
Maps:	Huntertown USGS quad.
Permits/fees:	None.
Camping:	None permitted.
Trailhead facilities:	There is a small parking lot at the trailhead, but no potable water source.

Finding the trailhead: Go north for 8 miles on Indiana 3 from the Interstate 69 interchange in Fort Wayne to Shoaff Road and turn right (east). Go 1.5 miles to the Bicentennial Woods parking lot, passing West and Kell roads. The parking lot is on the right (south) side of the road.

Key points:
    0.0 Trailhead.
    0.1 Reach the Eagle Trail/Dogwood Trail juncture; Arnold's Oaks.
    0.2 Cross the Willow Creek footbridge.
    0.5 Take the wetland turnoff.
    0.7 Reach the marsh.
    0.9 Follow the steps to the lower leg of the Eagle Trail.
    1.3 Return to the Willow Creek footbridge.

The hike: Although this hike is not exactly in "lake country," it is close enough, and it is certainly worthwhile. As the city of Fort Wayne approached its 200th anniversary in 1994, a local land preservation group—Allen County Reserves (ACRES)—set about looking for an appropriate property to commemorate the historic occasion. This 80-acre tract is what the group selected, because the gigantic trees growing here are representative of what much of the area looked like before it was settled.

Only a few trees were ever removed from the property, which is believed to be the last stand of virgin timber in the county. Stately oak trees with trunks 4 feet in diameter, and huge sycamores dominate a small, heavily wooded area that is bisected by Willow Creek, a quiet tributary of scenic Cedar Creek. The property has two designated hikes—the Dogwood Trail and the Eagle Trail, which is described here. This is a very secluded area with little traffic.

To begin the hike, locate the path on the south edge of the parking lot. Walk 70 yards to a T intersection where the Eagle and Dogwood Trails begin.

Eagle Trail in Bicentennial Woods

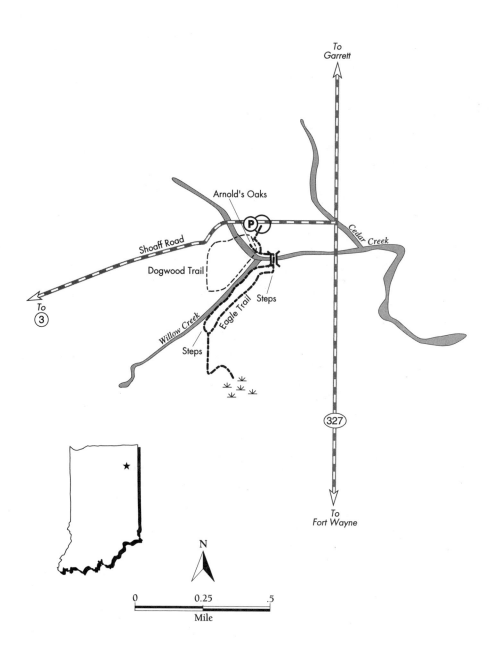

To
Garrett

Arnold's Oaks

P

Shoaff Road

Cedar Creek

Dogwood Trail

Steps

To
③

Willow Creek

Eagle Trail

Steps

327

To
Fort Wayne

N

0   0.25   .5
Mile

Turn left (south) on the Eagle Trail, and make a gradual descent along the face of a low ridge that slopes to the right. Reach another T intersection at 0.1 mile. Turn left (east) to the Willow Creek footbridge, or right (northwest) to Arnold's Oaks. The right turn is a one-way walk of only 20 yards that leads to a view of half a dozen gigantic trees that have been named in honor of the family that preserved the area before the land was purchased by ACRES.

From the T intersection, it is a 50-yard walk to the footbridge over Willow Creek. Cross the footbridge and climb a set of wooden steps. Follow the path as it curves right (south) along a ridge overlooking the creek, which is below and to the right (northwest).

At 0.5 mile, the path splits. Go straight, continuing through the woods as the trail curves left (east) and leads to a secluded wetland marsh at 0.7 mile. Retrace your steps to where the trail splits and turn left, going down wooden steps toward Willow Creek. The trail turns to the right (northeast) and proceeds along the creek to the footbridge at 1.3 miles. Cross the footbridge and return to the parking lot.

8   Crooked Lake Nature Preserve

Type of hike: Day hike, loop.
General description: A double-loop trail through fields, along a bluff, and along the lakeshore.
General location: North of Columbia City on Crooked Lake.
Total distance: 2 miles.
Difficulty: Easy.
Elevation gain: A 45-foot decline from the trailhead to the lakeshore.
Jurisdiction: Indiana Department of Natural Resources, Division of Nature Preserves, in association with ACRES, Inc.
Special attractions: The Phil M. McNagny Jr. Tall Trees Memorial Grove, the Leaman cemetery, and Crooked Lake.
Maps: Merriam USGS quad; Crooked Lake Nature Preserve brochure.
Permits/fees: None.
Camping: None.
Trailhead facilities: There is parking space for about six to eight vehicles. No potable water source is available.

Finding the trailhead: Go north from U.S. Highway 30 in Columbia City on Indiana 9 for about 7 miles to the Whitley-Noble county line. Turn left (west) on Noble County 600 South (also known as County Line Road), and go 0.5 mile. The nature preserve parking lot is on the left (south) side of the road as the road curves sharply to the right (north) and becomes Noble County 250 West.

Crooked Lake Nature Preserve

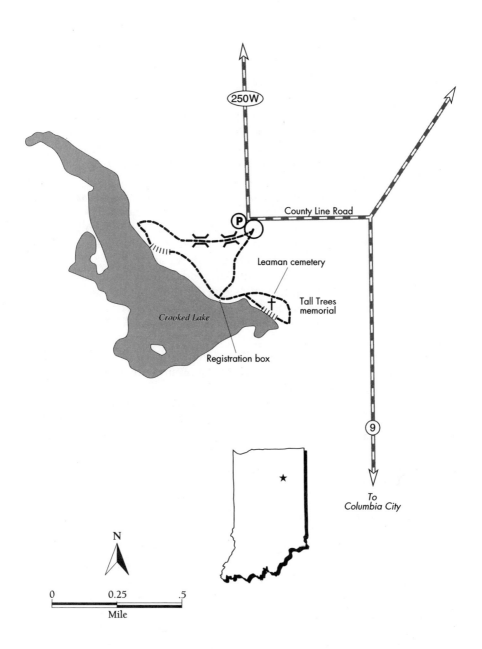

250W

County Line Road

P

Leaman cemetery

Tall Trees memorial

Crooked Lake

Registration box

9

To
Columbia City

N

0   0.25   .5
Mile

Key points:

0.0   Trailhead.
0.3   Pass the registration box at the start of the east loop.
0.6   Reach the Phil M. McNagny Jr. Tall Trees Memorial Grove.
0.7   Pass the Leaman cemetery.
0.9   Arrive at the registration box and the start of the west loop.
1.4   Reach the west end of the west loop trail.
1.9   Return to the juncture with main trail.

The hike: It is practically impossible to find a lake in northern Indiana that is not completely encircled by either summer cottages or year-round homes. This state-designated nature preserve protects about 3,500 feet of the north shoreline of Crooked Lake from such use. The spring-fed lake is one of the most pristine in Indiana, and one of the deepest at 105 feet.

It was on the shores of Crooked Lake that a pioneer family, the Leamans, were forced to interrupt their westward journey when a teenage daughter became ill. The daughter died, and legend has it the mother was so distraught at her tragic loss that she would not resume travel. The Leamans buried their daughter on a hillside overlooking the lake and built a home nearby. Over time, several other family members were buried in the small cemetery that is on the east loop of the nature preserve.

The 100-acre preserve features old farm fields, ridges, hardwood forests, a pine plantation, and a 0.5-mile walk along the shore of Crooked Lake. The woodlands feature green ash, beech, dogwood, hickory, ironwood, red oak, white oak, and sassafras trees.

Begin the hike by passing through the entry at the small parking lot. Pick up an interpretive brochure and walk the mowed path through fields that were farmed until the late 1970s. Already, the natural progression of vegetation is taking place as small trees pop up among the Queen Anne's lace, goldenrod, wild berries, and prairie grasses. It is about 0.3 mile from the trailhead through the fields and down a gradual slope to a registration box near the lakeshore. East and west loops begin here, and together they make a pleasant hike. Start with the east loop to keep in sequence with the numbered signs along the trail. Walk the shoreline for about a quarter of a mile, crossing boardwalks in two marshy areas before curving left for an uphill climb. Along the right side of the trail is a broad ravine featuring a winding creek and the Phil M. McNagny Jr. Tall Trees Memorial Grove, which is at the top of the ridge at 0.6 mile. Turn left (west), and at 0.7 mile pass by what remains of the Leaman cemetery along the left (south) side of the path.

Continue along the ridgetop, which features large red oak trees, before descending downhill toward the lake and to the registration box at 0.9 mile, where you will start the west loop. The path winds along the lakeshore, crossing two ravines and one boardwalk before turning right (east) and heading uphill at 1.4 miles. Cross a footbridge at the back end of a ravine before passing a pine plantation on the left (north). Just past the pines, cross another footbridge, then reenter the old farm fields. At 1.9 miles, link up with the main path and turn left to return to the parking lot.

9 Merry Lea Environmental Center

Type of hike:	Day hike, loop.
General description:	A network of trails through meadows and forests, past Bear and Cub lakes, and circling a large wetland.
General location:	North of Columbia City.
Total distance:	4.4 miles.
Difficulty:	Easy.
Elevation gain:	Minimal.
Jurisdiction:	Merry Lea Environmental Center.
Special attractions:	Peaceful meadows and wetlands.
Maps:	Ormas USGS quad; Merry Lea map sheet.
Permits/fees:	None required to use trails, but donations are encouraged.
Camping:	None permitted.
Trailhead facilities:	The Merry Lea Learning Center has nature displays as well as reference books, plus restrooms. There is a drinking fountain in the learning center.

Finding the trailhead: From Columbia City, drive north for 10 miles on Indiana 109, passing between Crooked Lake and Big Lake, to a directional sign pointing west to Merry Lea at Whitley County 350 South. Turn left (west) and go 1 mile to Whitley County 500 West. Turn right and go 0.4 mile to a T intersection with Whitley County 300 South. Directly across the intersection is the entrance to Merry Lea, a 1,150-acre complex managed and partly owned by Goshen College. Go 0.3 mile down the main lane to a parking lot near the learning center. The hike begins on a mowed path southwest of the learning center.

Key points:
- 0.0 Trailhead.
- 0.2 Pass Maple Bottom.
- 0.4 Reach Rieth Woods.
- 0.7 Skirt Bear Lake and Onion Bottom.
- 1.3 Arrive at Cub Lake.
- 2.5 Reach the Kesling Farm wetland.
- 3.8 Pass the picnic area.
- 4.2 Return down Luckey's Lane.

The hike: It was nearly 40 years ago that Mary Jane Rieth and her late husband, Lee A. Rieth, were inspired by their love for nature to establish the Merry Lea Environmental Center as a way of preserving habitat and creating a site for environmental study. Twenty years later, the Rieths began turning over the 1,150-acre property to Goshen College, which manages Merry Lea for educational and scientific purposes.

The area includes bogs, marshes, fields, meadows, and forest environments that are ideal for quiet hikes, wildlife watching, or plant study. The trails are generally well-groomed, but sometimes can be confusing to follow

Merry Lea Environmental Center

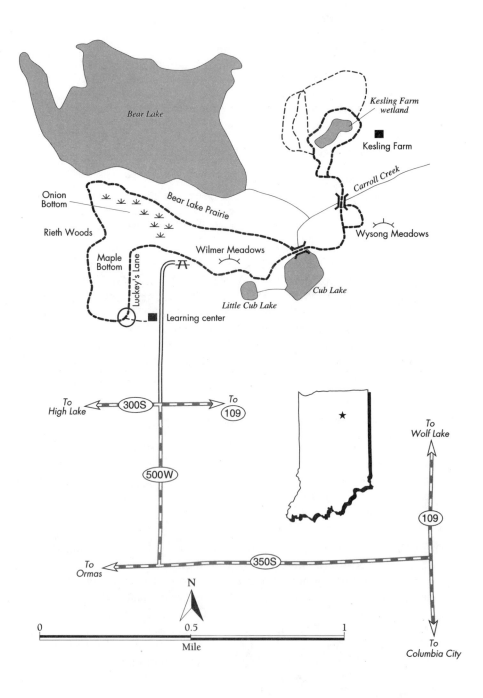

in spots where extra trails have been cleared by mowers. Merry Lea is a popular location for school trips, so weekdays can sometimes be quite busy.

Begin the hike by walking west past the learning center to a mowed path, and going about 0.1 mile to an intersection with a signpost marked A. It is the first of many signposts on the hike and is located in the southeast corner of Mary's Meadow. Take the left path and swing around the southwest corner of the meadow, turning north to enter the Maple Bottom at signpost E. The path can be muddy in wet weather.

At 0.4 mile, reach post H and turn right (east) on Hickory Ridge. Walk to post C and turn left (north) to wind through Rieth Woods toward Shrew Meadows. At 0.6 mile (post D), step onto a boardwalk that leads through a wooded wetland. At 0.7 mile and post O, a gravel path winds between two drastically different environments—dry and sparse Bear Lake Prairie on the left and Onion Bottom, a large wetland and pond, on the right.

At 0.9 mile (post M), turn left (east) and walk along the north side of Wilmer Meadows for a little more than 0.25 mile to post P, on the north shore of Cub Lake. Several paths merge here. Go east from Cub Lake and cross a bridge over a drainage ditch between Cub and Bear lakes. Continue east to post Q, where the trail turns north and passes Wysong Meadows.

At 1.8 miles, cross a footbridge over Carroll Creek to post R and turn left (west). Pass through another meadow to a pond, a wetland area, and post V at 2.1 miles. There are several trail options at this point. Stay to the right (north) to circle the pond in a clockwise direction, passing by the Kesling Farm before coming to post S at 2.7 miles. Turn left (south), and head back across the meadow to post R and the footbridge over Carroll Creek. After crossing the creek, turn left (east) and walk around the east side of Wysong Meadows.

At post Q and the 3.2-mile mark, retrace your steps west to Cub Lake and pick up the trail that runs along the south side of Wilmer Meadows. At post N, which is at 3.7 miles, cross the picnic area and locate an opening on the west side, where the path enters the woods. The Onion Bottom wetland is to the right. Cross a drainage ditch and walk to post J. Turn left (west) and continue through the woods. Cross a footbridge and pass by an observation deck on the right. At post F, which is at 4.2 miles, turn left (south) on Luckey's Lane and walk to post B. At post B, turn left and finish the hike by walking to the learning center.

10 Chain O'Lakes State Park

Type of hike:	Day hike, loop.
General description:	A connecting network of trails around a chain of glacier-formed lakes.
General location:	Near Albion in Noble County.
Total distance:	3.3 miles.
Difficulty:	Easy.

Chain O'Lakes State Park

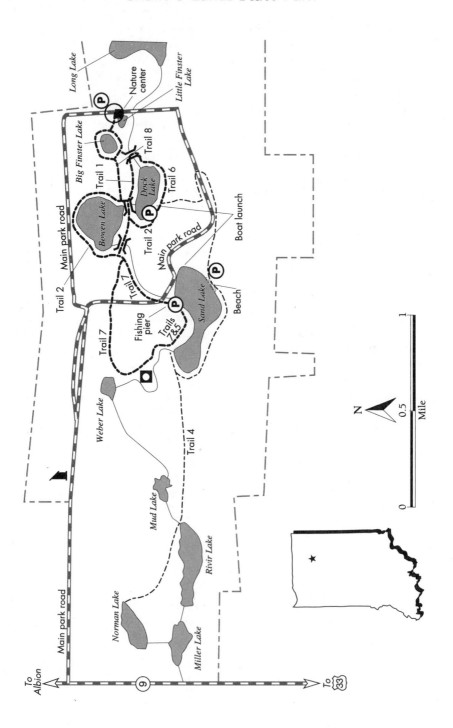

Elevation gain:	Minimal.
Jurisdiction:	Indiana Department of Natural Resources, Division of State Parks & Reservoirs.
Special attractions:	The kettle lake system.
Maps:	Merriam USGS quad; Chain O'Lakes State Park brochure.
Permits/fees:	There is a $2 entry fee for vehicles with Indiana license plates; $5 for out-of-state vehicles. Season passes are available.
Camping:	Chain O'Lakes State Park has 413 campsites, from modern to primitive, plus rally and youth tent areas.
Trailhead facilities:	A nature center is located in the old Stanley Schoolhouse, a one-room brick schoolhouse built in 1915. The nature center is open daily from Memorial Day through Labor Day. There is a drinking fountain outside the nature center and other water sources throughout the park.

Finding the trailhead: Chain O'Lakes State Park is located midway between Albion and Churubusco. From Albion, go 4 miles south on Indiana 9 to the park entrance and turn left (east). It is 1 mile to the park gate. From the park gate, go 1 mile on the main park road before taking a left (northeast) turn. Go another 1.25 miles to the nature center, which is on the right (west) side of the road. The parking lot is on the left (east) side of the road. The trail begins at the Trail 8 sign near the northeast corner of the nature center.

Key points:
- 0.0   Trailhead.
- 0.4   Circle Bowen Lake.
- 1.7   Reach Sand Lake.
- 2.2   Return to Bowen Lake.
- 2.4   Arrive at Dock Lake.
- 3.1   Reach Big Finster Lake.
- 3.3   Return to the nature center.

The hike: Chain O'Lakes State Park is exactly what the name implies—a park featuring a series of 11 small lakes connected to one another by channels. The trails are wide, well-maintained, and well-marked. There are a few potentially muddy spots near the lakes. The amount of trail traffic varies.

The lakes are what is left of the Pleistocene ice age, whose glaciers retreated from this area between 13,000 and 14,000 years ago. Beneath the melting glacier, streams deposited sand and gravel, while detached blocks of ice formed the steep depressions that became the kettle lakes in the park. Miami Indians settled here on the north shore of what now is Bowen Lake, which is named for William Bowen, one of the first white settlers in the area in the 1830s.

The hike begins near the east end of the park, at the nature center housed in a former one-room schoolhouse. First built in 1915, the Stanley Schoolhouse is the fourth school building at this site. Students attended the school until it closed in the early 1950s.

Begin the hike on the north side of the nature center at Trail 8, which is an interpretive nature trail that forms a loop around Big Finster Lake. Walk around the north side of Big Finster Lake, and at 0.2 mile, turn right on a path that leads across and down a ridge overlooking Dock Lake to the left (south).

At 0.4 mile, the path drops off the ridge and connects with Trail 2. Turn right (north) and walk counterclockwise around the shore of Bowen Lake. At the southwest corner of the lake, cross a footbridge and turn right (east) at the Trail 7 post. Go 20 yards and take another right (east) turn that leads along a flat ridge through upland woods to the main park road. Cross the road and continue the hike through a meadow as the path curves to the left (south). A creek is on the right side of the path and a small ridge on the left.

The path makes a gradual climb up to an overlook above the channel that connects Sand and Weber lakes. Drop off the ridge and walk toward the channel to the intersection of Trails 7 and 5 at 1.7 miles. Turn left (south) on Trails 7 and 5, walking along the north shore of Sand Lake, the largest of the 11 lakes in the park.

At 1.9 miles, the path reaches a small parking lot near a fishing pier. From the pier, walk the gravel road to the paved park road and cross over to pick up Trail 7 and reenter the woods. A channel between Sand and Bowen lakes runs along the right side of the trail.

At 2.2 miles, Trail 7 ends as it connects with Trail 2. Turn right (east) on Trail 2 and cross a footbridge over the Sand-Bowen channel. At 2.4 miles, turn right (south) off Trail 2 and onto Trail 1 as it skirts the west shore of Dock Lake. There is a boat launch on the south shore of Dock Lake. Walk through the parking lot toward pit toilets to pick up the marked trail. When Trail 1 joins Trail 6, turn left and follow Trail 6 around the south and east shores of Dock Lake to a footbridge that rejoins Trail 1 as it crosses the channel between Dock and Long lakes. Cross the bridge and turn left (west) along the north shore of Dock Lake. Take the path back toward a footbridge over the Dock-Bowen channel. About 10 feet before the footbridge make a 180-degree turn to head back uphill to the nature center. Approaching Big Finster Lake at 3.1 miles, turn right as the path reconnects with Trail 8. The nature center is at 3.3 miles.

11 Olin Lake Nature Preserve

Type of hike: Day hike, loop.
General description: An interlocking loop trail through mixed woods to a lake with an undeveloped shoreline.
General location: North of Kendallville in LaGrange County, northeast Indiana.

Total distance:	1.8 miles.
Difficulty:	Easy.
Elevation gain:	Minimal.
Jurisdiction:	Indiana Department of Natural Resources, Division of Nature Preserves.
Special attractions:	Olin Lake, the largest undeveloped lake in the state.
Maps:	Oliver Lake USGS quad; Olin Lake Nature Preserve brochure.
Permits/fees:	None required.
Camping:	None allowed.
Trailhead facilities:	There is a gravel parking lot for about a dozen vehicles. No potable water source is available.

Trillium.

Olin Lake Nature Preserve

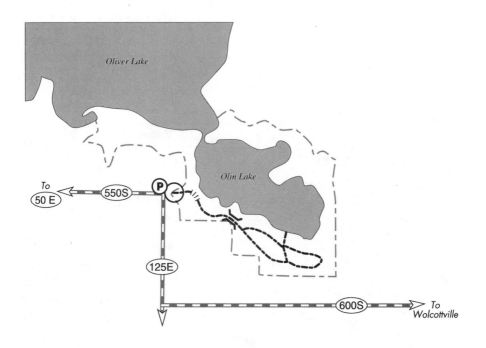

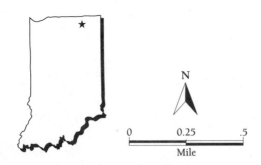

Finding the trailhead: From Kendallville, go west for 4 miles on Indiana 6 to Indiana 9. Turn right (north) on Indiana 9. Go north 7 miles, passing through Rome City and Wolcottville, and turn left (west) on LaGrange County 600 South. Go 2 miles to a T intersection with LaGrange County 125 East and turn right (north). Go 0.5 mile to LaGrange County 550 South. A parking lot for the nature preserve is on the right as the road curves to the left (west).

Key points:
    0.0   Trailhead.
    0.4   Reach the juncture with trail marker 2.
    1.4   Return to the juncture with trail marker 2.

The hike: Olin Lake is a rarity in Indiana because not one single cottage can be found on its entire shoreline. Although this 103-acre lake is 82 feet deep in one spot, its low, marshy shore contributed to its being the largest undeveloped lake in the state. State nature preserve status will keep it that way.

Olin is one of several lakes in a glacial chain connected by channels. To the northeast is tiny Martin Lake, and to the northwest is Oliver Lake, a popular fishing lake stocked annually by the state with rainbow trout and home to a remnant population of lake trout. Purdue University operates a summer camp on the northern border of the Olin Lake preserve.

The hike begins at the east end of the parking lot. Picture a figure eight on its side for a mental image of the trail layout. The east loop of the figure eight is lightly used since the main attraction, Olin Lake, is near the midpoint of the trail. Traffic is minimal, with the most use coming in spring when the wildflowers put on an early show.

Walk between the fence posts to a registration box, where you can pick up a copy of the interpetive brochure. The preserve is abundant with wildflowers—large-flowered trillium, false rue anemone, trout lily, Dutchman's breeches, bloodroot, spring beauty, hepatica, cut-leaved toothwort, and Jack-in-the-pulpit. At 0.3 mile, the trail crosses a boardwalk through a mucky area where two other plants are prominent—jewelweed, also called touch-me-not, and skunk cabbage. Look for a small tree that has smooth, gray bark with ripples; it is called musclewood. Many other trees grow in the low, wet soil, including basswood, red maple, black ash, and red elm.

After crossing a footbridge, come to signpost 2 at 0.4 mile, where the trail splits. Turn right (southeast), and walk through an upland woods featuring large beech, sugar maple, tulip, walnut, and oak trees.

At 0.6 mile, a crossroad marks the center point of the figure-eight trail. Turn right (southeast) and follow the east half of the figure eight as it loops counterclockwise through more upland woods before returning to the crossroad at 1 mile. Turn right (north) and walk less than 0.1 mile through a thick zone of shrubs to Olin Lake. Retrace your steps to the crossroad one more time and turn right (west) to walk the west loop of the figure eight in a counterclockwise direction.

At 1.4 miles, come to signpost 2 again and turn right (northwest), heading back over the footbridge and the boardwalk to the parking lot.

12 Pokagon Trail

Type of hike:	Day hike, loop.
General description:	A hike over varied terrain that skirts the outer perimeter of Pokagon State Park.
General location:	West of Angola.
Total distance:	8 miles, with an optional 2-mile addition.
Difficulty:	Mostly moderate, except for the distance, and the stairway at Hell's Point.
Elevation gain:	135 feet from Lake James to Hell's Point.
Jurisdiction:	Indiana Department of Natural Resources, Division of State Parks & Reservoirs.
Special attractions:	Hell's Point and Lake Lonidaw.
Maps:	Angola West USGS quad; Pokagon State Park brochure; Pokagon Trail brochure.
Permits/fees:	There is a $2 entry fee for vehicles with Indiana license plates; $5 for out-of-state vehicles. Season passes are available.
Camping:	Pokagon State Park has 310 individual campsites, from modern to primitive.
Trailhead facilities:	There is a large, paved parking lot at the nature center, which is open daily year-round. The nature center has restrooms and water. There are numerous other water sources in the park, including campgrounds, picnic areas, and the Potawatomi Inn.

The east end of the Pokagon Trail is spotted with wetlands like this.

Pokagon Trail

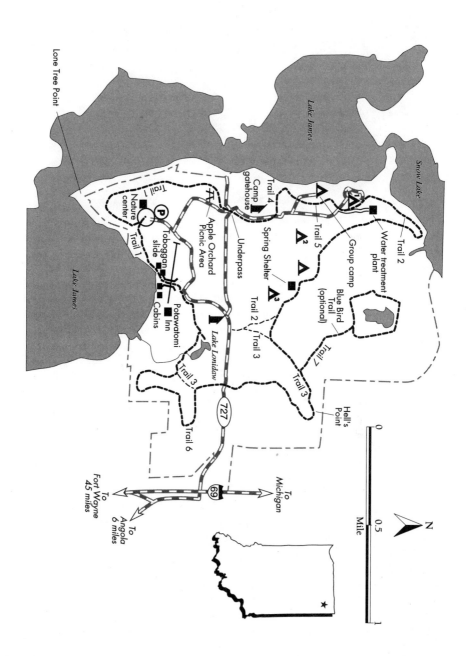

A young hiker taps the water spraying from a spring along the Pokagon Trail. The spring is tested weekly for water quality.

Finding the trailhead: From exit 154 on Interstate 69 near Angola, turn left (north) on Indiana 127 and go about 100 yards to its intersection with Indiana 727. Turn left (west) and pass underneath I-69, and follow Indiana 727 about 1 mile to the park gatehouse. Follow park signs to the nature center. The trail begins behind the nature center on a paved path.

Key points:
- 0.0   Trailhead at the nature center.
- 1.3   Reach the Apple Orchard Picnic Area.
- 1.8   Pass the campground gatehouse.
- 5.0   Reach the Spring Shelter.
- 5.8   Climb to Hell's Point.
- 7.0   Visit Lake Lonidaw.

The hike: Pokagon State Park may be one of the smallest state parks in Indiana at 1,203 acres, but it is also one of the most popular. More than one million annual visitors come to partake of its various attractions—hiking trails, camping, horseback riding, cross-country skiing, an 1,800-foot refrigerated toboggan slide, the Potawatomi Inn and cabins, and one of the largest natural lakes in the state—Lake James.

The park is named for Simon Pokagon, a Notre Dame–educated Potawatomi Indian chief who sold about 1 million acres of land to the U.S. government for three cents an acre, including a deed to the site of present-day Chicago. Pokagon State Park was established in 1925, and several of its buildings were constructed by the Civilian Conservation Corps in the 1930s and 1940s. The park owes its geographic legacy to the ice age, which left in its tracks piles of rocky debris known as glacial till, and the many lakes that dot the Steuben County landscape. Two of the most noticeable ice age remnants in the park are Hell's Point, located in the park's northeast corner, and Lake Lonidaw, named for Simon Pokagon's wife.

The hike described visits both locations and covers all or part of Trails 1, 2, 3, 4, 5, and 6, plus an optional 2-mile loop on Trail 7. The park trails are heavily used and, thus, easy to follow. Some segments of the trail—around the nature center, campgrounds, and Lake Lonidaw—can be busy, but other areas can seem remote. Major holiday weekends are the busiest.

To begin the hike, walk around to the back side of the nature center and down a paved path that joins a dirt trail marked Trail 1. Turn right and hike south and then north as the trail runs parallel to privately owned cottages that line Lone Tree Point on Lake James.

Just beyond the 0.5-mile mark, hike uphill into a clearing that at one time was a fenced pen for bison and elk, which no longer exist in the wild in Indiana. Various trails converge on Trail 1 as it continues north to the Apple Orchard Picnic Area; ignore these and remain on Trail 1.

You will reach the picnic area at 1.3 miles. Cut northeast diagonally across the picnic area to a path that leads downhill to a bridge passing over the main park road. Go under the bridge to find a bridle trail that parallels the paved road leading to the park campground area. Continue north, pass the

Someone made the most of this tree stump at Pokagon State Park.

campground gatehouse at 1.8 miles, and walk about 50 yards to Trail 4. Turn left (west) on Trail 4, cross the campground road, and climb a short set of wooden steps. Walk northwest on the trail, crossing a path that connects the group camp to the park's general store. Trail 4 heads downhill and twice connects with other paths. Stay to the right each time and connect with Trail 5 near the shore of Lake James. Turn right (north). The fenced plot of ground here is a deer enclosure, used to study the deer's impact on park vegetation. Trail 5 heads uphill, crosses a paved road, and passes along the east edge of a string of small cabins that are the group camp. Trail 5 ends at the paved road leading to Campground 1.

Cross the road and pick up Trail 2 on a gravel road that passes the park's water treatment plant and swings out to a point overlooking Snow Lake, one of a handful of smaller lakes in the James chain of lakes. When Trail 2 turns south away from Snow Lake, you are about 3 miles into the hike. Continue along Trail 2 as it slips behind the tent camp area. At 5 miles, you reach the Spring Shelter, a small shelter next to a natural spring that produces drinkable water. The water is checked for purity each week by park personnel.

Southeast of the shelter, Trail 2 forks; take the left fork, which leads to Trail 3. Turn left (northeast) on Trail 3 and walk about 0.25 mile to the intersection with Trail 7. Also known as the Blue Bird Trail, Trail 7 leads to a large meadow and wetland area in the north side of the park. Turn left (northwest) to take the optional loop on Trail 7, or continue straight (east) on Trail 3 for another 0.25 mile to Hell's Point, the highest point in the park and the third-highest point in the county (5.8 miles). A wooden staircase of 83 steps makes the climb easier, plus cuts down on erosion of the hill, a glacial deposit of stone known as a kame. The elevation change from the top of Hell's Point to the shore of Lake James is 135 feet.

From Hell's Point, hike south as Trail 3 descends into a series of small marshes and streams that dot the eastern area of the park. Cross Indiana 727, the entry road to the park, and walk less than 0.25 mile to the intersection with Trail 6. Turn left (east), and take Trail 6 as it skirts the park border for 1 mile before rejoining Trail 3. Turn left (west) on Trail 3 as the trail enters the Potawatomi Nature Preserve, a 208-acre preserve featuring cattail marshes, sedge meadows, and a tamarack-black ash swamp. The high glacial ridges that surround this area feature stands of red and white oak, shagbark hickory, and sugar maple trees. Lake Lonidaw, at 7 miles, is a deep, glacier-formed kettle lake that is another feature of the preserve. From Lake Lonidaw, walk southwest and then west to the main park road. Turn left (south) and walk along the road past Potawatomi Inn to a parking lot entrance with a boat rental sign. Turn left (south) and cross the parking lot to a bridge across the toboggan slide. Cross the bridge to a set of cabins. Walk between cabins 64 and 65, cross the parking lot, and pick up Trail 1 behind the parking space for cabin 73. Turn right (southwest) and follow Trail 1 for a little more than 0.25 mile along the shore of Lake James to the paved path that leads back to the nature center.

13   Trillium Woods Trail at Wing Haven Reserve

Type of hike:	Day hike, loop.
General description:	A short stroll through upland and lowland woods to a secluded lake, then back through a quiet ravine along a stream.
General location:	On the north outskirts of Angola in northeast Indiana.
Total distance:	0.9 mile.
Difficulty:	Easy.
Elevation gain:	20 to 30 feet.
Jurisdiction:	ACRES, Inc.
Special attractions:	Little Gentian Lake, one of seven small lakes in the Seven Sisters chain, a log cabin, and the possibility of seeing sandhill cranes.
Maps:	Angola East USGS quad; Wing Haven Reserve information sheet.
Permits/fees:	None required.
Camping:	None allowed.
Trailhead facilities:	There is a parking area at the trailhead, but nothing else. No potable water source is available.

Finding the trailhead: Take exit 154 from Interstate 69 near Angola to Indiana 127, and turn right (south) toward Angola. At the first road, Steuben County 400 North, turn left (east). Drive about a quarter of a mile to the parking lot on the left (north) side of the road.

Key points:
   0.0   Trailhead.
   0.5   Reach Little Gentian Lake.
   0.6   Pass the Wing Haven log cabin.
   0.8   Leave the ravine.

The hike: Wing Haven Reserve is a 160-acre holding of the ACRES Land Trust, a private preservation group that received the land as a gift from the estate of Helen Swenson. The property is about half the size of the original Wing Haven Resort, opened in 1950 by Swenson and her husband, Ben. The resort closed in 1970, after which part of the property was sold and is now a conference and retreat center.

There are three short trails at Wing Haven, including the Trillium Woods Trail described here. The trail is well-maintained and well-marked.

Begin the hike at the east end of the parking lot near a kiosk that displays information about Wing Haven and ACRES. The trail skirts the eastern edge of the meadows as it curls northward. At 0.1 mile, the trail splits, with the left fork continuing along the meadow's edge and the right fork slipping into the woods. Either option will do, since they rejoin after a very short distance, after which the trail crosses a footbridge and heads north and

Trillium Woods Trail at Wing Haven Reserve

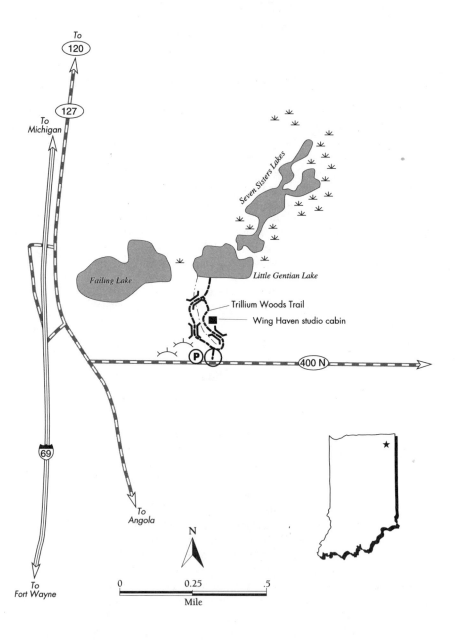

uphill into an upland woods featuring a blend of oak and hickory trees.

At 0.3 mile, Little Gentian Lake becomes visible as the trail curves right and drops downhill to cross another footbridge at 0.4 mile. Just past the footbridge, come to a T intersection. Take a left (north) turn and walk less than 0.1 mile to an observation pier on Little Gentian Lake at 0.5 mile. It is worth a moment to pause here and soak up the solitude. Fishing is prohibited. Canada geese and other waterfowl frequent the tiny lake, which is part of the Seven Sisters chain. Also, in recent years, sandhill cranes have begun to nest in the area—the first time this has happened in Indiana since 1929.

From the lake, head south to the T intersection, and continue uphill to the rustic log cabin that Helen Swenson used as an art studio. Today it serves as a gathering place for ACRES meetings and as a visitor center during open houses held the first Sunday of each month. Reach the cabin at 0.6 mile and walk to the right (west) side to locate the trail as it descends into a ravine. Crisscross the stream four times on footbridges before coming to a stairway out of the ravine at 0.8 mile. Turn left (south) upon reentering the meadow to return to the parking lot.

Wabash Valley

"Oh, the moonlight's fair tonight along the Wabash,
From the fields there comes the breath of new-mown hay;
Through the sycamores the candle lights are gleaming,
On the banks of the Wabash far away."

With these lines, Paul Dresser celebrated the Wabash River in his 1913 song, "On the Banks of the Wabash," which was named the official state song the same year. The river, on the other hand, has endured years of neglect. That changed in 1996, when Indiana's General Assembly declared the Wabash the "official state river," a deserving title for a variety of reasons.

From its origin just over the Ohio border, the Wabash cuts a swath across north-central Indiana to its western border, and then flows south past Terre Haute and Vincennes to where it merges with the Ohio River. The third-longest tributary of the Ohio River, the Wabash covers 475 miles from start to finish. The Wabash watershed drains nearly two-thirds of the state and forms almost 200 miles of the border with neighboring Illinois.

The river has played an integral role in Indiana history. Long before the French and the British arrived, Native Americans were drawn to the fertile river valley, which was home to bountiful wild game, including buffalo and deer. The Miami, Shawnee, Wea, Piankashaw, Kickapoo, Pepikokia, and Osage all established villages along the Wabash. They were not the first. Archaeological evidence indicates Native Americans lived along the Wabash as far back as 10,000 years ago.

The name given to the river by local indigenous peoples, Wah-bah-shik-a, means "water flowing over white stones." The French, who had arrived as fur traders by 1700, altered the river's name, calling it Ouabache. Later on, pioneer settlers kept the French pronunciation but changed the spelling to Wabash.

Because the river provided an obvious transportation route, the French established trading posts and military forts at Kekionga (now Fort Wayne), Ouiatenon (near Lafayette), and Sackville (near Vincennes). Replicas of those forts remain today as historic sites where the past is celebrated. One of the biggest annual events is the Feast of the Hunter's Moon at Fort Ouiatenon, held each October, which re-creates an eighteenth-century gathering of French and Native Americans.

Over time, more than two dozen towns were located along the Wabash, including Harmonie near the southern terminus. Harmonie was established in 1814 as a religious commune.

About the same time, state leaders embarked on their own dream—a statewide network of canals for transporting farm goods as well as people. It was several decades before work actually began in 1832 in Fort Wayne, and it took just over 30 years to finish. Areas that were completed flourished, but soon after the Wabash & Erie Canal was finished, it was rendered obsolete by the development of railroads.

The river has not always been a friendly neighbor. Massive floods have wreaked havoc on river towns, but flooding is minimized today by three dams. One dam forms Roush Lake (formerly Huntington Lake), and the others are on tributaries of the Wabash—the Mississinewa and Salamonie rivers.

Damaged by agricultural and industrial runoff, the Wabash River has become a focal point of a different sort in recent years. The Wabash River Heritage Commission is a coalition of groups working to develop recreational opportunities along the river, including hiking trails.

Also in the developmental stages is Prophetstown State Park, featuring the Museums at Prophetstown. The 300-acre museum site within the park will include a 1920s-era farm, Native American living history villages, and the Woodland Native American Cultural Center. Part of the museum is scheduled to open in the summer of 2000, and the park is on track to open within the next few years.

Trails in this section are presented from Fox Island Park near Fort Wayne, south to the Ouabache Trail near Bluffton, then west to the Portland Arch Nature Preserve near Lafayette.

14 Fox Island Park

Type of hike:	Day hike, loop.
General description:	Loop trail along wooded dune to marsh overlook and back.
General location:	Southwest side of Fort Wayne.
Total distance:	3.4 miles.
Difficulty:	Easy.
Elevation gain:	A minor elevation increase at the upper dune.
Jurisdiction:	Allen County Parks & Recreation Department.
Special attractions:	A bog and marsh.
Maps:	Fort Wayne West USGS quad; Fox Island Park trail sheet.
Permits/fees:	There is a gate entry fee of $2 per vehicle, and a $3 fee to hunt mushrooms.
Camping:	None permitted.
Trailhead facilities:	There is a nature center that has a restroom and drinking fountains.

Finding the trailhead: Go 0.4 mile west from Interstate 69 on U.S. Highway 24 to the third stoplight and turn left (south) on Ellison Road, following the directional signs pointing to Fox Island Park and the state police post. Follow Ellison Road for 1.9 miles as it parallels I-69, crosses over the interstate, and becomes Yohne Road. Go another 0.8 mile to the park entrance and turn left (north). From the gatehouse, turn right (east) to the nature center parking lot.

Fox Island Park

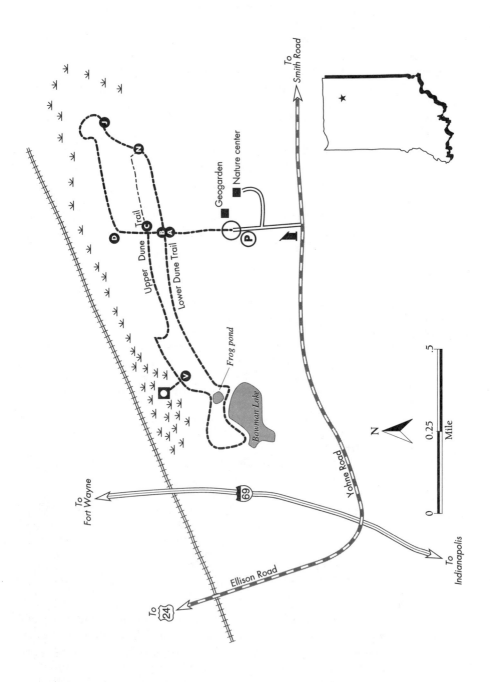

Key points:

- 0.0 Trailhead.
- 0.1 Turn right (north) at the geogarden.
- 0.3 Turn right (east) at the Lower Dune crossroads and post B.
- 0.6 Reach the post N intersection and go straight (north) past posts O and K.
- 0.7 Go right at post J to the bog.
- 1.2 Go left at post D.
- 1.3 Go right at post C.
- 1.6 Go right at post W.
- 1.8 Go right to marsh observation deck at post V.
- 2.1 Reach post U; go straight to post S and turn right.
- 2.7 Turn left to post S, then turn right past the frog pond.
- 3.1 Go right at post A.
- 3.3 Return to the geogarden; go straight and then left to the nature center.

The hike: When the Wisconsin glacier began its retreat more than 10,000 years ago, wind shaped a sand dune rising 40 feet high in the heart of a sluice that carried away glacial meltwaters. That dune is at the heart of Fox Island Park, a 600-acre county park that today is the largest continuous woodland in Allen County.

Almost half the park is protected as a state nature preserve. A marsh, wetlands, meadows, a peat bog, and the surrounding dune forest create varied habitat for wildlife and an abundance of wild plants. Nearly 200 species of birds have been seen at Fox Island. The forest features black oak trees along the upper dune; white oak, walnut, and black cherry trees along the dune slopes; and cottonwood, sycamore, and willow trees in the bottomland near the marshes and bogs. Fox Island has well-groomed and well-marked trails, which get a lot of use during the summer season.

Morel mushrooms are a coveted prize in springtime.

Go west from the nature center for a little more than 0.1 mile on a crushed stone pathway, past a bird observation building, and turn right (east) to the park's geogarden and a picnic shelter. The rock garden was made using granite, basalt, gneiss, and quartzite samples found in the park or donated by nearby stone companies. Most of the rocks on display were formed 1 to 3 billion years ago during the Precambrian Era, and carried here by glaciers.

From the geogarden, walk north along the wide pathway that leads to the dune trail. Know the alphabet for this hike because all trail junctures are marked by letters. Pass the A signpost on the left (west), and the nature preserve sign on the right (east) to reach post B at 0.3 mile. Turn right (east), following the Lower Dune Trail for about a quarter of a mile before turning left (north) and climbing to post N at the top of the dune. Go straight (north) and downhill, passing post O, post K, and post J—all less than 0.1 mile apart.

At post J at 0.7 mile, turn right (northeast) to make a short loop down to the peat bog, and continue counterclockwise to posts H and G. Turn right (west) at post G to hike through a forest of walnut and oak trees, passing posts E and F to reach post D at 1.2 miles. Turn left (south), walk back up the dune to post C at 1.3 miles, then turn right (west) to walk the Upper Dune Trail as it gradually slopes downhill toward the marsh in the northwest corner of the park. Pass post X at 1.4 miles, and continue to post W at 1.6 miles. Turn right, looping counterclockwise for a little less than 0.25 mile to post V. Turn right (north) to a long pier and an observation deck at the marsh at 1.8 miles, an excellent place for bird watching. Retrace your steps to post V and turn right (south), crossing a boardwalk and passing post U. At 2.1 miles, turn right at post S to make a 0.5-mile counterclockwise loop that leads past Bowan Lake.

Return to post S. Go past a frog pond to post R at 2.7 miles and continue straight, passing posts Q and P. Pick up the return leg of the Lower Dune Trail, which leads to post A at 3.1 miles. Turn right and follow the main trail back to the geogarden at 3.3 miles and the nature center at 3.4 miles.

15 Oubache State Park

Type of hike:	Day hike, loop.
General description:	A combination of park trails forming a perimeter loop through reforested sections in various stages of regrowth.
General location:	East of Bluffton in northeast Indiana.
Total distance:	6 miles.
Difficulty:	Easy.
Elevation gain:	Minimal.
Jurisdiction:	Indiana Department of Natural Resources, Division of State Parks & Reservoirs.

Special attractions:	A small herd of bison kept in a 20-acre pen.
Maps:	Linn Grove USGS quad; Ouabache State Park brochure.
Permits/fees:	There is a $2 park entry fee for vehicles with Indiana license plates; $5 for out-of-state vehicles. Season passes are available.
Camping:	Ouabache State Park has 124 campsites modern to primitive.
Trailhead facilities:	A gravel parking lot on the south edge of Kunkle Lake will accommodate two dozen vehicles. Although there is no potable water at the trailhead, there are water fountains around Kunkle Lake and near the swimming pool at the midway point of the hike.

Finding the trailhead: From Indiana 1 in Bluffton, go east 2 miles on Indiana 124 to the junction with Indiana 201. Turn right (south) on Indiana 201, and drive a little more than 0.5 mile to a four-way stop. Indiana 201 turns left (southeast) and goes directly into Ouabache State Park. It is 0.8 mile from the park gatehouse to a parking lot on the south edge of Kunkle Lake. Facing the lake levee, the trail begins on the right (east) side of the parking lot.

Key points:

- 0.0 Trailhead.
- 0.3 Cross the main park road.
- 0.8 Cross the youth camp road.
- 1.3 At the Trail 5/Trail 3 juncture, go right (east).
- 1.8 At the Trail 5/Trail 3/Trail 2 juncture, go right (north) on Trails 5 and 2.
- 2.4 At the Trail 2/5 juncture, go right (north) on Trail 5.
- 3.1 Trail 5 meets Trails 1 and 4. Go straight (south) around bison pen.
- 3.8 At the Trail 5/4/1 juncture, go left on Trails 5 and 4.
- 4.2 Trails 5 and 4 split; go straight on Trail 5.
- 5.5 At the junction of Trails 5 and 4, go straight.

The hike: The area around Ouabache State Park was once the home of Miami Indians, whose villages flanked the banks of the nearby Wabash River. Ouabache is the French Jesuit spelling of the Miami pronunciation of Wabash, but most people today mispronounce it "Oh-BA-chee."

The present property was acquired by the state in the 1930s and established as the Wells County State Forest and Game Preserve. The area had been stripped of its mature timber and was heavily eroded, but the Civilian Conservation Corps (CCC) and the Works Progress Administration (WPA) reforested the area. Other projects included construction of buildings and development of a game preserve. It was considered the "greatest wildlife laboratory in the United States," in which pheasant, quail, rabbits, and raccoons were raised for release elsewhere in the state.

The state phased out the game-raising program in the early 1960s and eventually converted the property to a state park. Remnants of the game pens can still be seen along some portions of the trail. Another key attraction is a 20-acre wildlife exhibit pen near the midway point of the trail. The

Ouabache State Park

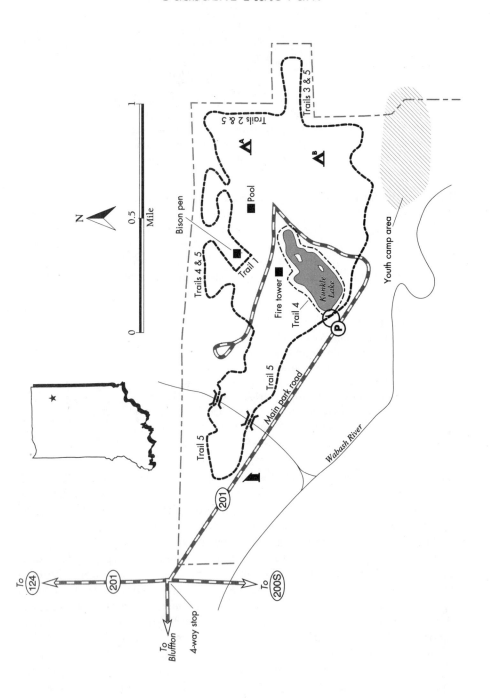

pen is home to American bison, an animal that roamed freely across Indiana years ago.

From the Kunkle Lake parking lot, pick up Trail 5 at the east edge of the lot and walk east. The flatness of the trail that greets the hiker does not change much over the next 6 miles, but the trail surface does—sometimes it is gravel, sometimes crushed stone, sometimes grass, and sometimes just dirt.

Almost immediately, you will come to the first of several footbridges, but most are not as elaborate as this one. In the first 0.5 mile, there are three spur trails that join the main trail from the left (north). Disregard them and keep to the right. At 0.3 mile, cross the main park road and pick up Trail 5 on the other side. At 0.5 mile, the trail passes an area where some of the old game-farm pens were located; look to the right of the trail for wooden posts about 7 feet tall with short boards angled at the top.

At 0.8 mile, the trail crosses another paved road, which leads to the youth camping area. At 1 mile, the trail turns north and squeezes between Campground B and the east boundary of the park.

At 1.3 miles, Trail 5 takes a right (east) turn and merges with Trail 3 as both trails swing out and back through a stand of mature hardwood trees. At 1.8 miles, the trail turns right (north) as it reaches another intersection—Trail 5 drops Trail 3 and picks up Trail 2. Trails 5 and 2 continue due north along the park boundary to the northeast corner of the park; take a left (west) turn.

At 2.4 miles, the trail reaches an open field just north of the park swimming pool. At this point, Trail 2 turns left. Trail 5 continues on with two

One of the bison on exhibit at Ouabache State Park. The small herd is a popular drawing card at the park.

options—go straight and take more than 0.5 mile off the hike, or turn right (north) as the trail takes a wide sweep through the open field along a wide, grass pathway. This is another place to look for concrete or metal remnants of the former game-rearing operation. The open field is also a good area to spot white-tailed deer if you are on an early morning hike.

The outer loop will pass the 3-mile mark before connecting with the shortcut trail again. At 3.1 miles, Trail 5 hooks up with Trails 1 and 4 at the wildlife exhibit pen, home to about a half-dozen American bison. Trail 1 makes a 0.75-mile circle of the pen, providing an opportunity to track down the bison.

Trails 5 and 4 continue from the northwest corner of the bison pen, heading west on a winding course through periodic stands of pine trees. Near the 4-mile mark, the trail crosses a paved road that was the entry road into the park until 1995.

At 4.2 miles, Trail 4 breaks off to the left (south) as Trail 5 continues toward the west boundary of the park. The trail crosses a creek at 4.5 miles, swings left (southeast) to parallel the main road as it passes the gatehouse, crosses the creek again, and continues toward the parking lot. At 5.5 miles, Trail 5 links again with Trail 4; Trail 4 then breaks off to the left (north) near the parking lot, and makes a 1-mile loop around Kunkle Lake.

16 Kekionga Trail

Type of hike:	Day hike, loop.
General description:	A loop trail around J. Edward Roush Lake, a flood-control reservoir on the Wabash River.
General location:	3 miles south of Huntington in northeast Indiana.
Total distance:	11 miles.
Difficulty:	Moderate.
Elevation gain:	No more than 50 feet from the trailhead to the bottom of some ravines.
Jurisdiction:	Indiana Department of Natural Resources, Division of Parks & Reservoirs.
Special attractions:	Ravines, Tah-Kum-Wah Creek, and scenic views of Roush Lake.
Maps:	Majenica USGS quad; Huntington Reservoir bike trail pamphlet.
Permits/fees:	None required.
Camping:	There are 130 sites at two campgrounds at the lake, plus a youth tent area.
Trailhead facilities:	There are restrooms, a water fountain, and a picnic shelter.

Finding the trailhead: From Interstate 69, take exit 86 and go west on

U.S. Highway 224 for 5.7 miles to the intersection of US 224 and Indiana 5. Turn left (south) on Indiana 5 and go about 1 mile to the Observation Mound picnic area on the left. The trailhead sign is about 100 yards east of the picnic shelter.

Key points:
- 0.0   Trailhead.
- 1.1   Pass the Little Turtle State Recreation Area entrance.
- 2.5   Reach the model airplane airport.
- 5.2   Cross Division Road.
- 6.0   Arrive at Huntington County 200 East and the New Hope Cemetery.
- 7.6   Turn right at the juncture with the exercise trail.
- 9.0   Cross the Kilsoquah Campground road.
- 10.0   Cross the boat ramp road.

The hike: After opening in 1970 as Huntington Reservoir, the lake has since been renamed in honor of former U.S. Congressman J. Edward Roush, who served the northeast Indiana district. The earthen dam was built as a U.S. Army Corps of Engineers flood-control project on the Wabash River. It is smaller than two other flood-control projects in the Upper Wabash Valley, but the 870-acre lake and surrounding 7,400-acre property provide a variety of recreational opportunities.

The Kekionga Trail initially was established for hikers, but mountain bikers were granted access in 1995. Hikers still have the right of way on the trail, but be alert for these faster trail users. An additional trailhead for bikers is located in the Little Turtle State Recreation Area. Disregard mile-

Trail sign and overlook of Roush Lake.

age posted on trail markers because it is measured from the bike trailhead. High water can block sections of this trail, so check for conditions at the reservoir office. The trail is well-marked, although it can be confusing at the trail juncture near Kilsoquah Campground. Remember to stay right (northwest). Traffic is heaviest near the Kilsoquah and Little Turtle camgrounds.

From the Observation Mound parking lot, walk back to Indiana 5, turn left (south), and hike along the left side of the road to cross over the dam. It is not very scenic (except for the view of the lake from the dam), and it requires caution because of vehicular traffic, but the 1.1-mile trail section along the road provides a good warm-up for the rest of the hike.

At the Little Turtle State Recreation Area entry road, turn left (east) and follow the orange trail markers that veer southeast away from the road to a wooded ravine. Continue to skirt the edge of the ravine as the trail alternates between wooded areas and open fields for the next mile. Reach the model airplane field at 2.5 miles. Cut across the gravel road and walk along the left (north) side of a fence row that bisects two farm fields. Locate a trail marker at the east end of the fields and turn left (north).

Go about 0.5 mile before turning right and crossing a deep gully. Near the 3-mile mark, pass a marker that points left. Cross another gully before coming to a paved road that leads to the Little Turtle boat ramp.

The trail resumes across the road, turning left at 3.2 miles and descending into a broad ravine that crosses a creek at 3.5 miles. Here you can catch a glimpse of Roush Lake to the left. Head uphill out of the ravine to an old roadbed. Turn left and continue to switch between gullies, open fields, and woods over the next mile. Several old Boy Scout trail markers can be seen along the way.

After crossing the north end of an open field, turn right (south) at 4.4 miles and follow an old road back into a stand of older trees. The trail leaves the roadbed and turns left to take a winding course along a couple of ravines before exiting the woods onto Division Road at 5.2 miles. (Again, disregard the mileage on the trail marker.)

Cross to the south side of the gravel road and locate an orange trail sign, then turn left to hike through an old field. Pine trees form a barrier between the field and the road to the left (north). Come to a gravel road at the east end of the field and take the road right (south) as it passes a pond and descends into a wide ravine. Climb up the other side of the ravine to paved Huntington County 200 East at 6 miles. New Hope Cemetery is to the right.

Turn left (north) and cross the bridge that essentially is the barrier between the lake and the Wabash River. It is also the halfway point of the hike. Walk on the left side of the road for a little more than 0.5 mile before turning left to begin the westbound leg of the hike. Drop into another broad ravine before hiking back uphill and into the woods.

At 7.2 miles, come to a large pond and stay to the left. The trail takes a winding course before reaching a footbridge at 7.6 miles. Just beyond the footbridge is a trail juncture with the exercise trail. Turn right (northwest), and follow the trail marked for bikers to avoid having to walk

Kekionga Trail

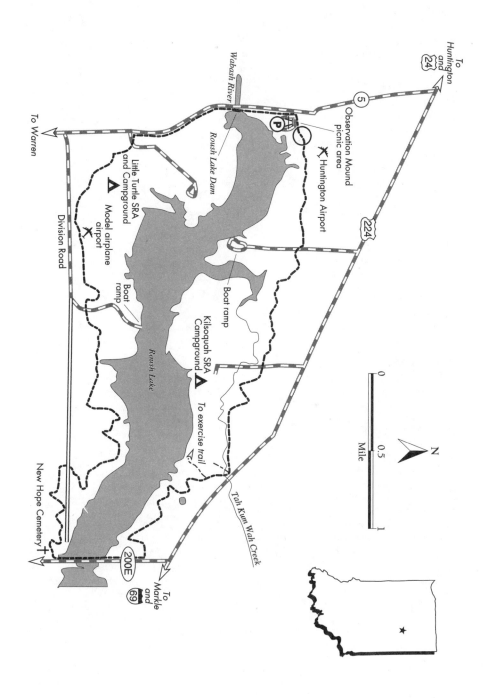

A ravine shows its greenery along the north shore of Roush Lake.

through the Kilsoquah Campground.

At about 8 miles, you come to Tah-Kum-Wah Creek, which enters the reservoir property from the northeast. Turn left (west) and follow the creek for about 0.5 mile before passing through another ravine.

Just past the 9-mile mark, cross the paved road that leads to the Kilsoquah Campground and turn right (north). Walk along the road a short distance and turn left (west) at the trail sign marked 8. Cross two more ravines before entering a prairie grass restoration project that was begun in 1992. The area straddles a north-south paved road leading to a boat ramp.

Cross the road to resume the hike, with less than 1 mile remaining. Over the next 0.25 mile, you can catch glimpses of the lake to the left (south) and the Huntington Municipal Airport to the right (north). Walk down the steepest drop of the hike—about a 50-foot descent into and out of a ravine. There is one final ravine to cross over the last 0.25 mile before you end up at the Observation Mound Trailhead.

17 Lakeview and Boundary Trails at Salamonie Reservoir

Type of hike: Day hike, loop.
General description: A loop hike of two trails that leads through meadows, over ravines, and along bluffs overlooking Salamonie Reservoir.
General location: South of Huntington in Huntington County.
Total distance: 9 miles.
Difficulty: Easy to moderate.
Elevation gain: Minimal.
Jurisdiction: Indiana Department of Natural Resources, Division of State Parks & Reservoirs.
Special attractions: The bluffs at Salamonie Reservoir.
Maps: Andrews and Mount Etna USGS quads; Salamonie Reservoir brochures.
Permits/fees: None required.
Camping: There are 246 modern campsites at the Lost Bridge West State Recreation Area, plus 242 primitive sites at Lost Bridge West, Lost Bridge East, Mount Etna, and Apple Orchard state recreation areas.
Trailhead facilities: Although restrooms and water fountains are available at both ends of the loop, Lost Bridge East offers the most conveniences.

Finding the trailhead: Go 9 miles south on Indiana 9 from its intersection with U.S. Highway 24 near Huntington. Turn right (west) on Indiana 124 and go 2.5 miles to Indiana 105. Turn right (north) on Indiana 105 and go 1.8 miles to Huntington County 400 South. Turn right (east) and go 1.2 miles to

Lakeview and Boundary Trails at Salamonie Reservoir

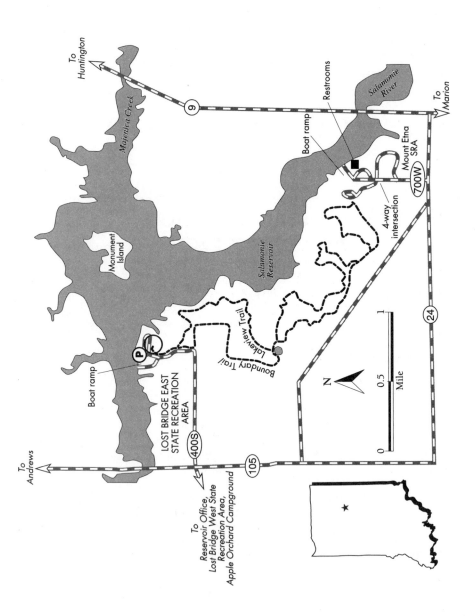

the Lost Bridge East parking area, which is above the boat ramp. The trail begins off the southwest corner of the brick restroom building.

An alternate trailhead is at Mount Etna State Recreation Area. From its intersection with Indiana 9, go west on Indiana 124 for about 0.4 mile and turn right (north) on Huntington County 700 West. Go 0.4 mile to a crossroad and turn left (west) to a small parking lot. The trailhead sign is off the west side of the parking lot.

Key points:
   0.0   Trailhead.
   0.4   Go right at the Lakeview and Boundary trails sign.
   1.6   Trails join near the pond; go right.
   3.0   The trails join again; go right.
   3.5   Reach the turnaround at the Lakeview and Boundary trails east sign, and go right.
   8.0   Reach the Monument Island vista.
   8.6   Reach the Lakeview and Boundary trails sign at the trails' west end.

The hike: Both the Lakeview and Boundary trails are part of the larger 22-mile Salamonie Snowmobile Trail, but they are also designated for hikers. The trails form a loop along the south side of the reservoir, a flood-control impoundment of the U.S. Army Corps of Engineers. The surrounding land, however, is managed by the Indiana Department of Natural Resources (DNR). The reservoir extends 17 miles during summer months.

Although DNR brochures and signs list the Lakeview and Boundary trails as a 12-mile hike, the loop is closer to 9 miles. Though both are easy trails to follow, they sometimes look as if they need attention. Grass sometimes grows knee-high in the meadow segments along the Boundary leg, while footbridges are susceptible to stormwater damage. Neither are impassable, however. With only modest use, the trail provides ample opportunity to see wildlife. State-regulated hunting is permitted in some areas of the trail corridor.

Begin the hike on a mowed pathway leading back along the entry road. In a small gravel parking lot at 0.4 mile, a wooden sign marks the starting point of the two trails—Boundary to the right (south) and Lakeview to the left (north). Opt for the Boundary Trail, leaving the most scenic spots for the return hike, not to mention the more shaded path.

The Boundary leg lives up to its name by skirting the edge of a patchwork of meadows and farm fields, occasionally slipping into the woods. At 1.6 miles, the two trails link for a short distance while passing a large pond. As the trail splits again, the Boundary leg is marked by twin yellow arrows and two white arrows pointing to the right (south).

Zigzag along meadow boundaries for another 0.5 mile before crossing a gully. At 2.7 miles, cross another gully, and at 3 miles reach the second spot where the two trails join. Continue straight, dipping into another gully, before reaching the trail turnaround at the Mount Etna State Recreation Area at 3.5 miles. The spot is marked by a sign matching the one at the west end of the trails.

Follow the paved road to the right (south) to reach the Mount Etna State Recreation Area facilities, which include a water supply, restrooms, and a primitive campground. Go 0.2 mile on the road to a four-way intersection and turn left (north). Go 0.1 mile and turn right (east) to reach the facilities.

Back at the Boundary and Lakeview trails sign, go right (northwest). You will immediately find that the Lakeview Trail also lives up to its name. At 0.1 mile from the eastern trailhead, the lake comes into view for the first time. The trail scallops the edge of several gullies over the next 4 miles, crossing footbridges at the high ends of the gullies and occasionally offering glimpses of the lake. The best views come near the 8-mile mark, where Monument Island can be seen. The island marks the previous location of Monument City, most of which is now under water. A monument to 27 men from Polk Township who died in the Civil War, and the town cemetery, were moved 1 mile north when the reservoir was built.

Go another 0.5 mile before crossing the last footbridge. Go uphill through a stand of young trees to the west-end trail sign at 8.6 miles. Turn right (north), and return to the parking lot.

18 Switchgrass Marsh and Tree Trails at Salamonie Reservoir

Type of hike:	Day hike, loop.
General description:	A double-loop trail, first through a marsh meadow, then a forest, and then back to the marsh meadow.
General location:	Salamonie Reservoir, southwest of Huntington.
Total distance:	2.5 miles.
Difficulty:	Easy to moderate.
Elevation gain:	Mostly level, except for a 40-foot ravine on Tree Trail.
Jurisdiction:	Indiana Department of Natural Resources, Division of State Parks & Reservoirs.
Special attractions:	The viewing area at Switchgrass Marsh, and identifying markers for about 50 native Indiana trees.
Maps:	Lagro USGS quad; Salamonie Reservoir trail pamphlets.
Permits/fees:	None if parking at the visitor center. There is a $2 entry fee to the Lost Bridge West State Recreation Area for vehicles with Indiana license plates; $5 for out-of-state vehicles. Season passes are available.
Camping:	There are 246 modern campsites at the Lost Bridge West State Recreation Area, plus 242 primitive sites at Lost Bridge West, Lost Bridge East, Mount Etna, and Apple Orchard state recreation areas.

Switchgrass Marsh and Tree Trails at Salamonie Reservoir

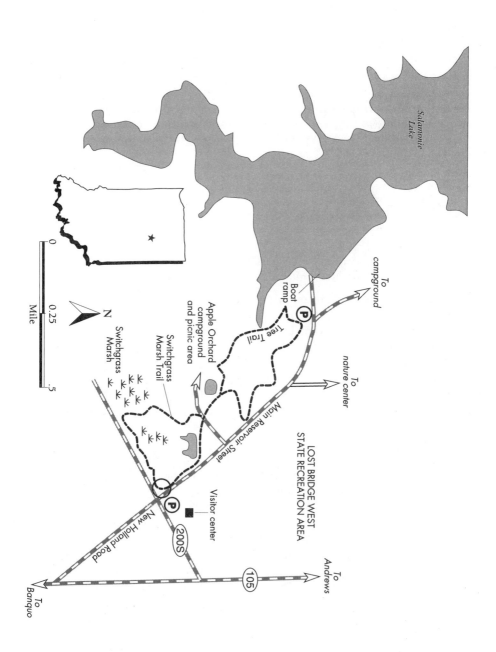

Trailhead facilities: The Lost Bridge West State Recreation Area visitor center has restrooms and water fountains. It is open 8 A.M. to 4 P.M. daily from Easter weekend through the weekend before Thanksgiving, and weekdays through the winter. Besides the visitor center, there are water sources in the campground area.

Finding the trailhead: Go south on Indiana 9 from its intersection with U.S. Highway 24 southwest of Huntington. Take Indiana 9 for about 5.5 miles to Huntington County 200 South and turn right (west). Follow CR 200 South for 1 mile, where the county road merges into Indiana 105. Follow Indiana 105 3.2 miles west and south before turning right (west) at the sign pointing to Lost Bridge State Recreation Area. Go 0.1 mile to the visitor center parking lot. The trailhead, which also marks the beginning of a cross-country ski trail, can be accessed without entering the state recreation area. It is west of the parking lot and across the main road to the state recreation area.

Key points:
- 0.0   Trailhead.
- 0.3   Reach Switchgrass Marsh.
- 0.6   Link to the Tree Trail.
- 0.8   Reach the Tree Trail.
- 2.0   Return to the link to Switchgrass Marsh Trail.
- 2.2   Reach the Switchgrass Marsh Trail.

The hike: In 1961, construction began on Salamonie Reservoir, part of a three-stage U.S. Army Corps of Engineers flood-control project in the Upper Wabash Valley. Salamonie is situated between Roush Lake to the northeast and Mississinewa Reservoir to the southwest. The $17 million earth-fill dam at Salamonie became operational in 1966, and created a lake that at its fullest is 17 miles long.

Three small towns were removed when the lake was built, including Monument City, so-named because of a monument listing the names of 27 men from Polk Township who died during the Civil War. The monument and cemetery were relocated 1 mile north of the lake.

The lake is surrounded by almost 12,000 acres of state-managed recreational land open to hiking, camping, cross-country skiing, horseback riding, hunting, and snowmobiling. There are two longer hikes at Salamonie—the 22-mile Snowmobile Trail, and the Lakeview and Boundary trails, which connect the Lost Bridge East and Mount Etna state recreation areas (Hike 17).

The Switchgrass Marsh and Tree trails are separate, but can be linked together for a 2.5-mile hike through vastly different environments. Switchgrass Marsh Trail is lightly used in spring, summer, and fall, while the Tree Trail gets slightly more traffic. Number markers make the Tree Trail easy to follow, and the Switchgrass Marsh Trail is equally easy to follow because of mowed paths surrounding the marshes.

From the visitor center parking lot, head west across a paved road and walk through a stand of pine trees to a sign marking the trailhead. Continue west along a row of pine trees on the mowed path for 0.3 mile to reach the first marsh pond. Follow the path as it turns right to slip between the pond and a larger pond on the left. A bench for viewing marsh wildlife—including birds—is at 0.4 mile. As the trail circles clockwise to the north side of the marsh pond, turn left to pass through the Apple Orchard primitive campground. Cross the paved road at 0.6 mile, and go northwest on the link path that will connect to the Tree Trail near a small pond at 0.8 mile.

The Tree Trail is easy to follow because of its numbered markers, beginning with post 6 by the pond. Go left (northwest) to walk the Tree Trail in a clockwise direction. Along the way, about 50 trees native to Indiana are identified with small signs. How many can you name without looking at the signs? Can you find shagbark hickory or pignut hickory, flowering dogwood, American hornbeam, slippery elm, honey locust, black walnut, white or burr oak, hackberry, sweetgum or sweet cherry, or osage orange trees?

Walk a little more than 0.25 mile and drop into a ravine. Cross a short metal footbridge and climb up the other side of the ravine, after which the remainder of the hike is on fairly level terrain.

Upon reaching the parking lot for the picnic area, veer right (northeast) to the marked trailhead for the Tree Trail. Follow the path north over a boardwalk as it enters the woods, and pass white ash, white pine, and Virginia pine trees. A water tower is on the left.

Cross four footbridges before coming back to the small pond at post 6 (2 miles). Turn left (southeast) and go 0.2 mile back to the Switchgrass Marsh Trail at 2.2 miles. Turn left (southeast), and proceed the remaining 0.3 mile to the trail's end.

19 Boy Scout Trail

Type of hike:	Day hike, loop.
General description:	A loop trail through ravines and over logging roads with its closing stretch along the Mississinewa River.
General location:	Southeast of Peru.
Total distance:	5 miles.
Difficulty:	Moderate.
Elevation gain:	Several 100-foot climbs.
Jurisdiction:	Indiana Department of Natural Resources, Division of State Parks & Reservoirs.
Special attractions:	Deep ravines, a pine forest, and the Mississinewa River.
Maps:	Peoria USGS quad; Pokagon-Kekionga Trails, Inc. brochure.
Permits/fees:	None.
Camping:	There are 637 sites at two campgrounds: the Frances Slocum State Recreation Area on the north side of the reservoir and the Miami State Recreation Area.

Boy Scout Trail

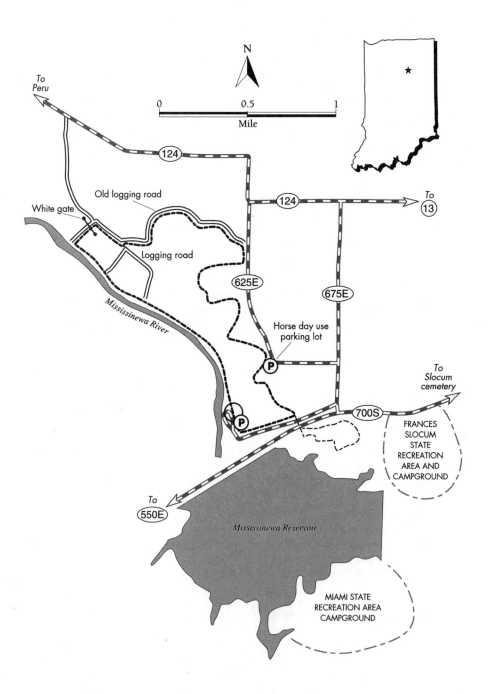

Trailhead facilities: There is a large, paved parking lot; pit toilets; and a public fishing site at the trailhead. There is no water supply at the Peoria Fishing Site, but water can be found nearby at the Observation Pavilion overlooking the dam.

Finding the trailhead: Go 0.2 mile south on Indiana 19 from the courthouse square in downtown Peru, cross a bridge over the Wabash River, and turn left (east) onto Indiana 124. Go about 6 miles to where Indiana 124 makes a 90-degree right turn, and then a left turn. Go another 0.5 mile on Indiana 124 to Miami County 675 East, and turn right (south). Go 1 mile to the turnoff for the Peoria Fishing Site. Turn right (southwest) and go downhill about half a mile before turning right (east) into a parking area. Disregard the trailhead sign and hike in a counterclockwise direction.

Key points:
    0.0   Trailhead.
    0.4   Turn left at the Scout Trail marker.
    0.9   Reach the horse day-use parking lot.
    2.2   Arrive at the old logging road.
    3.1   Turn right at the gravel crossroad.
    3.3   Turn left at the white gate.
    3.5   Reach the Mississinewa River.
    5.0   Return to the parking lot.

The hike: It might seem that the name Frances Slocum is on everything around here—a bank, a cemetery, a road, a state recreation area, and the state forest in which this hike is located.

Frances Slocum was five years old when she was kidnapped by Delaware Indians from her Quaker home in Pennsylvania in 1778. The Delaware named her Weletawash and raised her to adulthood, later changing her name to Maconaquah, meaning Little Bear Woman. She married the war chief Shepconnah, and lived among the Indians until she was found in 1837 by her brother, Isaac, who was able to identify her by a scar on her left hand. Once it was revealed that she was a white woman, Frances Slocum lost her claim to government payments to Indians proscribed in the Treaty of 1826, but John Quincy Adams took her case to Congress. Slocum and her family were allowed to remain in Indiana, and two daughters were granted almost 650 acres of land, including the original homesite. A memorial marks the homesite, which is adjacent to the Slocum cemetery, 4.3 miles east of the Boy Scout Trailhead on Mississinewa Road. Frances Slocum died in 1847, and is buried about 8 miles from the dam on the Mississinewa River.

The Boy Scout Trail that passes through Frances Slocum State Forest is no longer maintained by the Indiana Department of Natural Resources, but it is still a good hike. About one third of the hike is on old logging roads, another third is along the Mississinewa River, and the Boy Scouts of America recently marked the trail with yellow blazes, so it is easy to follow. Although some sections are marked for foot traffic only, horseback riders make regular use of some sections, so the path is relatively clear of debris. Still, the trail is scenic and remote from beginning to end. The trail can be hiked either direction from the parking lot, but the yellow blazes are placed only for the counterclockwise circuit.

Begin at the parking lot below the dam. Hike back up the paved road for 0.4 mile to a Boy Scout Trail sign on the left (north) side of the road. Although yellow markers indicate the trail continues east, turn left (north) at the trail sign to enter the woods.

The next 2 miles are the most rugged part of the hike, as the trail negotiates waves of ravines and ridges. Parts of this section of the trail lead through hardwood forests, and other parts weave through thick stands of pine. Complete the second ravine-ridge combination at a day-use parking lot for horseback riders at 0.9 mile. Turn left (northwest) to exit the lot, and cross a flat plateau before descending into the third ravine. The trail turns right (northeast) at the bottom of the ravine and works uphill before cutting left (west) to parallel private property.

After dropping into and climbing out of one more ravine, hike along the north side of a field while heading east to the edge of a county road. Turn left (north) at the road and go 0.1 mile to link with the old logging road at 2.2 miles. Follow the road west and downhill for almost 1 mile to a metal gate, and the intersection of another gravel road at 3.1 miles. Turn right (northwest) and go 0.2 mile to a white metal gate on the left (southwest) side of the road at 3.3 miles. Turn left (southwest) and follow the gravel road 0.2 mile to reach the banks of the Mississinewa River at 3.5 miles. Turn left (southeast) for a leisurely finish that passes beneath steep bluffs and deep ravines before reaching the parking lot.

20 Delphi Canal Trails

Type of hike: Day hike, loop.
General description: This is a loop trail, with short spurs at the beginning and end of the hike.
General location: On the outskirts of Delphi in west-central Indiana.
Total distance: 2 miles.
Difficulty: Easy.
Elevation gain: Less than 10 feet except for the Deer Creek Falls overlook.
Jurisdiction: Carroll County Wabash & Erie Canal Association.
Special attractions: Access to a remnant section of the historic Wabash & Erie Canal.
Maps: Delphi USGS quad; Wabash & Erie Canal Association brochure.
Permits/fees: None.
Camping: None.
Trailhead facilities: There are restrooms, a water pump, and a small shelter house at the trailhead.

Delphi Canal Trails

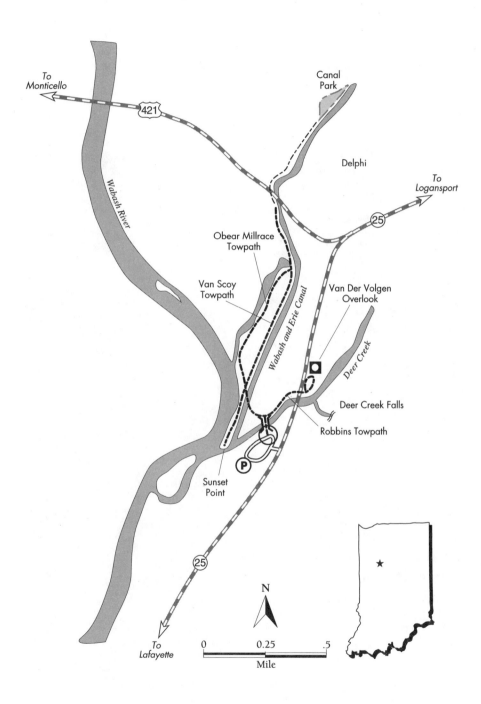

To Monticello

Canal Park

Delphi

421

To Logansport

25

Wabash River

Obear Millrace Towpath

Van Scoy Towpath

Van Der Volgen Overlook

Wabash and Erie Canal

Deer Creek

Deer Creek Falls

Robbins Towpath

P

Sunset Point

25

To Lafayette

N

0   0.25   .5
Mile

Finding the trailhead: Go 1.4 miles southwest from downtown Delphi on Indiana 25.

Key points:
- 0.0   Trailhead.
- 0.2   Reach Sunset Point.
- 0.3   Arrive at the VanScoy Towpath junction.
- 0.4   Reach the Obear Millrace Towpath junction.
- 0.9   Take the VanScoy Towpath return leg.
- 1.5   Cross the footbridge at the Robbins Towpath junction.
- 1.8   Arrive at the Deer Creek Falls overlook.

A wintry stroll along the towpath at Delphi Canals, site of a section of the Wabash & Erie Canal.

The hike: These interconnecting trails provide a glimpse of a bygone era, when farm products and other goods were transported over the Wabash & Erie Canal. The canal was a system of locks built between 1832 and 1863 to link Lake Erie to Evansville. The 468-mile stretch from Fort Wayne to Evansville was the largest manmade structure in the country at the time, and its construction and operation plunged the state into bankruptcy.

The area near Delphi is the only accessible location where water still flows through the historic canal, which went out of business in the 1870s as railroad transportation expanded. These are well-marked and well-maintained trails over pea gravel. Traffic is generally light most of the year.

The hike begins in Trailhead Park at a footbridge across Deer Creek. After crossing the bridge, turn left (west) for a short walk to Sunset Point, an overlook where Deer Creek and the canal spill into the Wabash River. Canal builders constructed a dam here to create a pool of water deep enough for barges to cross Deer Creek. The towpath at the confluence collapsed in 1874, sweeping mules and a driver into the river, where they drowned.

From Sunset Point, retrace your steps to the junction with the VanScoy Towpath, which horses and mules once used while towing barges through the canal. At 0.4 mile, turn left (northwest) off the VanScoy Towpath to follow the Obear Millrace Towpath northeast along a millrace that once fed water to two paper mills on the outskirts of Delphi. The Obear path reconnects to the VanScoy path at 0.9 mile. The trail network continues for another 0.75 mile to Canal Park in Delphi, but turn right (south) instead and follow the VanScoy Towpath back along the Wabash & Erie Canal to the footbridge. Turn left (northeast) at the footbridge at 1.5 miles and follow the Robbins Towpath for 0.25 mile along Deer Creek. Pass under Indiana 25 before turning left and climbing a slight incline to the Lawrence Van Der Volgen Overlook at 1.8 miles. Return down the same path to the trailhead.

21 Wabash Heritage Trail

Type of hike:	Day hike, shuttle.
General description:	A linear trail along the Wabash River that is full of historic locations, from Battle Ground to Tapawingo Park.
General location:	Near Lafayette in west-central Indiana.
Total distance:	9.5 miles.
Difficulty:	Moderate.
Elevation gain:	Minimal.
Jurisdiction:	Tippecanoe County Historical Association and the parks departments for Tippecanoe County, Lafayette, and West Lafayette.
Maps:	Brookston, Lafayette East, Lafayette West USGS quads; Wabash Heritage Trail brochure.
Permits/fees:	None.

Camping: None permitted.

Trailhead facilities: The battlefield museum is open from 10 A.M. to 5 P.M. Mondays through Saturdays, and from noon to 5 P.M. on Sundays. Admission is $3 for adults and $2 for students and seniors. The nature center is open seasonally. There is a drinking fountain at the museum, but no other potable sources of water are available until Tapawingo Park in West Lafayette.

Finding the trailhead: Go 3 miles northeast on Indiana 25 from the Interstate 65 interchange to Indiana 225. Turn left (northwest) on Indiana 225 and go over the one-lane bridge that crosses the Wabash River. The highway passes between the two sections of Prophetstown State Park before reaching the village of Battle Ground. Cross the railroad tracks at the center of town, take an immediate left (southwest) turn, and go 0.4 mile to the Tippecanoe Battlefield Memorial. The trailhead is at the Wah-bah-shik-a Nature Center at the north end of the parking lot.

Key points:

0.0	Trailhead.
0.1	Reach the Prophet's Rock Trail juncture.
1.4	Reach the Interstate 65 underpass.
1.8	Arrive at the Burnett Road underpass.
3.6	Cross the Davis Ferry Bridge.
4.1	Pass the Heron Island Wildlife Preserve.
5.8	Take the U.S. Highway 52 underpass to Lafayette Municipal Golf Course.
6.5	Reach McAllister Park.
9.3	Cross the John T. Myers pedestrian bridge.
9.5	Reach Tapawingo Park.

The trailhead of Wabash Heritage Trail at Burnett Creek, its northern terminus.

Wabash Heritage Trail

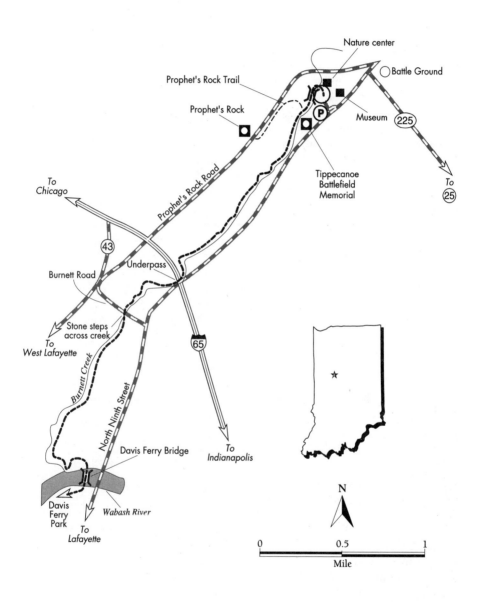

Nature center

Prophet's Rock Trail

Prophet's Rock

Battle Ground

Museum

225

To
Chicago

Prophet's Rock Road

Tippecanoe
Battlefield
Memorial

To
25

43

Underpass

Burnett Road

65

Stone steps
across creek

To
West Lafayette

Burnett Creek

North Ninth Street

Davis Ferry Bridge

To
Indianapolis

Davis
Ferry
Park

Wabash River

To
Lafayette

N

0   0.5   1
Mile

The hike: In 1811, Shawnee leader Tecumseh attempted to establish a confederacy of Native American tribes to resist the advancement of white settlers. Fourteen tribes gathered at a site known as Prophet's Town, named for Tecumseh's brother, The Prophet. Military forces directed by General William Henry Harrison were attacked by the Indians at Prophet's Town on November 7, 1811, and quickly crushed the uprising to effectively end Tecumseh's ambition. Harrison was elected U.S. president in 1839 but died after only 30 days in office.

Thirteen miles downstream from the battlefield is Fort Ouiatenon, the first military outpost in Indiana. It was established in 1717 by the French to counter British expansion. Explore the 104-acre battlefield or visit the museum or the nature center to learn more.

The linear nature and distance of this trail will require you to arrange a vehicle shuttle or be willing to backtrack. There are additional trailheads along the route, at Davis Ferry Park, Lafayette Municipal Golf Course, and Tapawingo Park. Spring rains can flood out some sections of the trail, but rerouting has taken care of most of the problems. Trail conditions sometimes are posted at the nature center. The busiest segments are at the battlefield and paved areas in downtown Lafayette.

To start the hike, walk down a concrete stairway near the nature center to a footbridge over Burnett Creek, named for William Burnett, a French trader and early settler. Just short of 0.1 mile, arrive at a marked juncture of the Wabash Heritage Trail and Prophet's Rock Trail. An optional side trip, Prophet's Rock Trail leads 0.2 mile one-way to the rock. Popular legend relates that The Prophet chanted encouragement and instructions to the Indian warriors from the rock during the 1811 battle. Native American historians dispute this tale.

From the juncture with Prophet's Rock Trail, turn left (southwest) at the Wabash Heritage Trail marker and follow a path that hugs the north bank of Burnett Creek as it cuts a southwesterly path toward its confluence with the Wabash River. Interpretive signposts help mark the way on what is an easy walk, with only three minor inclines over the entire stretch to Fort Ouiatenon.

Two short footbridges cross drainage ditches that feed Burnett Creek before the path passes under Interstate 65 at 1.4 miles. Go 0.1 mile to another footbridge, followed by a climb of 30 feet up a steep bank. Drop back down to the creekbed and pass under a bridge at Burnett Road at 1.8 miles.

The trail crosses Burnett Creek on round concrete stepping stones, then continues along the southeast bank of the creek for another 1.8 miles to Davis Ferry Bridge (3.6 miles). You will pass behind private homes and along a farm field to a paved road, and following trail markers that point to the iron suspension bridge built over the Wabash in 1912. John Davis, who married William Burnett's daughter, operated a ferry at this location until the bridge was built. Davis charged $.06 per person and $.12 per car or horse. The bridge is restricted to pedestrian use. Cross the bridge and turn right (west) as the path proceeds along the southeast bank of the Wabash. At 4.1 miles, pass Heron Island, a 12-acre wildlife preserve in the

Wabash Heritage Trail (part 2)

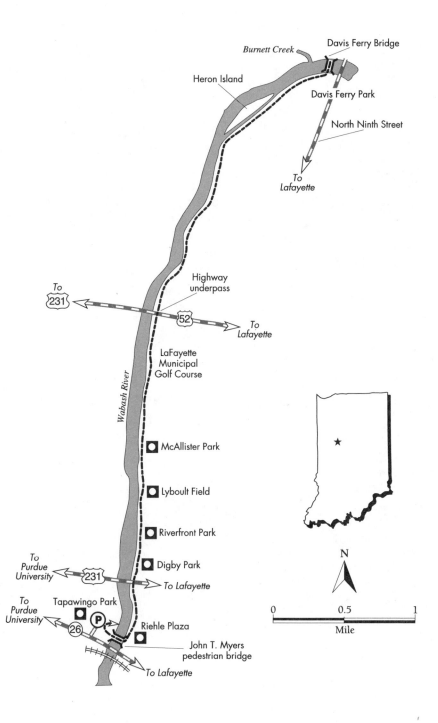

Burnett Creek

Davis Ferry Bridge

Heron Island

Davis Ferry Park

North Ninth Street

To Lafayette

Highway underpass

To 231

52

To Lafayette

Wabash River

LaFayette Municipal Golf Course

McAllister Park

Lyboult Field

Riverfront Park

Digby Park

To Purdue University

231

To Lafayette

To Purdue University

Tapawingo Park

26

P

Riehle Plaza

John T. Myers pedestrian bridge

To Lafayette

N

0   0.5   1
Mile

Concrete pilings provide the stepping stones to cross Burnett Creek on the Wabash Heritage Trail.

Wabash that is accessible only by boat. Continue along the banks of the Wabash for about 1.7 miles to another footbridge before passing under the U.S. Highway 52 bridge at 5.8 miles.

From here, the trail is unmarked but follows a service road that parallels the river and Lafayette Municipal Golf Course and an open field that is home to a local model airplane club. At 6.5 miles, you will come to McAllister Park and a paved section of trail that is also open to bicycles. Walk past several ballfields on the left (east), and under another bridge, to reach the final leg into downtown Lafayette.

At 9.3 miles, reach the Big Four Depot, a restored train stop at the foot of the John T. Myers pedestrian bridge, which crosses the Wabash into West Lafayette, home of Purdue University. After crossing the bridge, turn right into Tapawingo Park at 9.5 miles.

Option: It is possible to continue another 3.5 miles south along the west bank of the Wabash to Fort Ouiatenon, but the trail may be washed out in some locations, and the last 0.25 mile is along busy South River Road. Efforts are underway to upgrade the trail between Tapawingo and the fort.

22 Portland Arch Nature Preserve

Type of hike:	Day hike, loop.
General description:	A short loop trail.
General location:	Southwest of Lafayette (near Attica) in west-central Indiana.
Total distance:	0.8 mile.
Difficulty:	Moderate.
Elevation gain:	Less than 50 feet.
Jurisdiction:	Indiana Department of Natural Resources, Division of Nature Preserves.
Special attractions:	Portland Arch and Bear Creek ravine.
Maps:	Stone Bluff USGS quad; Portland Arch Nature Preserve brochure.
Permits/fees:	None.
Camping:	None.
Trailhead facilities:	There is a small gravel parking lot. No potable water source is available.

Finding the trailhead: Go south from Attica on Indiana 41 for 4 miles to the intersection of Indiana 41, 55, and 28. Continue south for 5 miles to Fountain County 650 North, and turn right (west). Go about 5 miles on CR 650 North to Walnut Street, which is on the west edge of Fountain. Turn left (southwest) on Walnut Street and go one block to Scout Camp Road. Turn left (southeast) onto a gravel road. Go 0.4 mile to a parking lot on the right (west) side of the road. The trailhead is on the west side of the parking lot.

Portland Arch Nature Preserve

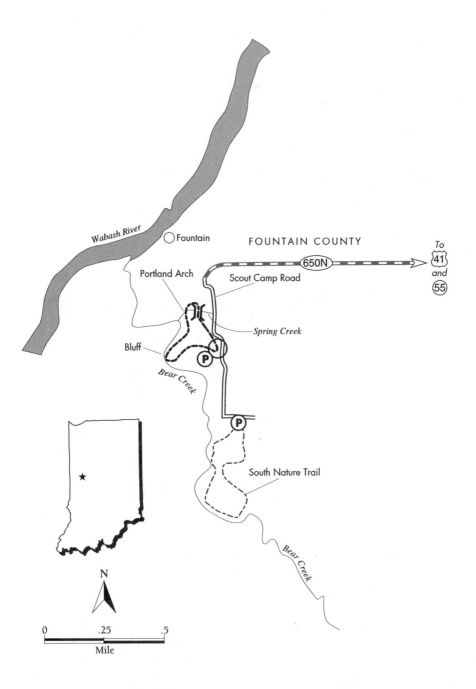

Wabash River

Fountain

FOUNTAIN COUNTY

650N

To
41
and
55

Portland Arch

Scout Camp Road

Spring Creek

Bluff

Bear Creek

P

P

South Nature Trail

Bear Creek

★

N

0   .25   .5
Mile

Key points:
   0.0   Trailhead.
   0.3   Reach Portland Arch.
   0.6   Climb the rocky ledge on Bear Creek.

The hike: Legend has it that following the defeat of his Indian confederacy at the Battle of Tippecanoe in 1811, Shawnee chief, Tecumseh, sought refuge at this site. If true, it was a good hiding place. Bear Creek already had carved a deep but narrow channel through layers of rock when a small adjoining stream—Spring Creek—punched a hole in the sandstone to create a natural bridge.

The archway that Spring Creek formed is the focal point of the hike, but not the only attractive feature of the state-protected nature preserve, which is listed as a national natural landmark by the U.S. Department of Interior. Plant life is abundant in the moist ravine environment, where steep slopes host a mix of oak, hickory, and native white pine trees. Berry bushes, lichens, and mosses grow in the thin soil, and a variety of other plants cling to small crevices in the surrounding cliffs. Bush honeysuckle makes a rare appearance here, and it is the only place in the state where Canada blueberry grows.

The trail alternates between being rugged, muddy, steep, and level. Designed as an interpretive nature trail, several markers are missing.

Begin the hike by passing through the opening in the fence at the west end of the parking lot, and picking up an interpretive trail brochure at the registration box. Turn right (north) and begin a short walk toward the ravine before making a sharp descent at 0.1 mile. Cross a footbridge and continue downhill to Spring Creek at 0.2 mile. The trail turns left (west) beside a cliff, with Spring Creek on the right (north). Walk over two footbridges to reach the sometimes muddy passageway beneath the arch.

Once through the archway, turn left (south) and follow the pathway beside the sandstone ridge to a fairly straight stretch alongside Bear Creek. At about 0.6 mile, turn left and climb uphill to a ledge along the east side of the ravine, eventually turning east to return to the parking lot.

Option: A second trail, the 0.9-mile South Nature Trail is also available in the preserve. It is accessed by turning right (south) from the Portland Arch parking lot, and going 0.3 mile to its parking area.

Central

Among the various geographic regions in Indiana, this is the largest. It also gives the impression of being the most featureless area of the state. Nothing could be further from the truth.

Three of the more unique properties in Indiana are located here—Shades and Turkey Run state parks, and Pine Hills Nature Preserve. Each is marked by deep ravines, canyons, flowing water, and lush vegetation.

Even the state capital, Indianapolis, has its share of scenic locations, including those along Fall Creek at Fort Ben Harrison State Park and at Eagle Creek Park on the northwest side.

The area is bounded on the north by the Wabash River, and on the south by a jagged line just below midstate that marks the farthest advance of the last glacier thousands of years ago. Rolling plains and flat farmland typify most of the Central Plains, but the Shades and Turkey Run parks, on the western edge of the region, are notable exceptions.

Sandy sediment was dumped here, at the mouth of the ancient Michigan River, and it solidified like cement. Later, the exposed sandstone was carved and gouged by glacial meltwaters to create a maze of canyons and ravines.

Nearby, Pine Hills further exemplifies the erosive power of water. Two small, winding creeks—Clifty and Indian—have sliced through the bedrock to create four narrow backbone ridges. The formations are 100 feet high and as much as 1,000 feet long. Devil's Backbone is a scant 6 feet wide at one spot.

The splendor and abundance of the scenery of Shades, Turkey Run, and Pine Hills parks is unmatched in the state.

The trails in this section are presented in a clockwise sweep heading south from Mounds State Park near Anderson to Indianapolis, and west from Indianapolis toward Crawfordsville.

23 Mounds State Park

Type of hike:	Day hike, loop.
General description:	Loop trail past prehistoric earthworks and burial mounds.
General location:	Near Anderson.
Total distance:	1.5 miles.
Difficulty:	Easy to moderate.
Elevation gain:	About 70 feet from White River to the Great Mound.
Jurisdiction:	Indiana Department of Natural Resources, Division of State Parks & Reservoirs.

Special attractions:	The Great Mound and several smaller earthworks.
Maps:	Anderson South and Middletown USGS quads; Mounds State Park brochure.
Permits/fees:	There is a $2 gate fee for vehicles with Indiana license plates; $5 for out-of-state vehicles. Season passes are available.
Camping:	The park has 75 modern campsites, plus a youth camp area.
Trailhead facilities:	There is a large parking lot near the Pavilion. Water and restrooms are located throughout the park.

Finding the trailhead: Go 1.1 miles north on Indiana 9 from Interstate 69 to Indiana 232 and turn right. Go about 0.75 mile to the Mounds State Park entrance on the left (northwest). After passing the gatehouse, follow the main park road less than 0.1 mile to the Pavilion parking lot on the left.

Key points:
- 0.0 Trailhead.
- 0.2 At the junction of the bridle path (Trail 2) and Trail 1, turn left on Trail 1.
- 0.5 At the trail juncture, turn left and go uphill on Trail 1.
- 0.7 At the junction of Trails 1 and 4, turn left on Trail 4.
- 1.2 Trails 4 and 1 meet again; turn left on Trail 1.
- 1.5 Reach the Pavilion.

The hike: As state parks go in Indiana, Mounds is a tiny one. At just over 280 acres, it is about one-tenth the average size of Indiana parks. It is one of the busiest, though, with an average annual visitation of about 500,000 people, which ranks in the top ten.

The trail entrance sign at Mounds State Park.

Mounds State Park

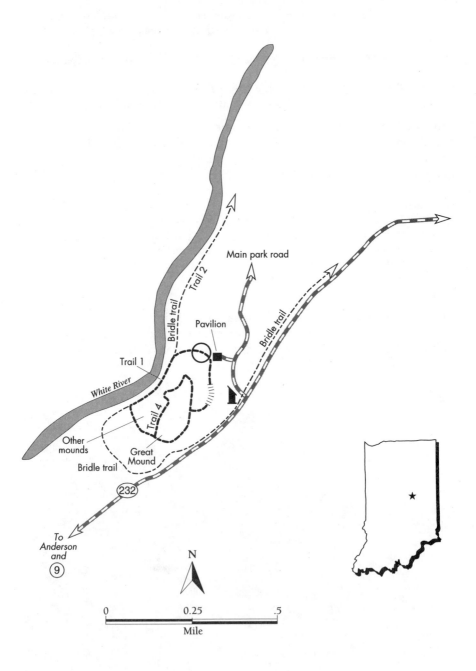

The Great Mound is 1,200 feet around and 9 feet high.

Despite its size, the park has several attractions—picnic areas, bridle trails, a swimming pool—plus the extensive mounds and earthworks believed to have been constructed about 150 B.C. by the Adena and Hopewell peoples. The largest is the Great Mound, more than 1,200 feet around, 9 feet high and 60 feet wide at the base. An archaeological excavation in the late 1960s uncovered bone awls, a stone pipe, pot shards, projectile points, and two human skeletons. Other mounds in the park are circular, fiddle-shaped, or rectangular.

These trails get heavy use, and erosion is evident at the downhill and uphill sections near the White River. Crowds normally can be avoided by visiting the park on weekdays. People are not alone in swarming this small park. Mosquitoes can be a problem too.

Trail 1, which leads to the Great Mound, begins across a grassy area behind the Pavilion. Go downhill over wooden steps and across a small creek to the White River; at 0.2 mile, Trail 1 joins with a bridle trail that circles the perimeter of the park. Turn left (south) and go 0.3 mile along the riverbank to where Trail 1 turns left (southeast) and goes uphill to a plateau where most of the mounds are located.

Between the Fiddleback Mound and Great Mound, at 0.7 mile, turn left (north) on Trail 4 for a winding walk along bluffs and around the high side of a ravine. Circle back to a juncture with Trail 1 at 1.2 miles, near the northeast side of the Great Mound.

Turn left (east) on Trail 1, and cross a multi-tiered, suspended boardwalk and staircase above a moist ravine through which a small creek flows. At the end of the boardwalk at 1.5 miles, enter the grassy area near the Pavilion.

24 Fall Creek Trail at Fort Harrison State Park

Type of hike: Day hike, loop.
General description: A loop trail along the banks of Fall Creek.
General location: The east side of Indianapolis in central Indiana.
Total distance: 2.2 miles.
Difficulty: Moderate.
Elevation gain: 75 feet.
Jurisdiction: Indiana Department of Natural Resources, Division of State Parks & Reservoirs.
Special attraction: The secluded woodland along Camp Creek.
Maps: Fishers, Indianapolis East USGS quads; Fort Harrison State Park brochure.
Permits/fees: There is a $2 entry fee for vehicles with Indiana license plates; $5 for out-of-state vehicles. Season passes are available.
Camping: None available at the park.
Trailhead facilities: There is a large parking lot, with nearby modern restrooms equipped with drinking fountains and vending machines.

Finding the trailhead: From Interstate 465, exit 40, go 2 miles on 56th Street east to Post Road. Turn left (north) and go 0.5 mile to the main park road. Turn left (northwest) and go to the park gatehouse. From the gate, go 0.7 mile to a T intersection. Turn right (east) and go 0.2 mile to the Delaware Lake Picnic Area parking lot.

Key points:
0.0 Trailhead.
0.7 Reach the trail intersection and go left (northeast).
1.4 Cross the Harrison Trace Bike Trail.
1.5 Pass the duck pond.
1.8 Reach the gravel road; follow Camp Creek west.

The hike: Fort Benjamin Harrison, or "Fort Ben" for short, is Indiana's newest state park, established in 1996 after the Indiana Department of Natural Resources acquired about two-thirds of the former military post from the U.S. government. Fort Ben was dedicated in 1906 by President Teddy Roosevelt, and was used by the military until its closure in 1991.

The 1,700-acre state park contains several large tracts of hardwood forest, three small lakes, Fall Creek, Lawrence Creek, and a championship golf course. Low spots along Fall Creek can be muddy in wet weather. A popular new urban park, Fort Ben draws a lot of visitors, and the trails get considerable use.

Leave the northeast corner of the main parking lot at Delaware Lake Picnic Area and walk 0.25 mile on the crushed stone path to the junction

Fall Creek Trail at Fort Harrison State Park

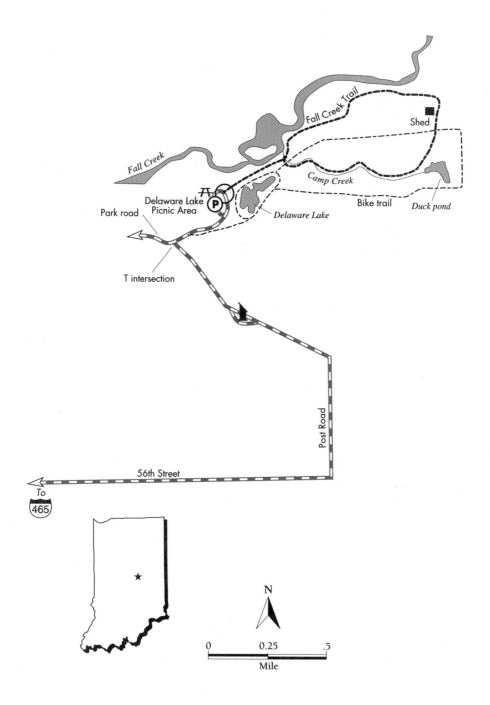

Fall Creek Trail

Fall Creek

Shed

Camp Creek

Delaware Lake
Picnic Area

Park road

Bike trail

Duck pond

Delaware Lake

T intersection

Post Road

56th Street

To
465

N

0   0.25   .5
Mile

with the loop trail. Take the left (northeast) path, sticking to the south bank of Fall Creek.

At 0.7 miles, the connector trail from the paved Harrison Trace Bike Trail joins on the right (southeast) side. Continue straight ahead for 0.1 mile to where the trail bends right (south). Climb over an undulating, tree-rooted section to a flat ridgetop and the highest point on the trail—about 75 feet above Fall Creek. Look for signs of the former military post—a sandbag bunker or concrete marker.

At 1.2 miles, pass a large shed and reach a gravel road that crosses over the Harrison Trace Bike Trail at 1.4 miles. Walk through a series of small forest openings to the duck pond and cross a small footbridge at 1.5 miles, then reenter the woods on a gravel lane.

At 1.8 miles, begin a downhill walk on the winding gravel lane to a quiet ravine containing Camp Creek. The area is home to some of the largest trees—oak, hickory, and maple—in the park, plus a variety of wildflowers.

Cross the bike path one more time at 2 miles, and turn left (southwest) at the connecting leg of the Fall Creek Trail to return to the parking lot.

25 Pine Hills Nature Preserve

Type of hike: Day hike, lollipop loops.
General description: A passage over two backbone ridges above a deep gorge in the state's first dedicated nature preserve.
General location: Near Shades State Park, southwest of Crawfordsville.
Total distance: 1.8 miles.
Difficulty: Moderate to strenuous.
Elevation gain: 100 feet to Devil's Backbone.
Jurisdiction: Indiana Department of Natural Resources, Division of Nature Preserves.
Special attractions: Turkey Backbone, Devil's Backbone, and Honeycomb Rock.
Maps: Alamo USGS quad; Pine Hills Nature Preserve brochure.
Permits/fees: None.
Camping: None permitted.
Trailhead facilities: There is a water fountain and pit toilet in the parking lot located across the road from the trailhead.

Finding the trailhead: Go 7.5 miles southwest from Crawfordsville on Indiana 47 to Indiana 234 and turn right (west). Go 6 miles to a gravel parking lot on the left (west) side of the road. Cross the road and climb over a stile to access the trailhead.

Key points:
0.0 Trailhead.
0.4 Reach the Turkey Backbone.

Pine Hills Nature Preserve

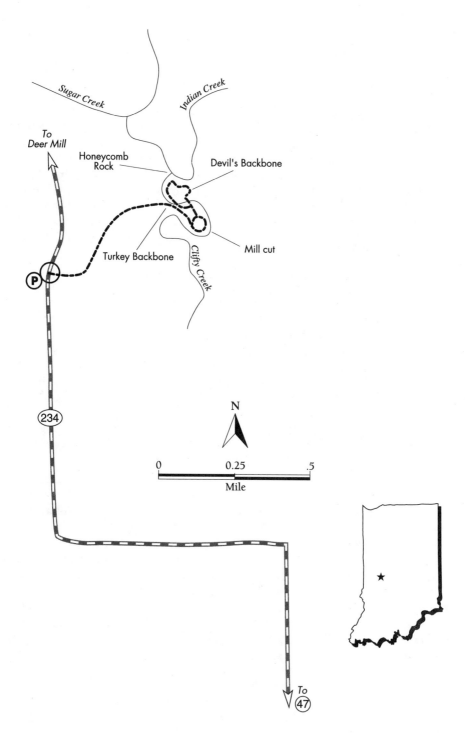

Sugar Creek

Indian Creek

To Deer Mill

Honeycomb Rock

Devil's Backbone

Turkey Backbone

Mill cut

Cliffy Creek

234

N

0   0.25   .5
Mile

To 47

0.6   At the base of gorge, turn right.
0.8   At the trail junction, turn right (north).
0.9   Turn right (northeast) at the trail fork.
1.0   Reach the Devil's Backbone.
1.1   Arrive at Honeycomb Rock.
1.3   Reach the Turkey Backbone staircase.

The hike: Don't be fooled by the easy pace with which this trail begins. The deep gorge that the entry trail leads to may be the most spectacular piece of natural landscape in Indiana.

Dedicated in 1971 as the first state nature preserve, Pine Hills presents perhaps the finest examples of "incised meanders" in the eastern United States. Glacial meltwater formed two meandering streams—Clifty Creek and Indian Creek—which carved a deep gorge through the bedrock, leaving four narrow ridges or backbones that rise 70 to 100 feet. The pathway over Devil's Backbone is a mere 6 feet wide, with a sheer dropoff on both sides. Caution should be used in this hazardous area.

Two other geological features in the preserve are The Slide, a smooth patch on Clifty Creek created by constant rock slides, and Honeycomb Rock, a wall of sandstone where the two creeks meet.

There is more to the preserve than rocks, however. When the last glacier receded thousands of years ago, Indiana had a Canadian-like appearance in which white pine, hemlock, and Canada yew trees prospered. These trees remain as prominent features of the preserve.

Despite its uniqueness, the area did not avoid human intervention. Timber interests removed many large hardwoods in the 1850s, and in 1868 the Pine Hill Woolen Company dammed Clifty Creek and cut a notch in one of the backbones through which water flowed to power its mill. The business pulled out five years later, and the area has been mostly undisturbed since then.

Often considered a part of adjacent Shades State Park, the site covers 480 acres. Portions of this trail are steep and hazardous so proceed with caution.

An entrance trail begins at the stile and proceeds along a gravel road for 0.4 mile to the Turkey Backbone. At the east end of the backbone, descend a set of wooden steps to the floor of the gorge at 0.6 mile. Turn right (southeast) to make a loop along the banks of Clifty Creek past the old woolen mill site, the mill cut, and The Slide. At 0.8 mile, the loop intersects with the trail leading to Devil's Backbone. Go right (north) to another trail fork at 0.9 mile. Take the right (northeast) fork and scramble up the steep slope to the east end of the Devil's Backbone at 1 mile.

Use extreme caution in crossing the narrow band to a hemlock grove. Descend the western slope of the ridge to Honeycomb Rock at 1.1 miles, where the two creeks merge and flow north to Sugar Creek. Turn left (south) and follow the path along Clifty Creek before crossing the creek to link up with the main trail near the base of Turkey Backbone. Climb the staircase at 1.3 miles to begin backtracking to the trailhead parking lot.

26 Ravine Trails at Shades State Park

Type of hike:	Day hike, lollipop loops.
General description:	A combination of loop trails that follow the streambeds of rocky ravines.
General location:	Southwest of Crawfordsville.
Total distance:	3.5 miles.
Difficulty:	Strenuous.
Elevation gain:	A drop of 150 feet from the trailhead to Sugar Creek.
Jurisdiction:	Indiana Department of Natural Resources, Division of State Parks & Reservoirs.
Special attractions:	Kintz, Frisz, and Kickapoo ravines, Inspiration Point, Silver Cascade Falls, and Devil's Punch Bowl.
Maps:	Alamo USGS quad; Shades State Park brochure.
Permits/fees:	There is a $2 gate fee for vehicles with Indiana license plates; $5 for out-of-state vehicles. Season passes are available.
Camping:	The park has 105 campsites, plus a youth camp area.
Trailhead facilities:	There is a water spigot at the trailhead parking lot, plus a pit toilet nearby. Water supply and restroom facilities are also located elsewhere in the park.

Finding the trailhead: Go 7.5 miles southwest on Indiana 47 from Crawfordsville to Indiana 234. Turn right (north) and go 5 miles to where Indiana 234 curves to the right (north). Turn left (west) onto Montgomery County 800 South, passing a Shades State Park sign. Go 0.8 mile to the entrance road to the park. From the gatehouse, take the first paved road to the right (north) and go 0.4 mile to a parking lot northwest of Dell Shelter at the end of the road. The trail begins at a metal gate.

Key points:
- 0.0 Trailhead.
- 0.1 Reach the Devil's Punch Bowl overlook.
- 0.2 Turn left (west) on the trail to Trail 7.
- 0.4 Turn right at the Trail 7 juncture.
- 1.3 Turn left at the Trail 8 juncture.
- 1.4 Turn left at the Trail 4 juncture.
- 2.0 Turn left at the trail juncture.
- 2.1 Turn left at the Trail 5 juncture.
- 2.9 Reach the Hickory Shelter.
- 3.0 Visit Prospect Point and Inspiration Point.
- 3.1 Go down the stairs to Silver Cascade Falls.
- 3.4 Reach the Devil's Punch Bowl

The hike: Long before it became a state park in 1947, the dark, shadowy forest along the banks of Sugar Creek was called "Shades of Death." Stories vary on the origins of the name, but the eerie legends it evoked led to it being simplified to "The Shades."

Ravine Trails at Shades State Park

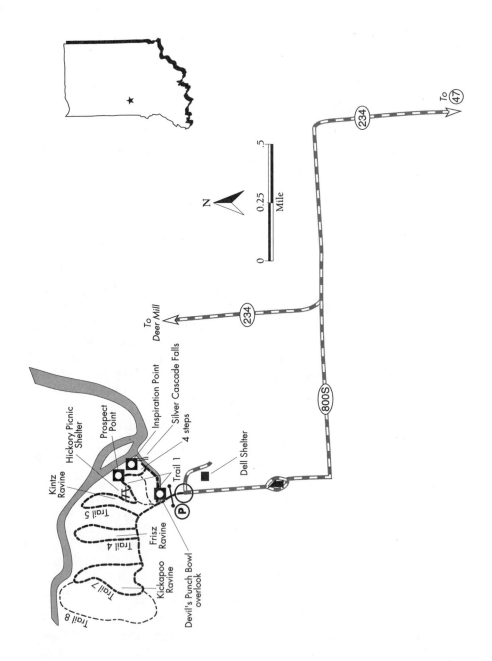

In 1887, a 40-room inn was built as part of a health resort on a hill just south of the Devil's Punch Bowl. The inn later closed due to fire damage, but Joseph W. Frisz gained financial control of the association that owned the surrounding property. Frisz protected the natural features while adding more land.

Acquired by the state in 1947, the park now covers nearly 3,100 acres, and includes the adjacent Pine Hills Nature Preserve. The remote location of Shades, and the popularity of nearby Turkey Run State Park, make Shades an overlooked jewel in the state park system. Although fifth in size among Indiana parks, Shades ranks 15th in annual visitation with about 20 percent of the attendance at Turkey Run. Perhaps another reason for the park's relative lack of visitors is that hiking the trails at Shades is a challenge, particularly along the ravine streambeds.

Shades is popular with hard-core hikers, but the rugged ravines are a limiting factor. Most visitors congregate at the Devil's Punch Bowl and

A hiker climbs one of the ladders in the Kintz Ravine at Shades State Park.

Hikers work their way along the canyon from Devil's Punch Bowl at Shades State Park.

Silver Cascade Falls, where multi-tiered wooden staircases reduce the difficulty of the steep climbs. Trail sections that follow ravine streambeds can be wet and hazardous after heavy rain. The following hike links Trails 1, 4, 5, and 7, traveling through four ravines and passing two scenic overlooks more than 200 feet above Sugar Creek.

Begin at the parking lot just north of Dell Shelter, site of the old inn, pass a metal gate on Trail 1, and go 0.1 mile to a wood deck above the Devil's Punch Bowl. From the deck, go left (west) over two gullies on a pair of footbridges. Climb a set of stairs to a gravel road that circles Hickory Shelter. Turn left (west) on the gravel road at 0.2 mile, and follow markers leading to Trail 7, passing the starting points of Trails 5 and 4.

Turn right (north) at the Trail 7 juncture at 0.4 mile to make a counterclockwise loop of Kickapoo Ravine. The narrow, dirt path descends to Sugar Creek through a dense forest. The downhill walk is aided by stairs in a couple of places, including one set that has 85 steps. Two sets of steps go uphill; take the left set to continue uphill through Kickapoo Ravine (the right set leads to Shawnee Canyon and Trail 8). Stay left (east) when the trail joins Trail 8 at 1.3 miles, and return to the starting point of Trail 7.

Backtrack to the first Trail 4 marker at 1.4 miles, and turn left (north) on Trail 4, which begins as a wide gravel path leading downhill. Upon reaching Sugar Creek, turn right (east, then south) to Frisz Ravine, a more rugged uphill scramble than Kickapoo Ravine. The narrow passage of Frisz Ravine follows a streambed and requires climbing a staircase and two ladders in some of the roughest spots.

After exiting the top of the ravine at 2 miles, turn left (east) on the feeder trail and go to the first Trail 5 marker at 2.1 miles. Turn left (north) and go back downhill once more to Sugar Creek. Several sets of steps lead to the creek. Turn right (east, then south) at the creek and begin another scramble through Kintz Ravine. Frisz and Kintz ravines are similar in that they are narrow and littered with boulders and fallen trees that must be climbed over. A set of stairs bypasses a small waterfall in Kintz Ravine.

Climb a ladder near the top end of the ravine and enter an open area near Hickory Shelter at 2.9 miles. Rejoin the feeder trail at a Trail 5 marker on the right (west) side of the shelter restroom and turn left (southeast) to backtrack to Trail 1. Follow Trail 1 uphill to the east side of the Hickory Shelter area and take the left fork of Trail 1 (northeast) to Prospect Point, the first of two overlooks high above Sugar Creek. After passing the second overlook—Inspiration Point—at 3 miles, turn left and go down the stairs to get a view of Silver Cascade Falls at 3.1 miles. At the base of the stairs, turn left (northeast) and take a spur trail about 30 yards to get a full view of the falls. Backtrack on the spur trail to the main trail, and follow the creek through a sandstone canyon to get a ground-level view of Devil's Punch Bowl at 3.4 miles. A set of stairs leads up from the canyon to the wood deck above the canyon. Backtrack from here to the parking lot.

27 Pearl Ravine at Shades State Park

Type of hike:	Day hike, loop.
General description:	A loop trail through a rugged ravine, with a spur trail to the scenic Lover's Leap overlook.
General location:	Southwest of Crawfordsville.
Total distance:	1.3 miles.
Difficulty:	Strenuous.
Elevation gain:	A loss of 150 feet from the trailhead to Sugar Creek.
Jurisdiction:	Indiana Department of Natural Resources, Division of State Parks & Reservoirs.
Special attractions:	Lover's Leap, Pearl Ravine, and Maidenhair Falls.
Maps:	Alamo USGS quad; Shades State Park brochure.
Permits/fees:	There is a $2 gate fee for vehicles with Indiana license plates; $5 for out-of-state vehicles. Season passes are available.
Camping:	The park has 105 campsites, plus a youth camp area.
Trailhead facilities:	There is a parking lot, with water and pit toilets, about 100 yards north of Dell Shelter.

Finding the trailhead: Go 7.5 miles southwest on Indiana 47 from Crawfordsville to Indiana 234. Turn right (north) and go 5 miles to where Indiana 234 curves to the right (north). Turn left (west) onto Montgomery County 800 South, passing a Shades State Park sign. Go 0.8 mile to the entrance road to the park. From the gatehouse, take the first paved road to the right (north) and go 0.4 mile, turning right (east) to the parking lot below Dell Shelter. The trail begins east of the shelter house.

Key points:
- 0.0 Trailhead.
- 0.1 Turn left on the Lover's Leap spur.
- 0.3 Follow stairs down to Pearl Ravine.
- 0.4 Turn right in Pearl Ravine.
- 0.6 Reach Maidenhair Falls.
- 0.7 Climb the stairway out of Pearl Ravine.
- 1.1 At the trail juncture, turn left to parking lot.

The hike: If the Ravine Trails (Hike 26) were not enough, Trail 2 at Shades State Park provides the finishing touch with a hike up Pearl Ravine. Most visitors congregate at the Lover's Leap overlook or return from Pearl Ravine via the stairs. The trail section following the ravine streambed can be wet and hazardous after heavy rain.

Begin by heading northeast from the Dell Shelter parking area to a Trail 2 sign. At 0.1 mile, a spur trail leads to Lover's Leap, a superb overlook 200 feet above Sugar Creek. Backtrack to the main trail and turn left (east). Go 0.2 miles to a staircase, then cross a footbridge over a ravine to a trail juncture. Turn left (northeast) and proceed to a long staircase at 0.3 mile. There are 180 steps to the bottom of the ravine; of

Pearl Ravine at Shades State Park

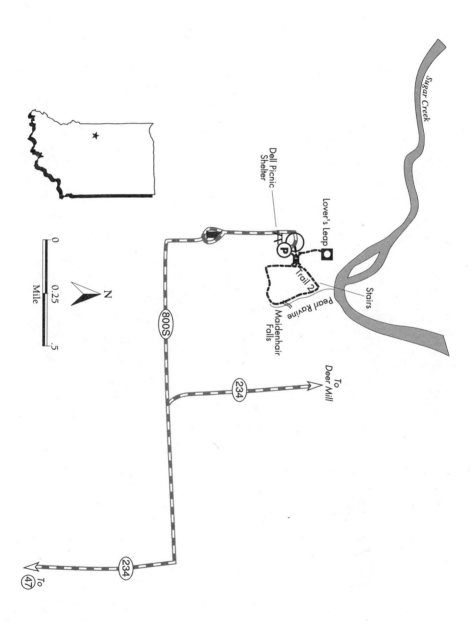

Maidenhair Falls is 6 feet wide and about 6 feet high. The falls are situated on the Pearl Ravine Trail in Shades State Park.

The author steps over a pile of rocks and logs that clog the way on one of the ravines in Shades State Park.

which the last couple of sections are very steep.

Turn right (south) at the bottom and work up Pearl Ravine. Take notice along the way of the layered bedrock of sandstone, limestone, and siltstone that has been exposed over time by the eroding forces of water.

At 0.6 mile, reach Maidenhair Falls, a fitting name for the delicate waterfall that is only 6 feet wide and 6 feet high. A stairway bypasses the falls, and at about 0.7 mile, you should take another set of stairs out of the ravine. The trail loops west and then north to rejoin the entry trail that leads back to the footbridge and stairway leading to the parking lot.

28 Turkey Run State Park

Type of hike:	Day hike, loop.
General description:	A combination of park trails looping through canyons and along scenic Sugar Creek.
General location:	Southwest of Crawfordsville.
Total distance:	3 miles.
Difficulty:	Strenuous.

Elevation gain:	About 150 feet from the north bank of Sugar Creek to the ridgetops above the various canyons.
Jurisdiction:	Indiana Department of Natural Resources, Division of State Parks & Reservoirs.
Special attractions:	Devil's Ice Box, Falls Canyon, Boulder Canyon, 140 Steps, Punch Bowl, Rocky Hollow, and Wedge Rock.
Maps:	Wallace USGS quad; Turkey Run State Park brochure.
Permits/fees:	There is a $2 gate fee for vehicles with Indiana license plates; $5 for out-of-state vehicles. Season passes are available.
Camping:	The park has 253 campsites, primitive or modern, plus a youth camp area. The campground entrance is about half a mile west of the main park entrance on Indiana 47.
Trailhead facilities:	The parking lot can accommodate cars and buses. Water is available at the nature center and at other locations throughout the park. Restrooms are also located around the park, although there are no water supplies or restrooms on the north side of Sugar Creek.

Finding the trailhead: Go 23 miles west on Indiana 47 from Crawfordsville to the Turkey Run State Park entrance on the right (north) side of the highway. Go about a quarter of a mile from the gatehouse to the main parking lot near the nature center. The trailhead is on the north side of the nature center and leads to a suspension bridge that crosses to the north bank of Sugar Creek.

Key points:
- 0.0   Trailhead.
- 0.1   Cross the suspension bridge.
- 0.2   Reach Devil's Ice Box.
- 0.9   Walk through Falls Canyon.
- 1.2   Arrive at Boulder Canyon.
- 1.8   Descend 140 Steps.
- 2.4   Reach Rocky Hollow Canyon.
- 2.8   Return to the suspension bridge.

The hike: The sandstone cliffs of Turkey Run State Park have their origins 300,000 years ago, when the ancient Michigan River left sandy deposits as it spilled into a great inland sea. Post-glacial streams then carved the canyons that are distinguishing characteristics of the park. The retreating glacier left two other notable features—boulders carried here from Canada and the eastern hemlock. A native species in colder regions of North America, this tree makes one of its rare Indiana appearances here.

Turkey Run was set aside as a state park in 1916. Pioneers probably are responsible for the name. Wild turkeys were once abundant, and were known to congregate in the warmer canyon bottoms during winter. The pioneers took advantage of the situation by herding the turkeys together for an easy hunt.

Turkeys still roam the park, as do white-tailed deer. Pileated woodpeckers are common. Warblers pass through during their spring and fall migrations, and turkey vultures have used the park as a winter roost since the late

Turkey Run State Park

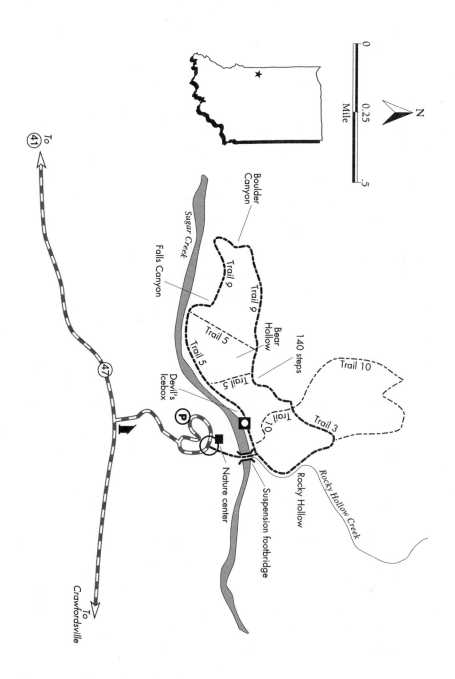

1800s. The park contains sycamore, walnut, oak, and hemlock trees that are several hundred years old. Wildflowers are abundant, and more than half of the mosses and lichens in the state can be found here. The park is bisected by scenic Sugar Creek, considered one of the cleanest streams in the state. The fish population of the creek is quite diverse, including seven different species of darters—further evidence of a clean, cool aquatic environment.

There are 11 trails in the park, and elements of three are included in this hike. The spectacular nature of the sandstone canyons and their accessibility are major factors in the popularity of Turkey Run State Park. Although smaller than neighboring Shades State Park, Turkey Run draws five times as many annual visitors. Trails can be jam-packed on weekends, especially at features in the vicinity of the suspension bridge. At the busiest times, lines form to pass through some areas.

To begin, follow the path from the north side of the nature center and cross the suspension footbridge at Sugar Creek to a Trail 3 marker on the north bank. Turn left (west), climb over a large rock formation, and then over a boardwalk. A gravel path leads uphill to a platform overlook above Sugar Creek. The trail descends from here across a footbridge and downhill over stone steps to the Devil's Ice Box, an eroded opening in the cliff at 0.2 mile.

Continue west along Sugar Creek, walking over a couple of footbridges and through virgin forest featuring gigantic beech and walnut trees. Where Trails 3 and 5 intersect at 0.6 mile, continue straight (west) on Trail 5. Hike along the creek through pine and hemlock stands to where Trails 5 and 9 intersect in a hemlock grove. Go straight (west and north) on Trail 9 to the first of two ravines at 0.9 mile. Falls Canyon, a moss- and fern-covered ravine, follows the creekbed uphill to wooden steps that lead to a ridgetop. At 1.2 miles, head downhill on wooden steps to Boulder Canyon. Passing through this canyon requires climbing over large boulders and exposed tree roots.

Stone steps lead out of the canyon to an upland forest. Head right (east) from the canyon across a broad ridge to a wooden staircase with 64 steps. At the junction with Trail 5, which comes in from the right (south), stay left (east) and go about 0.1 mile to 140 Steps at 1.8 miles. This stone staircase descends to the end of Trail 5 at its junction with Trail 3, and a set of ladders at the north end of Bear Hollow. Skip the ladders and stay left (northeast) on Trail 3, passing through a canyon and streambed before climbing over a ridge to the first of two junctions with Trail 10.

Go straight (north and then east) on Trail 3, and cross several footbridges and stairways to the second Trail 10 junction on the left (north). Go straight (east) on Trail 3 to the wooden steps leading into Rocky Hollow Canyon at 2.4 miles, and the junction with Trail 4, which breaks off to the left (north). Go right (south) on Trail 3, and proceed through Rocky Hollow, passing the Punch Bowl, a pothole scoured by glacial boulders, on the left (east) side of the trail.

Slip through narrow passages in which you can either walk through the stream or along a sometimes slippery ledge of sandstone. The canyon becomes wider, and the walls steeper. Pass Wedge Rock on the left (east) side of the canyon before you arrive at the end of Trail 3 near the suspension bridge over Sugar Creek at 2.8 miles.

Southeast

Diversity is the calling card of this region of the state.

Whether it is the rugged hills of Clark State Forest, the marshes and meadows of Muscatatuck National Wildlife Refuge, the waterfalls and deep canyons of Clifty Falls State Park, or the rivers and bluffs of Harrison-Crawford State Forest, southeast Indiana has a bit of everything.

Much of this area escaped the influences of the last glacial advance, which accounts for the variety in landscape.

The most recognizable feature is the Knobstone escarpment, a steep slope that runs up from the Ohio River at a northwest angle for more than 100 miles. The ridge separates two land features—the Norman Upland to the west and the Scottsburg Lowland to the east. The southeast region chapter of this book encompasses both areas.

This chapter includes hikes in several of Indiana's state forests, which were established in the early 1900s to protect the state's dwindling woodlands. The initial intention of the Indiana legislature, which created a State Forestry Board in 1901, seemed to be directed toward ensuring Indiana's place in the timber industry. The goals were twofold—to preserve remnants of Indiana's once-great forests and to explore methods of reforestation. Purdue Univeristy in West Lafayette began offering courses in forestry in 1905, and Charles C. Deam was named the state's first forester in 1909.

Clark State Forest, located southwest of Scottsburg, was established in 1903. When created by the state legislature, the forest covered only 2,000 acres. It now exceeds 24,000 acres. Harrison-Crawford State Forest, located west of Corydon, was established in 1926 and now has 26,000 acres within its boundaries. Both forests, along with Jackson-Washington State Forest to the north, are comprised primarily of hardwoods with occasional stands of white pine.

The Indiana Department of Natural Resources Division of Forestry still operates with the primary mission of managing sustainable forests, but it also has embraced many recreation opportunities that state forests can provide, including hiking, camping, hunting, fishing, and horseback riding.

Clifty Falls, outside Madison, was dedicated as a state park in 1920. Five waterfalls splash over the cliffs of the 3-mile-long canyon. The four primary falls—Big Clifty, Little Clifty, Hoffman, and Tunnel falls—range from 60 to 83 feet high. The exposed limestone and shale of the canyon is among the oldest bedrock in the state—425 million years old.

John Brough, a local railroad company owner, tried to take advantage of the canyon and its access to the Ohio River during the 1850s. Brough attempted to build two tunnels through the canyon for a rail system. It was a financial failure that became known as Brough's Folly.

Muscatatuck National Wildlife Refuge may lack the geographic splendor of Clifty Falls, but it certainly makes up for it in other ways. A variety of wildlife species make the refuge a year-round home, while hundreds of migratory bird species pass through during spring and fall migrations.

Hikes are presented heading south in a clockwise sweep from Muscatatuck National Wildlife Refuge near Seymour toward the Ohio River.

29 Muscatatuck National Wildlife Refuge

Type of hike: Day hike, double loop.
General description: A double loop trail through meadows and along river bottoms.
General location: Near Seymour in Jackson County.
Total distance: The East River Trail is 2.8 miles; West River Trail is 3.9 miles. The combination described here totals 5.5 miles.
Difficulty: Easy.
Elevation gain: Minimal.
Jurisdiction: Muscatatuck National Wildlife Refuge.
Special attractions: Muscatatuck River and Myers Cemetery.
Maps: Chestnut Ridge USGS quad; Muscatatuck National Wildlife Refuge brochure and trail information sheet.
Permits/fees: None.
Camping: None permitted.
Trailhead facilities: There is a small parking lot at the trailhead with restrooms. There is no water at the trailhead, but water can be obtained at the visitor center.

Finding the trailhead: From Interstate 65 near Seymour, go 2 miles east on U.S. Highway 50 to the Muscatatuck National Wildlife Refuge entrance on the right (south) side of the highway. Go 0.5 mile south on the main refuge road to the visitor center. From the center, go 3 miles south on the main refuge road, passing Richart and Stanfield lakes, to a gravel parking lot on the right (west) at a T intersection. From the parking lot, go south to the T intersection and begin the trail at the gated entrance to an old farm lane.

Key points:
0.0 Trailhead.
0.5 Go left (east) at the East River Trail intersection.
1.5 Reach the optional spur to Half-Moon Lake.
1.6 Pass Myers Cemetery.
2.4 Go left (south) at the old farm road.
2.5 Reach the West River Trail intersection and go right (west).

The hike: Muscatatuck is the first national wildlife refuge established in Indiana and one of more than 500 across the country whose purchase was funded by revenue from federal duck stamps. Land acquisition at

Muscatatuck National Wildlife Refuge

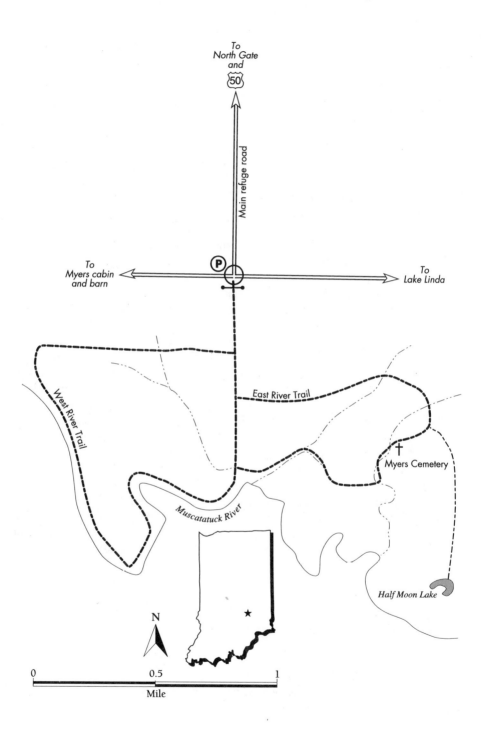

Muscatatuck began in 1966 and encompasses 7,700 acres of varied habitat providing sanctuary for an abundance of wildlife. Birds are particularly noteworthy inhabitants, with more than 250 species observed at the refuge, including uncommon Indiana birds such as the least bittern and the yellow-crowned night heron.

Spring and fall bring migrating waterfowl to Muscatatuck by the thousands, and sandhill cranes, ospreys, and bald eagles can be seen during the fall. Deer, wild turkeys, rabbits, beavers, muskrats, quail, and raccoons are common, and Muscatatuck was the site at which restoration efforts for river otters and trumpeter swans were launched in recent years. Another common inhabitant of the refuge is the nonpoisonous copperbelly watersnake, so rare nationwide that it was considered for federally listed threatened status by the U.S. Fish and Wildlife Service.

There are eight maintained hiking trails at the refuge, but most are less than 1 mile long. The two river trails are the longest, and together make a substantial hike through meadows and along the river. Distance and location make both loops the least-traveled trails in the refuge. Both trails can be closed during periods of high water on the Muscatatuck, usually in the spring. There are very few markers along either trail.

Start at the gated entrance and follow an old farm lane south for 0.5 mile to the beginning of the East River Trail. It is a wooded pathway at the outset, but soon opens into rolling meadows; more than half the refuge consists of grasslands and abandoned farm fields.

At 1.2 miles, the trail curls to the south and meanders through a meadow before intersecting with an optional spur to Half-Moon Lake at 1.5 miles. At 1.6 miles, pass the Myers Cemetery, a small graveyard of the family that settled in this river bottom in the early 1800s. The Myers cabin and barn are located 0.25 mile west of the gated entrance to the river trails.

From the cemetery, continue west, crossing a couple of shallow gullies and intermittent streams. The trail parallels the streams at times before coming back to the old farm road at 2.4 miles. Turn left (south) and go 0.1 mile to the start of a clockwise loop of the West River Trail. Unlike the East River Trail, the West River Trail actually follows the Muscatatuck River, winding along its banks for a little more than 1.5 miles before turning north to a service road. Turn right on a straight, east-bound stretch that borders the south side of the waterfowl sanctuary for almost 1 mile before reaching the old farm road. Turn left (north) and return to the trailhead.

30 Versailles State Park

Type of hike: Day hike, loop.
General description: A loop trail circling upland woods, ravines, and sinkholes along the eastern bluff of Laughery Valley.

General location:	Southeast Indiana, 24 miles north of Madison.
Total distance:	2.4 miles.
Difficulty:	Easy to moderate.
Elevation gain:	One climb of 80 feet.
Jurisdiction:	Indiana Department of Natural Resources, Division of State Parks & Reservoirs.
Special attractions:	Overlook of Laughery Valley and sinkholes.
Maps:	Milan USGS quad; Versailles State Park brochure.
Permits/fees:	There is a $2 entry fee for vehicles with Indiana license plates; $5 for out-of-state vehicles. Season passes are available.
Camping:	Versailles State Park has 226 campsites, all modern, plus a youth tent area.
Trailhead facilities:	In addition to the ample parking space at Oak Grove Shelter, there are restrooms, but no water source. Water is available at other locations in the park, including at the campgrounds, plus at the nature center and camp store, which are open only during the summer.

Finding the trailhead: Go east from Versailles for 0.8 mile on U.S. Highway 50/Indiana 129 to the entrance road to the state park. Turn left (north) and go 0.7 mile to the gatehouse. Go straight for 0.4 mile, and turn right (east) toward the campgrounds. Go 0.6 mile to the Oak Grove Shelter parking lot, and turn left (northwest). The trailhead is located on the west side of the shelter house.

Key points:
- 0.0   Trailhead.
- 0.7   Reach the Laughery Creek overlook.
- 1.2   The trail turns north.
- 2.2   Go straight at the road crossing, then turn left.

The hike: Much of present-day Versailles State Park was marginal farmland when the National Park Service acquired it in the 1930s. The National Park Service teamed with the Civilian Conservation Corps (CCC) to develop the 5,900-acre property into the Versailles Recreation Demonstration Area, then turned it all over to the state of Indiana in 1943.

Despite being the second-largest state park, Versailles is largely undeveloped, with many of the facilities centralized around Versailles Lake. Two state nature preserves—Laughery Bluff and Versailles Flatwoods—lie within the park boundaries, but neither is easily accessible.

There are three hiking trails in the park, including Trail 1, which is described here. Because there are so few trails in Versailles, they get plenty of use. There is less traffic on this trail because the other two are closer to the restrooms.

Begin the hike by walking west from the parking area toward the Oak Grove Shelter, one of the original contributions constructed by the CCC. Locate the trail marker off the southwest corner of the building near an out-of-service stone drinking fountain. Descend the hill to the south and cross a footbridge, then the park road. On the opposite side of the road, walk up the

Versailles State Park

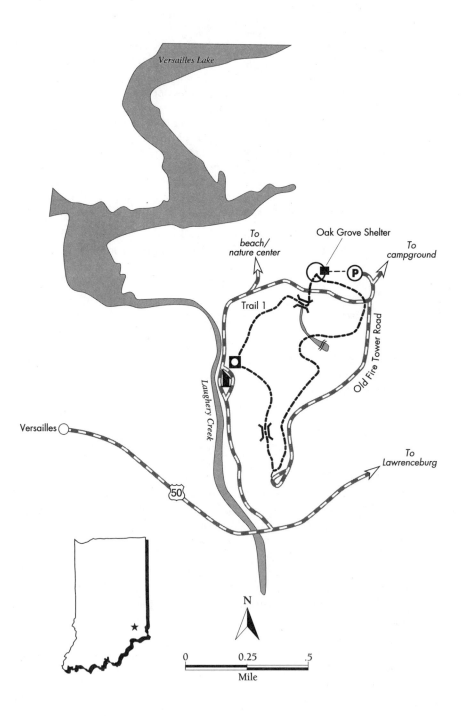

Versailles Lake

To beach/nature center

Oak Grove Shelter

To campground

Trail 1

Old Fire Tower Road

Laughery Creek

Versailles

50

To Lawrenceburg

N

0   0.25   .5

Mile

ravine, then turn east to cross another footbridge.

Hike uphill out of the ravine and turn south again. It is about an 80-foot climb. Once on top of the ridge, either begin looking along the left (east) side of the trail for some of the numerous sinkholes that are sprinkled throughout the woods, or, look right and soak up the view of Laughery Valley. There is an overlook at 0.7 mile for this purpose as well. Laughery, also the name of the creek below and to the west, actually is a misprint. The creek was named for Colonel Archibald Lochry, who was killed along with half his Pennsylvania volunteer army during a confrontation with Native Americans in 1781.

Cross over another bridge and head uphill. Reach the southern tip of the trail at 1.2 miles near an access path that leads to a parking area at the end of the Old Fire Tower Road. The trail turns north at this point and follows a level course for nearly 0.5 mile before dropping down into a ravine that features a picturesque little waterfall. Hike up the other side of the ravine onto a flat area before dropping down once more as the trail intersects with the park road at 2.2 miles. Cross the road, turn left (west) on the trail, and follow it for 0.25 mile parallel to the park road to the Oak Grove Shelter.

31   Clifty Falls State Park

Type of hike: Day hike, loop.
General description: A combination of park trails forming a loop hike through Clifty Falls Canyon.
General location: Southeast Indiana near Madison.
Total distance: 7 miles.
Difficulty: Strenuous.
Elevation gain: About 300 feet.
Jurisdiction: Indiana Department of Natural Resources, Division of State Parks & Reservoirs.
Special attractions: The Ohio River overlook, Hoffman Falls, Clifty Falls, Little Clifty Falls, and Wallace Falls.
Maps: Clifty Falls and Madison West USGS quads; Clifty Falls State Park brochure.
Permits/fees: There is a $2 entry fee for vehicles with Indiana license plates; $5 for out-of-state vehicles. Season passes are available.
Camping: Clifty Falls State Park has 165 individual campsites, from modern to primitive, plus a youth tent area.
Trailhead facilities: There is a parking lot and nature center that is open 9 A.M. to 4 P.M. Wednesdays through Sundays. Restrooms and drinkable water sources are available throughout the park at picnic shelter locations.

Finding the trailhead: Clifty Falls State Park has gatehouses at the north

Clifty Falls State Park

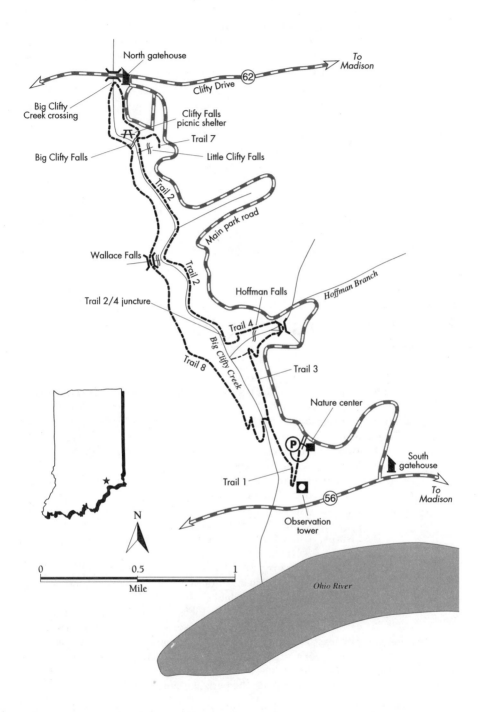

North gatehouse

To Madison

Clifty Drive

62

Big Clifty Creek crossing

Clifty Falls picnic shelter

Trail 7

Big Clifty Falls

Little Clifty Falls

Trail 2

Main park road

Wallace Falls

Trail 2

Hoffman Falls

Hoffman Branch

Trail 2/4 juncture

Trail 4

Trail 8

Big Clifty Creek

Trail 3

Nature center

Trail 1

P

South gatehouse

To Madison

56

Observation tower

N

0   0.5   1

Mile

Ohio River

and south ends. From U.S. Highway 421 in downtown Madison, go 2 miles west on Indiana 56 to the south entrance. From the south gatehouse, go 1.1 miles and turn left into the nature center parking lot. To reach the north entrance from US 421 in Madison, go 3.8 miles west on Indiana 62. From the north gate, go 4.2 miles and turn right into the nature center parking lot. Trail 1 begins at the south end of the parking lot.

Key points:
- 0.0   Trailhead.
- 0.2   Reach the Ohio River observation tower.
- 0.5   At the intersection of Trails 1, 2, and 3, take Trail 3 (the middle fork).
- 0.9   An unmarked trail goes left; turn right.
- 1.4   Reach the Hoffman Falls overlook.
- 1.5   Turn left at the "To Trail 2" marker.
- 3.0   Arrive at Big Clifty Falls.
- 3.4   Trail 8 begins near the gatehouse.
- 4.4   An unmarked trail goes left; stay straight.
- 4.8   Reach Wallace Falls.
- 6.0   Make a switchback descent to Big Clifty Creek.
- 6.4   Reach a marker for Trails 1, 2, and 8 over the creek; follow Trail 2.
- 6.5   Trail 2 joins Trails 1 and 3; turn right on Trail 1.

The hike: Most of Clifty Falls State Park's highlights can be seen by combining elements of five different park trails. In doing so, you will pass by four of the park's five major waterfalls, walk a rock-strewn portion of Clifty Creek, and see the sheer-walled canyon both from above and below.

Big Clifty Creek.

Hikers under the Big Clifty Falls at Clifty Falls State Park. Big Clifty is one of 5 major falls in the park.

The canyon is more than 300 feet deep, and so narrow in places that it is said sunlight can only reach the canyon floor at noon. Because the Trail 2 portion of this hike is along the streambed of Big Clifty Creek, it is sometimes impassable due to high water. Overall, it is a very rugged hike with difficult footing and some steep climbs. Traffic is heaviest around Hoffman Falls, Big Clifty Falls, and Little Clifty Falls, but it is noticeably lighter on Trail 8 along the west rim of the canyon.

Begin hiking at the nature center on Trail 1. Head south toward the Ohio River, coming to an observation tower at 0.2 mile. The tower provides a spectacular view of the Ohio and the nearby river town of Madison.

From the tower, head north on Trail 1 as the trail enters the canyon, hugging a ledge about midway between the top of the canyon and Big Clifty Creek below. The trail narrows and crosses a couple of footbridges over areas wet with water seeping from the shale and limestone that, at 425 million years old, is among the oldest exposed bedrock in the state.

At 0.5 mile, Trail 1 joins Trails 2 and 3 at a three-way fork in the path. Take Trail 3, the middle fork, and continue along the ledge toward Hoffman Falls, the third highest of the waterfalls at 78 feet. At 0.9 mile, an unmarked trail breaks off to the left. Stay right, climbing up a steep grade over stone steps toward the canyon lip. Go east along the ledge for another 0.25 mile and cross a footbridge over Hoffman Branch to connect with Trail 4. The trail turns left (west) along the north side of the creek and leads to a wooden walkway and platform that extends over the canyon to provide a clear view of Hoffman Falls.

Continue away from the falls on Trail 4 with the canyon to the left of the trail. At 1.5 miles, Trail 4 cuts right (north), but go left (south) on a downhill path marked "To Trail 2." This link is steep—a 150-foot drop to the canyon floor in the span of about one-tenth of a mile.

At the bottom of the canyon, turn right (north) to begin a rugged stretch of almost 1.5 miles over loose rocks and running water to the base of Big Clifty Falls. The best sign that the falls are getting closer is the size of the rocks in the stream. They are much bigger; some are as big as a compact car.

Just before you reach Big Clifty Falls, a branch of Little Clifty Creek breaks off to the right (east). Stay left (north) to get a look at Big Clifty Falls from below, then climb a 150-foot ladder and staircase system out of the canyon. It is a short, 20-yard hop over to Little Clifty Falls before you loop back to Big Clifty Falls at 3 miles. Trail 2 joins Trail 7 on a 100-yard jaunt to the Clifty Shelter picnic area. The shelter house is the last water source before heading out on the return leg to the nature center.

Turn left on the paved road and follow it north toward the gatehouse to pick up Trail 8, which is in a clearing just west of the gatehouse at 3.4 miles. Cross Big Clifty Creek just below a bridge on Indiana 62, and turn southward as the trail hugs the west rim of the canyon for the next 3 miles.

Before you reach Big Clifty Falls, look across to the east side of the creek to an abandoned stone building. This pump house, built by the Civilian Conservation Corps (CCC) more than 60 years ago, created a reservoir for a water supply for the CCC while they were working to develop the park. The building thus has historical significance, but it can not be restored because it now rests in a state nature preserve that encompasses the area north of the falls.

The west-rim hike begins on a relatively flat grade, but is punctuated by occasional cuts for small streams that spill and tumble down the canyon walls. Signs stating "No Hikers Beyond This Point" bear witness to the dangers of getting too close to the edge. Continue to ridge hop to an intersecting trail at 4.4 miles that goes left (east) and down to the canyon floor. Stay right, hugging the west rim for another 0.25 mile to Wallace Falls at 4.8 miles, which is unmarked on the state park brochure. At 79 feet, Wallace Falls is second in height only to Tunnel Falls.

Cross a footbridge over the creek feeding the falls and continue south over the humps and ridges of the canyon rim. The trail begins to slide easily down from the canyon rim, and reaches a switchback at 6 miles that leads down to Big Clifty Creek. At 6.4 miles, look for a sign hung across the creek with wire pointing to Trails 1, 2, and 8. Follow Trail 2, and begin the climb on the east side of the canyon. When Trail 2 joins Trail 1 at 6.5 miles, turn right (south) and continue uphill past the observation tower to the nature center parking lot.

32 Charlestown State Park

Type of hike: Day hike, loop.
General description: A loop trail through dense floodplain forest and along exposed rock outcroppings above Fourteenmile Creek.
General location: Southeast Indiana near the Ohio River.
Total distance: 2 miles.
Difficulty: Moderate to strenuous.
Elevation gain: The trail changes elevation several times but never by more than about 100 feet.
Jurisdiction: Indiana Department of Natural Resources, Division of State Parks & Reservoirs.
Special attractions: Fourteenmile Creek.
Maps: Charlestown USGS quad; Charlestown State Park brochure.
Permits/fees: There is a $2 gate fee for vehicles with Indiana license plates; $5 for out-of-state vehicles. Season passes are available.
Camping: None is available at Charlestown State Park, although campsites are being developed.
Trailhead facilities: Water pumps are located near the picnic shelters.

Finding the trailhead: From the Henryville exit on Interstate 65, go east 9.5 miles on Indiana 160 to its intersection with Indiana 403. Turn right

Charlestown State Park

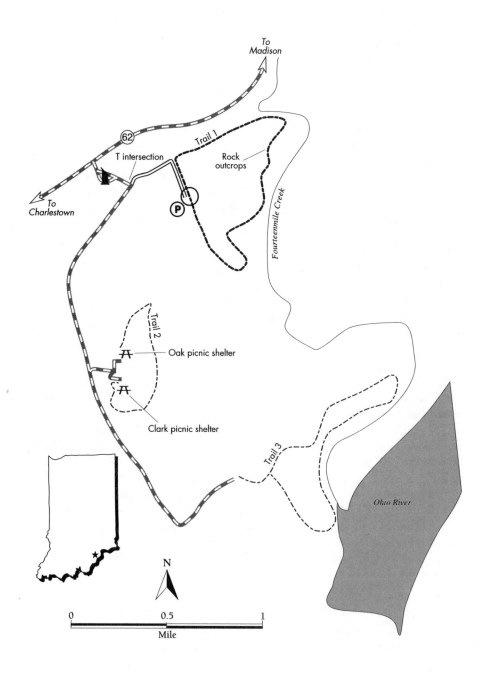

To
Madison

62

Trail 1

T intersection

Rock
outcrops

To
Charlestown

P

Fourteenmile Creek

Trail 2

Oak picnic shelter

Clark picnic shelter

Trail 3

Ohio River

N

0   0.5   1
Mile

(southeast), and go 0.8 mile to Indiana 62. Turn left (northeast), go 1.1 miles to the Charlestown State Park entrance on the right (south). From the park gatehouse, go 0.1 mile to a T intersection. Turn left (northeast), and go 1.1 miles to the Trail 1 parking lot.

Key points:
- 0.0   Trailhead.
- 0.2   Make a right turn from a gravel road to an old service road.
- 0.9   Leave the service road.
- 1.5   Cross a footbridge over the creek.
- 1.8   Reconnect to the service road.

The hike: Established in 1996, this park is so new that it has not yet caught on in popularity. Because of the floodplain environment, the trails can be muddy and slippery during and after periods of rain.

The beginning leg of this trail is less than impressive—a 0.25-mile jaunt back along the gravel entry road from the parking lot, followed by a slightly longer walk on an old service road as it descends toward Fourteenmile Creek. Depending on water levels in the creek, you are apt to catch sight of the creek before the trail takes a slow turn to the right (south). The creek winds through an unglaciated valley to the Ohio River. Locks and dams that control the Ohio River affect Fourteenmile Creek, giving it the appearance of a narrow lake rather than a flowing stream.

Once the turn is made at 0.9 mile, it is easy to see why the trail builders came this direction. The trail makes an uphill climb along a narrower path, crosses a footbridge, and meanders along the high ground past moss-covered rock abutments. As you work your way up and down the east-facing slope of the Fourteenmile Creek valley, you will pass by several rock slabs that have sheered off the cliff and tumbled toward the creek. This can be the trickiest part of the trail during wet weather, which can transform the rich soil into slippery muck.

The trail curves southwest away from the creek, crossing another creek via a footbridge near the 1.5-mile mark in the midst of a cedar thicket. Follow the trail as it swings back to the southeast below the ridgetop to a point overlooking Fourteenmile Creek. Here the trail curves back to the northwest on a 100-foot uphill climb over the next 0.25 mile.

The trail levels off at the 1.8-mile mark as it connects with the old service road. Look for the scattered concrete pilings that are remnants of buildings that date back to when the property was a U.S. Army munitions plant. It is a little more than 0.25 mile along a level grade to the Trail 1 parking lot.

Options: There are two other trails in the park, the most noteworthy being Trail 3, which begins with a steep, 250-foot descent to Fourteenmile Creek, then passes a small waterfall and rock outcroppings before concluding with a gradual ascent on an old roadbed.

33 Adventure Hiking Trail

Type of hike:	Backpack, loop.
General description:	A long-distance loop trail along forested river bluffs, ravines, sinkholes, and caves.
General location:	Southeast Indiana between Corydon and Leavenworth.
Total distance:	23 miles.
Difficulty:	Strenuous.
Elevation gain:	Eight elevation increases of over 200 feet, including two increases of 300 feet or more.
Jurisdiction:	Indiana Department of Natural Resources, Division of Forestry.
Special attractions:	Bluffs overlooking the Ohio River, Blue River, and Indian Creek, plus four overnight shelters.
Maps:	Leavenworth and Corydon West USGS quads; Indiana State Forest brochure.
Permits/fees:	There is a $2 entry fee for vehicles with Indiana license plates; $5 for out-of-state vehicles. Season passes are available.
Camping:	The Harrison-Crawford State Forest complex has 281 modern campsites, 25 primitive campsites, and a youth tent area.
Trailhead facilities:	There actually are several spots to access the Adventure Hiking Trail, but the preferred starting location is the large parking lot at the Ohio River Picnic Area. There is no water supply, but there are pit toilets. Water is available in the Wyandotte Woods Campground and at other locations in the state recreation area.

Finding the trailhead: Go west 6.8 miles on Indiana 62 from the Indiana 135 intersection in Corydon, turning left (south) at Indiana 462. Follow Indiana 462 south for 3 miles to the forest office and gatehouse. Go another 0.5 mile to the second paved road, turn left (southwest), and follow the main road past the nature center, group camp, and Potato Run Church. Go 0.9 mile past the church to the Pioneer Picnic Cabin Shelter on the left (east) side of the road. Post 1 for the Adventure Hiking Trail is located here. Additional parking is available at the Ohio River and Blue River picnic areas farther down the road to the southwest.

Key points:
- 0.0 Trailhead.
- 1.6 Reach post 2 and go straight to continue; turn right to reach Wyandotte Woods Campground.
- 2.8 Go right at post 3. *Do not cross the bridge.*
- 4.8 Reach the overnight shelter at post B.
- 7.4 Turn right at post C.
- 8.6 Reach post 8 and the junction with Indiana 462.

Adventure Hiking Trail

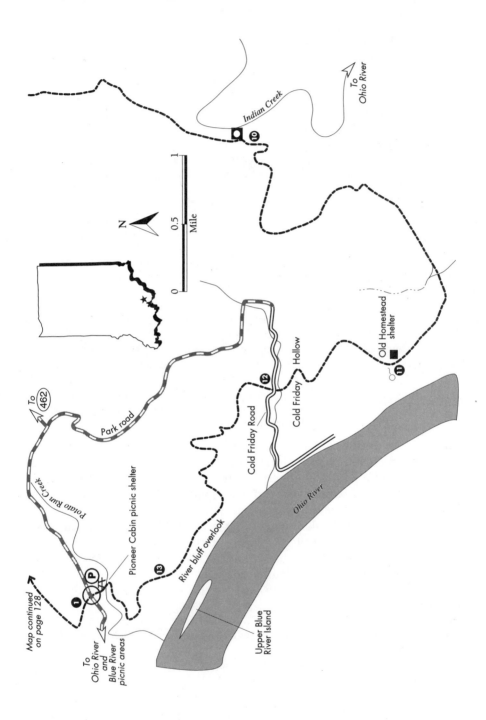

To
Ohio River

Indian Creek

N

0   0.5   1
Mile

To
462

Park road

Potato Run Creek

Pioneer Cabin picnic shelter

Cold Friday Road

Cold Friday Hollow

Old Homestead
shelter

River bluff overlook

Ohio River

Upper Blue
River Island

To
Ohio River
and
Blue River
picnic areas

Map continued
on page 128

10.2	Arrive at post 9 and the junction with an old forest road.
13.4	Reach post 10 and the Indian Creek overlook shelter.
17.8	The Old Homestead shelter is at post 11.
19.1	Go straight at post 12 and the junction with Cold Friday Road.
22.2	The Ohio River shelter is at post 13.
23.0	Reach post 1 and the Pioneer Cabin picnic shelter.

The hike: The Adventure Hiking Trail—or AHT—keeps getting shorter, but it is still the second-longest trail in the state next to the Knobstone Trail (Hikes 60–65). Once listed as being 27 to 30 miles long, the AHT now measures just more than 23 miles and is still under revision. Check with the property office, nature center, or gatehouse for updates.

The AHT has been shortened to eliminate dangerous crossovers of Indiana 62, and the entire trail now lies south of the highway in the 24,000-acre state forest complex. The terrain is similar to the Knobstone Trail—narrow ridgetops alternating with deep ravines. The major difference on the AHT is the breathtaking view from bluffs 300 to 400 feet above the Ohio River and two of its tributaries—Blue River and Indian Creek.

The AHT also features several overnight shelter houses along the way, plus the option of primitive camping along the trail, so long as camp is made on public land, is at least 1 mile from all roads and recreation areas, and can not be seen from the trail.

With 12 climbs of between 150 and 300 feet, the AHT typically takes three days to complete. It is marked with posts painted green and white, and with numbers and letters designating specific locations along the trail. The trail is definitely rugged, with numerous steep climbs. Once considered poorly marked and confusing to follow, the AHT has benefited from trail maintenance in recent years. Traffic is usually highest around the Pioneer Cabin and the Wyandotte Woods Campground. Overall, the AHT gets a modest amount of use.

The trail begins at the Pioneer Cabin, about half a mile northeast of the Ohio River Picnic Area. Locate post 1 near the cabin, and turn left (northwest) to begin the first uphill challenge—a 250-foot climb to a knob. Atop the knob, turn right (northeast) and follow the saddles that connect it to two more knobs.

At post 2—1.6 miles from post 1—turn right (northeast) to reach the Wyandotte Woods Campground, or continue on a northwest course down a ravine to connect with an old road that leads to post 3 at 2.8 miles. Previously, this is where the AHT crossed the Blue River via an iron bridge. The bridge fell into disrepair, providing another reason to close off the north section of the trail.

Instead of crossing the bridge, the AHT continues for about three-quarters of a mile along the east bank of the Blue River through a state wildlife management area. Head right (southeast) into a ravine and go uphill to follow a bluff overlooking a bend in the Blue River. Descend from the bluff on a steep grade to cross a creek and reach an old barn that now serves as an overnight shelter option. At 4.8 miles from the starting point, it is an unlikely place to stop on the first day.

Continue through Fox Valley, aptly named for its abundant red fox popu-

Adventure Hiking Trail (part 2)

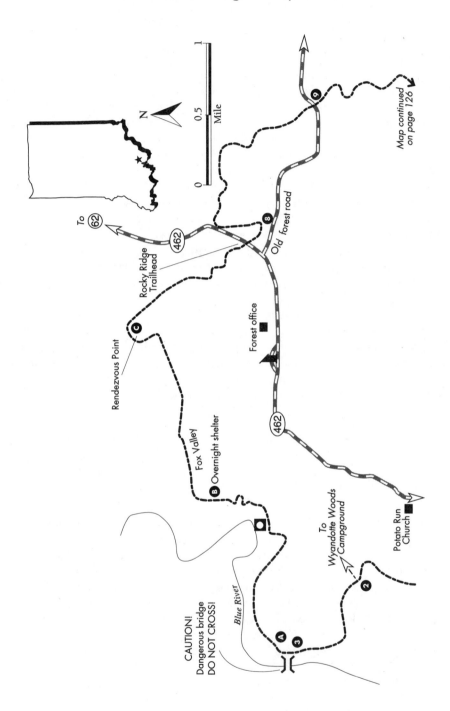

To 62

462

Rocky Ridge Trailhead

Old forest road

8

9

Map continued on page 126

Forest office

Rendezvous Point

C

Fox Valley

B Overnight shelter

To Wyandotte Woods Campground

462

Potato Run Church

2

A

3

Blue River

CAUTION! Dangerous bridge DO NOT CROSS!

N

0   0.5   1
Mile

lation. The valley once was a thriving farm. At post C, 7.4 miles into the trail, the AHT reaches the Rendezvous Point—a spot where hikers used to be able to turn left (north) and hike about 8 miles to Wyandotte Caves. All but 2 miles of that leg, however, is north of Indiana 62 and presently closed to hikers.

Turn right (south) at post C, and follow a ridgeline for 1.2 miles to a gravel parking lot at Indiana 462 (8.6 miles). A sign marks the spot as the Rocky Ridge Trailhead. Cross the highway to post 8.

There are two ravine crossings in the 1.6 miles between post 8 and post 9. The first is a drop of more than 200 feet, followed by a climb of about 250 feet, then a drop of 180 feet and a climb of 160 feet. Cross an old forest road just before reaching post 9 at 10.2 miles.

The next 3.2 miles to post 10 travel through a wildlife management area. The manipulated clearings and small ponds attract white-tailed deer, ruffed grouse, and wild turkeys. To improve chances of seeing wildlife, approach these areas quietly. The last 1.5 miles before Post 10 traverses a ridgetop that leads to a sheer bluff overlooking Indian Creek. The 300-foot drop is a good place to see turkey vultures and hawks as they soar near the cliff.

A trailside shelter is located at post 10 at 13.4 miles. From there, the trail descends gradually before skirting the high side of a ravine and passing several sinkholes. From a high knob, descend a wide ravine on a southeast course and cross a creek before embarking on a climb of nearly 300 feet to post 11 and the Old Homestead shelter. The shelter is located on a broad plateau at 17.8 miles and is built on the foundation of an 1860s-era log cabin, complete with the original chimney. Water can usually be obtained from a nearby spring.

Go northeast from post 11 for almost 0.5 mile before turning northwest to descend a broad ridge point into Cold Friday Hollow. Cross a creek and old Cold Friday Road in the hollow, as well as post 12 at 19.1 miles. Beyond the road, you will reach a demanding stretch of the trail—three ridge and two ravine crossings in the span of just over 1.5 miles. The last climb curls southwest around a ridge point and leads to the most scenic stretch of the AHT along a steep bluff overlooking the Ohio River.

The last overnight shelter is located at post 13, at 22.2 miles, and is the place to be in springtime when bald eagles frequent Upper Blue River Island almost 400 feet below. From post 13, go downhill 0.8 mile to the Pioneer Cabin, which is beyond the Potato Run Creek crossing.

34 Shaw Lake Loop

Type of hike: Day hike, loop.
General description: A trail over the rugged, hilly terrain of Clark State Forest.
General location: Near Henryville in southeast Indiana.

Total distance:	5.5 miles, with an optional 3.3-mile wildlife spur.
Difficulty:	Strenuous.
Elevation gain:	Two steep climbs of more than 250 feet.
Jurisdiction:	Indiana Department of Natural Resources, Division of Forestry.
Special attractions:	High knob vistas.
Maps:	Henryville USGS quad; Clark State Forest brochure.
Permits/fees:	None required.
Camping:	No camping is permitted on the trail, but there are 70 primitive campsites near the Clark State Forest office.
Trailhead facilities:	There is only a parking lot at the trailhead. No restrooms or potable water sources are available.

Finding the trailhead: From the Clark State Forest main entrance on U.S. Highway 31 on the north side of Henryville, go 0.5 mile to Brownstown Road and turn left (west). Go 3.4 miles, passing under Interstate 65, to the Shaw Lake parking lot on the right (north) side of the road. The trail begins in the northwest corner of the parking lot at a red metal gate.

Key points:
- 0.0   Trailhead.
- 0.2   At the trail juncture go straight over the dam.
- 1.2   Go right (northeast) at the trail juncture.
- 1.6   Reach Oak Knob; turn right (east) and go downhill.
- 2.2   Go straight at the trail juncture at the knob.
- 2.5   Reach the Leaf Run creek crossing and go straight.
- 3.0   Reach a trail juncture at a knob and go right. The 3.3-mile wildlife spur is to the left.
- 4.5   Descend from the ridgetop.
- 5.3   At the trail juncture turn left to the parking lot.

The hike: Established in 1903, Clark State Forest is the oldest in the Indiana system. Portions of the original forest are on land granted to General George Rogers Clark and his soldiers for their service during the Revolutionary War. Originally encompassing a mere 2,000 acres, Clark State Forest now covers 24,000 acres and is the third-largest forest in the state. The property was used as an experimental forest in its early years.

The forest has nine trails designated for horseback riding, but hikers are welcome to use them as well. Shaw Lake is typical of the trail system, with scenic vistas, narrow backbones, and steep hills. This is an easy trail to follow, but because it is shared with equestrians, the footing can be loose on steep slopes and muddy in low areas. It is definitely not a hike to take in wet conditions.

To begin the hike, pass by the gate and follow a path of crushed stone less than 0.1 mile to a trail juncture that forms the beginning and end points of the loop. Take the left (north) fork, which leads over a ridgetop and downhill to another juncture at 0.2 mile. Here, the left fork is marked with a green sign that directs horse traffic around the Shaw Lake Dam. Take the right fork down to the lake and cross over the dam to the northwest corner of the lake at 0.5 mile.

Shaw Lake Loop

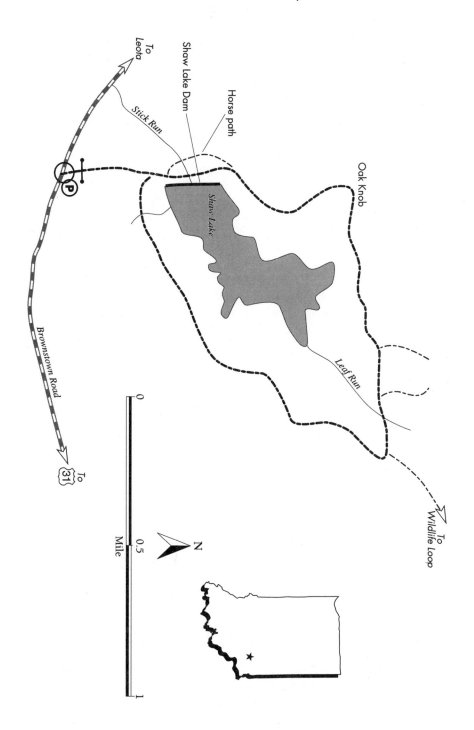

Reenter the forest and hike up and over a series of ridges as the trail turns northeast. In addition to green markers that help point the way, look for occasional green paint blazes on trees. At 1.2 miles, come to another split in the trail. Go right (northeast), following the green markers as the trail descends into and out of two deep gullies, both of which can be wet and muddy. From here, the hiking really gets tough, beginning with a steep climb to a narrow ridge. The trail stays suspended along the ridgetop, with sharp slopes dropping off on either side. Remember to follow the green trail markers or green blazes on the trees.

After climbing to Oak Knob at 1.6 miles, the trail splits once more at 2.2 miles. The left fork leads through an optional 3.3-mile wildlife management unit, but stay to the right (south) and hike down a steep incline to where the trail crosses Leaf Run at 2.5 miles. Head uphill at a steep angle to another high knob. At 3 miles, the main trail veers to the south, while the optional 3.3-mile Wildlife Loop branches off to the left (northeast).

Staying on the main trail, walk south along a narrow ridgetop that dips and rises for another mile or so. At 4.5 miles, begin an extremely sharp descent where the footing can be loose over dirt and stone depending on the amount of recent horse traffic. At the bottom of the hill, cross a rocky stretch and a stream before climbing over a small ridge and picking up a wider path that leads back to the intersection at the beginning of the loop. At the intersection at 5.3 miles, turn left (south) and return along the stone path to the parking lot.

35 Starve Hollow State Recreation Area

Type of hike:	Day hike, multiple loop.
General description:	A combination of three short trails, including a rugged section to ridgetop vistas.
General location:	South of Brownstown in Jackson County.
Total distance:	4.6 miles.
Difficulty:	Moderate to strenuous.
Elevation gain:	There is a 315-foot climb from Starve Hollow Lake to the top of the Vista Trail.
Jurisdiction:	Indiana Department of Natural Resources, Division of Forestry.
Special attractions:	An interpretive nature trail and Starve Hollow vistas.
Maps:	Vallonia USGS quad; Starve Hollow State Recreation Area brochure.
Permits/fees:	There is a $2 entry fee for vehicles with Indiana license plates; $5 for out-of-state vehicles. Season passes are available.

Camping:	Starve Hollow State Recreation Area has 219 individual campsites, all modern.
Trailhead facilities:	Restrooms and water are located near the campground gatehouse and between the campgrounds near the trailhead kiosk.

Finding the trailhead: From its intersection with U.S. Highway 50 on the west side of Brownstown, go 2.9 miles south on Indiana 135. Turn left on Jackson County 300 West (also known as Lake Road), and go south 2.3 miles to the Starve Hollow State Recreation Area entrance on the left (east). After entering through the first gatehouse, go to the campground gatehouse. Non-campers must park in the lot next to the gatehouse and walk from there to the trailhead.

Key points:
- 0.0 Trailhead.
- 0.7 Cross over the third footbridge.
- 1.4 Reach the intersection of Lakeshore Loop and Vista Trail; cross the road and turn left.
- 1.7 Turn right (south) on the Vista Trail ridgetop.
- 2.0 At the south vista, go downhill.
- 3.2 The Vista Trail ends; rejoin Lakeshore Loop.
- 3.9 Lakeshore Loop ends; rejoin Oak Leaf Trail.
- 4.6 Return to the campground gatehouse.

The hike: Starve Hollow State Recreation Area is part of Jackson-Washington State Forest, a 15,000-acre property noted for its "knobby" ridges. Two

A scenic overlook on the Vista Trail offers an almost unobstructed view of Starve Hollow Lake.

Starve Hollow State Recreation Area

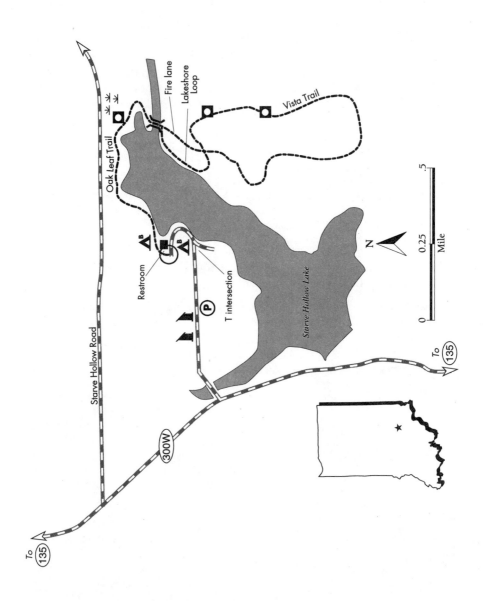

other Indiana Department of Natural Resources operations—Driftwood Fish Hatchery and Vallonia Nursery—are located in the valley below the high ridges of the Knobstone Escarpment. This hike features one of the knobs typical of this natural feature.

The first leg of this route, which is an interpretive nature trail, gets the most traffic. The Lakeshore Loop (marked by yellow blazes) can be muddy and wet at times, but the gravel fire lane provides an alternate route. The Vista Trail is the least traveled of the three, but is clearly marked with blue blazes.

The hike has a slow start due to the location of the trailhead in the campground. Go through the B campground to Starve Hollow Lake, a 145-acre reservoir constructed in 1938. Turn left (north) at the T intersection and follow the paved road as it goes north and then curves west to a brick restroom building. Turn right (north) at the building and go to the trailhead kiosk near campsite 42. All hiking options begin here.

What follows is a description of the three trails—Oak Leaf Trail, Lakeshore Loop, and Vista Trail—combined to create one hike. The Oak Leaf segment is an interpretive trail with a brochure that identifies numbered markers for plants or trees such as sumac, big tooth aspen, club moss, red pine, persimmon, bald cypress, horsetail or scouring rush, red cedar, sycamore, tulip poplar, and beech. Just past the second footbridge is a viewing platform for a woodland marsh. A third footbridge at 0.7 mile crosses one of the creeks that feeds the lake. Link with the Lakeshore Loop at this point.

The loop has two possible routes, both marked by yellow blazes. Follow the right (southwest) fork, which hugs the lakeshore, while passing up and over several fingerlike ridges before turning uphill to meet a fire lane. Cross the lane to a long, wooden bench and trail intersection at 1.4 miles. Turn left (north) to follow the blue-marked Vista Trail through a mature hardwood forest. A very steep climb covers the 315-foot elevation difference from the lakeshore to the top of the ridge at 1.7 miles and one of two vistas or overlooks. The trail bends south from here and follows a ridgeline that offers occasional glimpses of Starve Hollow Lake before coming to a nearly unobstructed view near the south tip at 2 miles. The trail makes a sharp descent from here into a ravine where streams run in intermittent fashion depending on rainfall. Hike through this area, which features a continual series of small fingerlike ridges and occasional stream crossings, to return to the end of the Vista Trail at the wooden bench at 3.2 miles.

Either retrace your steps along the lakeshore, or turn right (north) and follow the fire lane downhill to the footbridge and the end of the Lakeshore Loop at 3.9 miles. Walk back over the Oak Leaf Trail to the trailhead at 4.6 miles.

36 Knob Lake Trail

Type of hike:	Day hike, loop.
General description:	A loop hike, with a linear spur near the finish, that includes climbs up some of the highest hills in the Jackson-Washington State Forest.
General location:	East of Brownstown in south-central Indiana.
Total distance:	4.3 miles.
Difficulty:	Strenuous.
Elevation gain:	A difference of 345 feet between the low and high spots.
Jurisdiction:	Indiana Department of Natural Resources, Division of Forestry.
Special attractions:	High Point Knob, Old Tower Knob, and Pinnacle Peak.
Maps:	Tampico, Vallonia, and Seymour USGS quads; Jackson-Washington State Forest brochure.
Permits/fees:	None required.
Camping:	There are 65 primitive sites at the Knob Lake campground.
Trailhead facilities:	Pit toilets and drinking water are available in the Knob Lake campground area, and there is a well pump at the Oven Shelterhouse.

Finding the trailhead: From its intersection with U.S. Highway 50 in Brownstown, go 2 miles east on Indiana 250 to the Knob Lake turnoff. Turn left (northeast) off Indiana 250 and follow the paved road, passing the forest office and Knob Lake, and past the Museum Shelterhouse, to a parking lot near Oven Shelterhouse. Park in the lot and walk up the stone steps to the Oven Shelterhouse area. Walk to the south end of the playground to begin the trail.

Key points:
- 0.0 Trailhead.
- 1.0 Reach the service area.
- 1.5 Leave the stream and begin to climb.
- 2.5 Reach High Point Knob.
- 2.7 Arrive at Old Tower Knob.
- 3.3 Reach Pinnacle Peak.

The hike: This hike begins at a rather casual pace, but the last 3 miles are as challenging as it gets, with a string of high, round hills—or knobs—connected together like a backbone. The Trail 1 portion gets more traffic than Trails 2 and 3, largely because of the attraction of Pinnacle Peak. All trails are well-maintained, well-marked, and easy to follow.

Begin at the Oven Shelterhouse, a picnic area built by the Civilian Conservation Corps that was placed on the National Registry of Historic Places in 1997. Go to the southeast corner of the picnic area and continue along a wide gravel path to the first trail marker—a brown, plastic post. Cross over a stone bridge at the north end of Knob Lake, and turn right at the Trail 3

136

Knob Lake Trail

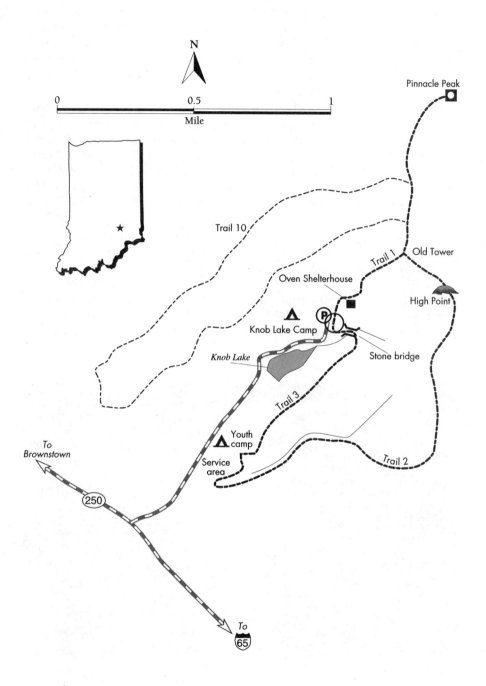

marker. After crossing a footbridge, the trail curves to the right and begins to climb nearly 100 feet to a ridge that runs southwest, gradually descending to a youth camp area.

At the camp, take a left turn on the gravel road and follow it around to a service area at 1 mile before turning left at a Trail 3 marker. This is a transition point from the end of Trail 3 to the south terminus of Trail 2. Walk a short distance to the first Trail 2 marker and head northeast up a ravine along a meandering stream. Crisscross from one side of the stream to the other several times before turning away from the stream at 1.5 miles to begin the toughest part of the hike.

What starts as a gradual climb turns into a demanding scramble that rises more than 250 feet over the next 0.5 mile to a knob that is 970 feet above sea level. It is not the highest knob on the hike, but it is a pretty good warm-up. Over the next mile, a series of knobs reaching from 910 to 985 feet are connected by saddles that drop no lower than 830 feet. The 985-foot knob is appropriately named High Point and is at 2.5 miles. It is followed by the Old Tower Knob at 2.7 miles, which is marked by the concrete footings of an old fire tower that was torn down years ago.

Turn right (north) from the Old Tower Knob, and proceed north, passing two points that intersect with another trail (Trail 10). After the second intersection, skirt the east side of a knob and walk along a ledge that leads to Pinnacle Peak (966 feet), an exposed face of loose rock that provides a spectacular scenic view to the south and east. From Pinnacle Peak at 3.3 miles, backtrack to the Old Tower Knob and turn right (southwest), descending a steep grade that eventually levels off before reaching the Oven Shelterhouse picnic area.

Trees frame High Point, the highest of several knob-like hills that are climbed on the rugged Knob Lake Trail.

Hill Country

Time has not stood still in the picturesque Hill Country of south-central Indiana, but in many ways the region and its residents have not completely outgrown the pioneer lifestyle. Instead they have capitalized on it.

The sleepy Brown County town of Nashville has been a tourist mecca since the 1930s because of its craft shops and artist galleries. An estimated four million visitors clog its streets each year in search of antiques, collectibles, or something that simply looks old or handmade.

The area's greatest ambassador was a cartoon character—Abe Martin. The creation of Indianapolis newspaperman and humorist Kin Hubbard, Martin spun folksy wisdom about life in fictional "Bloom Center" and its odd assortment of residents. "It ain't a bad plan to keep still occasionally, even when you know what you're talking about," is one of the 16,000 sayings attributed to Abe Martin. The lodge at nearby Brown County State Park is named for the popular cartoon character.

The park is the crown jewel of the state system. It is the largest, at about 16,000 acres, and annually draws more than 1.7 million visitors, many who come to enjoy the autumn colors of the hardwood forest. The park and the town of Nashville are often favorably compared to Great Smoky Mountains National Park and Gatlinburg, Tennessee. Authentic log cabin homes are a common sight, and colorful place names are plentiful—Graveyard Hollow, Deadman Hollow, Gnaw Bone, Weed Patch Hill, Hesitation Point, Scarce O' Fat Ridge, and Greasy Creek, to name a few.

Spared the forces of the last great glacier, the region is noted as much for its deep valleys and ravines as it is for its rolling hills. Stripped of its native timber a century ago, the land became an affordable dream for those hoping to carve out an existence on small farms. The thin rocky soil, coupled with the highly erodable terrain, proved unsuitable for agriculture, however, and most of the pioneer farms failed during the Great Depression.

The state acquired about 40,000 acres of abandoned farmland in 1929 and with it established Brown County State Park and Morgan-Monroe State Forest. Yellowwood State Forest was added to the picture in 1947, when the federal land was deeded to the state.

The northern boundary of the Hoosier National Forest abuts the three state properties, creating a massive block of public land available for outdoor recreation opportunities.

Farther south is Spring Mill State Park, which is noted for its karst cave topography. The area is riddled with sinkholes and caves.

Hikes in this section are presented in a clockwise sweep heading north from Bloomington.

37 Low Gap Trail in Morgan-Monroe State Forest

Type of hike:	Day hike or backpack, loop.
General description:	A loop trail covering steep, forested ridges, ravines, creeks, and the Back Country Area of Morgan-Monroe State Forest.
General location:	Midway between Bloomington and Martinsville in south-central Indiana.
Total distance:	10 miles, with an optional 1-mile round-trip spur to Draper Cabin.
Difficulty:	Strenuous.
Elevation gain:	Several changes of 200 to 270 feet from ridgetops to ravines and back.
Jurisdiction:	Indiana Department of Natural Resources, Division of Forestry.
Special attractions:	Draper Cabin and Rock cliffs in Sweedy Hollow.
Maps:	Hindustan USGS quad; Morgan-Monroe State Forest brochure.
Permits/fees:	None required.
Camping:	There are 32 primitive campsites in Morgan-Monroe State Forest—21 at Mason Ridge and 11 at Oak Ridge. Additional sites are located in the Scout Ridge youth tent area. The campgrounds are located on the main forest road north of the trailhead. Camping is also permitted in the Back Country Area crossed by the eastern section of Low Gap Trail.
Trailhead facilities:	There is only a small gravel parking lot at the trailhead, but water, restrooms, and picnic shelters are available at several locations along the main forest road.

Finding the trailhead: Go 13 miles north on Indiana 37 from Bloomington, and turn right (northeast) at the Morgan-Monroe State Forest signs. Go 0.6 mile to Old State Road 37 and turn right. Go 1.7 miles to the main forest road and turn left (northeast) to enter Morgan-Monroe State Forest. Go 4.5 miles to a parking area on the right (south) side of the main road. The trailhead is about 10 yards off the road.

Key points:

0.0	Trailhead.
0.1	Go left (south) on the Tincher Ridge logging road.
1.0	Go left (east) to Sweedy Hollow.
2.8	At the trail juncture, go right on the Landram Ridge logging road.
4.0	Cross over Low Gap Road to the parking lot and footbridge.
6.7	At the trail juncture, turn left on Orcutt Road.
7.8	Cross Low Gap Road and follow the gravel Orcutt Road uphill.
8.2	Go right on the logging road beyond the cable barricade.
8.7	Pass the radio tower on the left.

Low Gap Trail in Morgan-Monroe State Forest

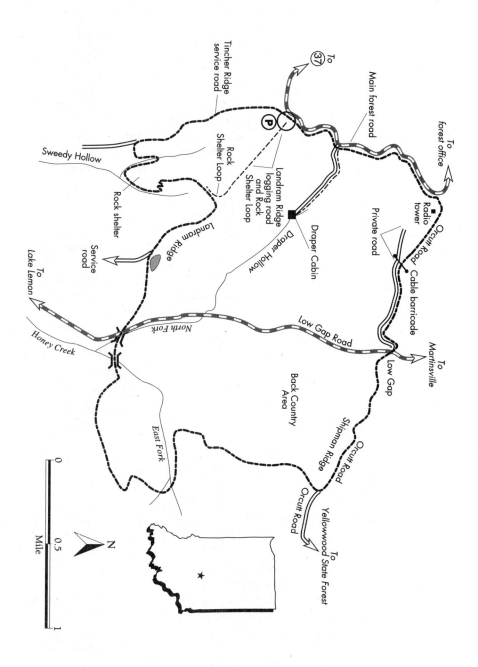

8.8   At the trail juncture, go left (west).

9.7   At the gravel road, go straight to complete the trail or go left (south) to Draper Cabin.

10.0   Reach the trailhead parking lot.

The hike: It is almost impossible to imagine this area devoid of trees, but it was, after the original settlers cleared it in a vain attempt to establish farms. The rocky soil proved unsuitable, and the land was abandoned. The state stepped in during the Great Depression to purchase 24,000 acres of the eroding hillsides, and established Morgan-Monroe State Forest.

The intervening years have allowed the lush forest to be reestablished, including 2,700 acres designated as the Back Country Area in 1981. Low Gap Trail passes through this area, which was set aside to provide a wilderness experience. Low Gap is one of two 10-mile hikes in Morgan-Monroe State Forest. It is well-marked with white blazes on trees, plus blue paint markings at mile intervals. Although a good part of the trail follows abandoned roads and service roads, the rugged segments through Sweedy Hollow and along Gorley Ridge and Shipman Ridge, discourage all but avid hikers.

The trail begins at a small, gravel parking lot just off the main forest road. Head west for 0.1 mile to connect with an old road and turn left (south), following the roadway and trail south along Tincher Ridge. At 1 mile, turn left off the trail and make the steep descent via a series of switchbacks over a fern-carpeted slope into Sweedy Hollow. At the bottom of the ravine, follow the creek, which the trail crosses several times, for almost another mile before passing below stone cliffs that overhang the west side of the ravine. Continuing on the trail, make the steep climb out of Sweedy Hollow to reach the 2-mile mark on a ridgetop.

At 2.8 miles, link up with Landram Ridge Road, a gravel service road. A sign marks the spot, pointing left (northwest) for the 3-mile Rock Shelter Loop and right (southeast) for the continuation of the Low Gap Trail. Go right, crossing the high end of a ravine while keeping on a southeast course. The service road soon breaks to the right (south), but the trail continues left (east) and downhill along a powerline corridor.

Pass a pond after another 0.5 mile, then leave the powerline corridor to enter the woods. Continue downhill to the first crossover of Low Gap Road at 4 miles. A gravel parking lot marks the entry to the Back Country Area. Cross a pair of footbridges over the North Fork and East Fork of Honey Creek before making a steep uphill march to the top of Gorley Ridge, which is about the midway point of the hike. Part of the climb is over an old roadbed, but the trail eventually leaves the roadbed to drop into a ravine to the East Fork of Honey Creek. Cross the creek a couple of times, passing through a pine plantation that is a popular Back Country camping site.

The last challenging portion of the trail begins with a climb to a narrow ridgetop that leads to Shipman Ridge and the linkup with Orcutt Road, a service road. At the intersection at 6.7 miles, turn left (northwest) and follow Orcutt Road as it winds gradually downhill to the second crossover of Low Gap Road. A small parking lot at 7.8 miles marks the spot, with the trail continuing uphill to the northwest along the gravel Orcutt Road, which

Rock overhangs are a rugged component of Sweedy Hollow, which is on the Low Gap Trail in Morgan-Monroe State Forest.

leads to private residences.

Stay on the road, splitting off to the right at a cable barricade at the 8.2-mile mark. The trail follows the service road past a radio tower, and continues toward the main forest road.

Low Gap Trail turns left (west) off the service road about 50 yards before the main forest road at 8.8 miles. Hike parallel to the main road, reaching a gravel road at the 9.7-mile mark. The gravel road leads south for 0.5 mile to the Draper Cabin, a rustic log home on the banks of the North Fork of Honey Creek. The cabin, which has stone floors and no plumbing, can be rented for overnight stays between April and Thanksgiving, and during the winter depending on weather conditions.

Visit the cabin, then backtrack uphill to the Low Gap Trail and turn left (south), following a path parallel to the main forest road for less than 0.5 mile to the trailhead parking lot.

38 Three Lakes Loop in Morgan-Monroe State Forest

Type of hike:	Day hike, loop.
General description:	This trail visits the steep, forested ridges, ravines, creeks, and lakes of Morgan-Monroe State Forest.
General location:	Midway between Bloomington and Martinsville in south-central Indiana.
Total distance:	10 miles.
Difficulty:	Strenuous.
Elevation gain:	Five descents of 140 to 250 feet, and four climbs of 140 to 200 feet.
Jurisdiction:	Indiana Department of Natural Resources, Division of Forestry.
Special attractions:	Lush woodland valleys, Bryant Creek Lake, creek banks, and a pioneer cemetery.
Maps:	Hindustan USGS quad; Morgan-Monroe State Forest brochure.
Permits/fees:	None required.
Camping:	There are 32 primitive campsites in Morgan-Monroe State Forest—21 at Mason Ridge and 11 at Oak Ridge. Additional sites are located in the Scout Ridge youth tent area. The campgrounds are located on the main forest road north of the trailhead. Camping is also permitted in the Back Country Area crossed by the eastern section of Low Gap Trail.
Trailhead facilities:	There is a small parking lot at the trailhead, but water and restrooms are located nearby at the Cherry Lake picnic shelter. Water and restrooms can also be found at other locations in the state forest.

Three Lakes Loop in Morgan-Monroe State Forest

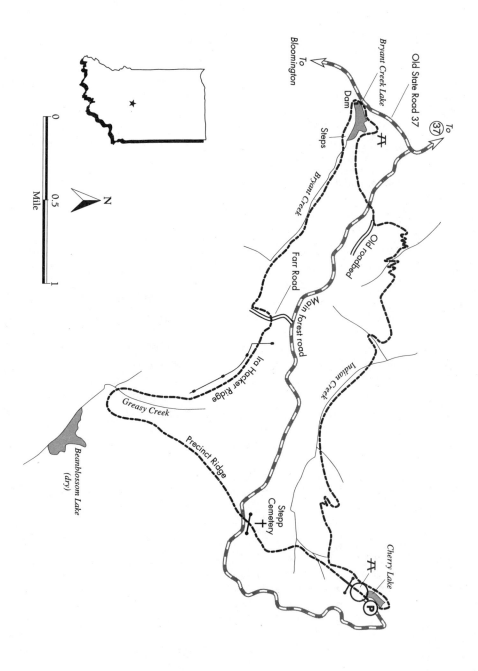

Finding the trailhead: Go 13 miles north from Bloomington on Indiana 37, and turn right (northeast) at the Morgan-Monroe State Forest signs. Go 0.6 mile to Old State Road 37 and turn right (southeast). Go 1.7 miles to the main forest road and turn left (northeast) to enter Morgan-Monroe State Forest. Go 4.8 miles to the first paved road to the left (north). Turn left and go 0.2 mile to a small paved parking lot on the right (northwest) overlooking Cherry Lake. The trail begins 0.1 mile down the road on the left (south) side at a metal gate blocking a forest service road.

Key points:
- 0.0   Trailhead.
- 1.0   Reach the Stepp Cemetery.
- 1.1   Go straight at the main road crossing.
- 2.3   Cross Greasy Creek.
- 3.5   Cross over Farr Road.
- 5.0   Reach Bryant Creek Lake.
- 6.0   Go straight at the main road crossing.
- 6.5   Cross Indian Creek.
- 9.6   Return to the Cherry Lake shelter house.

The hike: The name for this trail is no longer accurate because it actually only goes to two lakes—Bryant Creek and Cherry lakes. The third lake on the original triangular-shaped trail, Beanblossom Lake, has dried up. Regardless of name accuracy, the Three Lakes Loop is every bit as demanding as the Low Gap Trail (Hike 37), the other long-distance hike in Morgan-Monroe State Forest. The trail stretches along narrow ridgetops and through creekbeds in deep ravines, and requires a lot of up-and-down climbing. The seclusion of the hardwood forests, the abundance of wildflowers, and the opportunity to encounter wildlife makes the Three Lakes Loop a quality hiking opportunity.

Except for some areas in the valleys where vegetation grows thick, the trail is well-marked with white blazes and brown plastic markers. Direction changes are clearly marked with double blazes. Most traffic revolves around the shelter houses at Cherry and Bryant lakes, but the trail receives only modest use.

Begin the hike on an old roadbed that starts downhill after about 100 yards, and reaches the first of what will be several creek crossings over the next 10 miles. The creeks are small, however, and flow intermittently with seasonal rainfall, so they normally present little trouble.

Continue along the creek, breaking to the left (south) after about 0.75 mile to head up a ravine—again on an old roadbed. After leveling off, pass the Stepp Cemetery at 1 mile. Markers in the graveyard include at least three that memorialize Civil War veterans, and another is for Isaac Hartsock, a private in the Virginia Militia during the War of 1812. An inscription on the headstone for Jay Alberto Coffa reads, "The quiet man who is dreaming a clear labrynth (sic)."

Head southeast from the cemetery on the gravel road to the main forest road at 1.1 miles. Cross over, picking up the trail as it continues southeast over Precinct Ridge before dropping into a ravine to cross

Greasy Creek at 2.3 miles. You are about 0.25 mile north of the former Beanblossom Lake.

After crossing the creek, turn right (north) and begin a steep climb of 200 feet up Ira Hacker Ridge to follow a powerline easement. When the powerline takes a right (north) turn, the trail goes straight (northwest). At 3.5 miles, the trail crosses Farr Road. Look for trail markers on the trees directly across from the bend in the road. Weave through a stand of young trees before heading downhill to join up with Bryant Creek at 4 miles.

Follow the creek for almost 1 mile through heavy vegetation, climbing over a long, straight hump at one point before reaching a stand of pine trees near Bryant Creek Lake. At 5 miles, reach and circle the lake in a clockwise direction, climbing wooden steps around the high south shoreline. Cross the dam at the west end of the lake, and continue northeast to a picnic shelter in the woods north of the lake.

From the shelter, head east over a broad ridge to the main road near the 6-mile mark. Cross the road, and zigzag across an old roadbed to a double-blaze marker. Turn left and walk along a ridge before descending a switchback to cross a branch of Indian Creek at 6.5 miles. Head up the other side of the ravine, and cross a ridgetop. Descend once more to Indian Creek and follow its banks for almost 1 mile, crossing several side creeks before turning left (northeast) at the trail junction at 8.5 miles and heading uphill onto a steep ridge. Beyond the ridgetop, slip across a ravine to another ridgetop, and follow a winding path through the woods to Indian Creek. Turn left (northeast) at the creek and follow it to the Cherry Lake shelter house at 9.6 miles. Go to the north side of the shelter and proceed in a clockwise direction around the lake to the trailhead parking lot.

39 Scarce O'Fat Trail

Type of hike: Day hike, loop.
General description: A loop trail along a ridgetop, through a deep ravine, and over a steep hill featuring a north-facing vista overlooking Yellowwood Lake.
General location: Between Bloomington and Nashville in the Yellowwood State Forest.
Total distance: 4.5 miles.
Difficulty: Strenuous.
Elevation gain: About 290 feet from the trailhead to the highest point, which is just north of Caldwell Hollow.
Jurisdiction: Indiana Department of Natural Resources, Division of Forestry.
Special attractions: Caldwell Hollow and High King Hill.
Maps: Belmont USGS quad; Yellowwood State Forest brochure.

Scarce O'Fat Trail

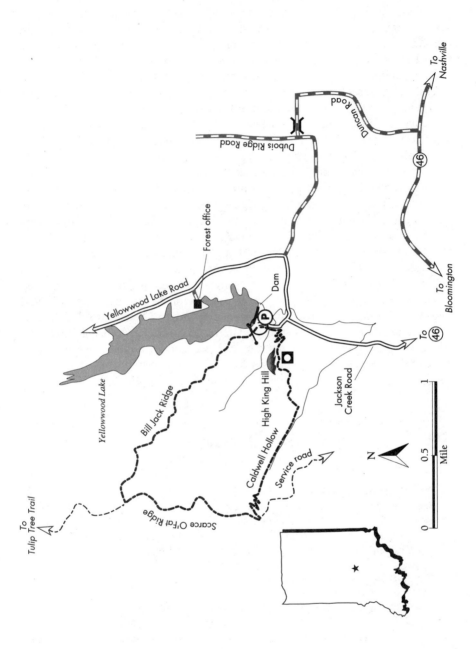

Permits/fees: None required.

Camping: Yellowwood State Forest has 80 primitive campsites and a rally camp area.

Trailhead facilities: There is a small parking lot, but no water supply or restrooms. Water and restrooms are available at the forest office on Yellowwood Lake Road.

Finding the trailhead: Go east from Bloomington for 10 miles on Indiana 46, toward Nashville. Turn left (north) on Duncan Road at the brown signs for Yellowwood State Forest. Follow Duncan Road for 1.3 miles until it crosses a bridge and deadends at a T intersection with Dubois Ridge Road. Turn left (south) and travel 0.9 mile to a Y intersection—the right (north) fork is Yellowwood Lake Road, and the left (west) fork is Jackson Creek Road. Take Jackson Creek Road 0.5 mile to signs pointing to Scarce O'Fat Trail. Turn right (north) on a gravel road, drive through a creekbed, and go 0.2 mile to the parking lot near the trailhead.

Key points:
- 0.0 Trailhead.
- 1.7 Turn left (south) onto Scarce O'Fat Ridge.
- 2.8 Turn left (east) to enter Caldwell Hollow.
- 3.8 Turn left (northeast) to climb High King Hill.
- 4.3 Reach the High King Hill vista.

The hike: After early settlers of this area found the rocky ground unsuitable for farming, they applied the name Scarce O'Fat Ridge to describe the difficulty of scratching out anything more than a meager living. While Scarce O'Fat lends its name to the trail, the trail's best features are actually the segments through Caldwell Hollow, and the finishing climb up and down High King Hill. Although High King makes for a clever play on words (High King/hiking), it actually was the highest point on property once owned by a man named King.

Also worth noting is the forest's name—Yellowwood. The yellowwood tree is a close cousin of the black locust and is common in the mid-South, but it is so rare this far north that it is on the Indiana endangered species list. The forest covers 23,200 acres, of which only 200 are suitable habitat for the yellowwood tree.

What the first two-thirds of this trail lacks in scenic splendor, it more than makes up for in hiking ease. Also, the first section sets the stage for the best features of Scarce O'Fat Trail—the solitude of Caldwell Hollow and the accomplishment of conquering High King Hill for a clear view of Yellowwood Lake.

The first two-thirds of the trail follows service roads through the forest (the Indiana Division of Forestry has plans to reroute the trail off these service roads). Brown plastic posts and wooden signs mark the early segments of the trail. White blazes on trees and boot outlines on wooden posts direct the way through Caldwell Hollow and over High King Hill. The entire trail gets limited use, with most visitors preferring only to climb High King Hill to enjoy the view before returning to the parking area.

The trail begins at the base of Yellowwood Lake Dam. From the small parking lot, it is easy to locate the marked trailhead at a gate that blocks a forest service road. The road is the trail for about the first 3 miles. It begins with a gradual climb of 140 feet to Bill Jack Ridge and winds through a forest of oak, beech, poplar, and shagbark hickory trees. If you schedule a hike for midsummer you will find wild raspberries in plentiful supply along the edge of the road.

Once on top of Bill Jack Ridge, the trail levels off for 2 miles. The trail is clearly marked along this portion with brown plastic signs. At 1.7 miles, turn left (south) as the trail connects with Scarce O'Fat Ridge. The turnoff is marked by a wooden sign with two white blazes. Be alert for occasional spurs that veer to the right (west) off the main service road; stay to the left (south). It is through this stretch that the trail reaches its highest point, but the elevation change is so slight that it is hard to notice.

At 2.8 miles, another double-blaze marker and brown plastic markers indicate a left (east) turn into the forest. This begins the descent into Caldwell Hollow. The trail follows a switchback that drops in elevation almost 220 feet in the span of 0.5 mile. Trail markers through Caldwell Hollow consist of white blaze markings on trees, and wood posts sporting the outline of a boot. Once at the bottom of the hollow, the trail crosses a creekbed several times as it meanders through a corridor of other ravines that converge with Caldwell Hollow.

At 3.8 miles, turn left (northeast) and begin the climb up High King Hill. The steepest part of this trail segment is over the next 0.25 mile as the elevation changes almost 150 feet. The remaining climb is much more gradual.

Technically, Scarce O' Fat Trail ends atop High King Hill, where it joins High King Trail for the final 0.25 mile. A series of switchbacks drops almost 200 feet to an intermittent streambed. Cross through the streambed to the road, turn left (north), and walk a few hundred feet back to the parking lot.

40 Trail 8 at Brown County State Park

Type of hike: Day hike, loop.
General description: A trail through the remote ravines of Brown County State Park.
General location: Outside Nashville in Brown County.
Total distance: 3.5 miles.
Difficulty: Moderate to strenuous.
Elevation gain: More than 300 feet from Hesitation Point to the low end of Upper Schooner Creek valley.
Jurisdiction: Indiana Department of Natural Resources, Division of State Parks & Reservoirs.

Special attractions:	The Hesitation Point vista and Upper Schooner Creek valley.
Maps:	Belmont and Nashville USGS quads; Brown County State Park brochure.
Permits/fees:	There is a $2 entry fee for vehicles with Indiana license plates; $5 for out-of-state vehicles. Season passes are available.
Camping:	Brown County State Park has 429 individual campsites, from modern to primitive, plus a rally and youth camping area.
Trailhead facilities:	There is a large parking area, but no potable water and no restrooms. Water is available at other locations in the park, including at the picnic area near Ogle Lake.

Finding the trailhead: From Nashville, go 2.5 miles south on Indiana 46 to Brown County State Park's west gatehouse. Go 1.2 miles to the West Lookout Tower parking lot. The trail begins on the east side of the stockade-shaped tower.

Key points:
- 0.0   Trailhead.
- 0.4   At the Trail 8 juncture, go straight.
- 1.5   Reach the Hesitation Point vista.
- 1.8   Enter the Upper Schooner Creek valley.
- 2.3   At the trail juncture, go straight to Ogle Lake.
- 2.4   Backtrack to the trail juncture and turn left.
- 3.1   At the trail juncture, turn left to the trailhead.

Dutchman's breeches.

Trail 8 at Brown County State Park

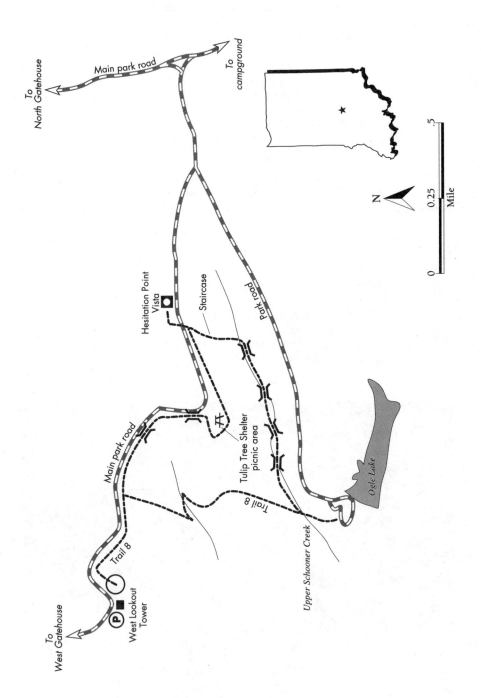

The hike: Although Brown County State Park is the largest state park in the Indiana system, it has a very limited supply of designated hiking trails—nine trails totaling just short of 15 miles. This is the longest hiking trail at 3.5 miles.

Visited by thousands of people in the fall because of the brilliant displays as leaves change color, Brown County State Park is just as colorful in the spring because of its abundance of wildflowers—toothwort, Dutchman's breeches, Jack-in-the-pulpit, spring larkspur, bluets, large-flowered trillium, wood sorrel, celandine poppy, fire pink, and prairie trillium. The entire park suffered from severe grazing damage inflicted by an overpopulation of deer until special hunts were implemented several years ago to cull deer numbers in the park. With fewer deer, the vegetation has recovered. The Upper Schooner Creek valley is flush with wildflowers and ferns, representative of the richness of this park.

Boardwalks and staircases take some of the difficulty out of the portion of the trail between Hesitation Point and the Upper Schooner Creek ravine. Although the trail is well-maintained, it gets less traffic than other trails in the park. It is busiest near the West Lookout Tower and around Ogle Lake.

From the West Lookout Tower, head east as the trail follows the main park road 10 to 20 feet down the side of the ridge. At 0.4 mile, the trail intersects with the inbound leg of Trail 8, which joins from the right (south). Stay left (east) and continue on a course parallel to the main road for another mile, passing over two footbridges and behind the Tulip Tree Shelter picnic area.

At 1.5 miles, Trail 8 turns right (south); before you make this turn, go left (north), and cross the main road to Hesitation Point at 1.5 miles. Soak up the views from this north-facing vista, then backtrack to the south side of the park road. Follow Trail 8 south for a little less than 0.25 mile to a wooden staircase with 153 steps leading down to Upper Schooner Creek (1.8 miles).

The Upper Schooner Creek valley is long and narrow, with an extremely steep bluff along the south side. The bluff on the north side of the creek starts out equally steep, but begins to flatten over the next 0.5 mile. Cross five footbridges as the trail switches from one side of the creek to the other.

Walk under a canopy of mature trees and cross a lengthy boardwalk to the trail juncture at 2.3 miles. Trail 8 turns north toward the West Lookout Tower. Instead, go straight (south) to the parking lot west of Ogle Lake, one of two small lakes within the park boundaries.

Backtrack to the trail juncture at 2.4 miles, turn left (north), and climb a ridge point before the trail makes a steep drop to the left (west) into another valley. Cross the creek at the bottom of the ravine and head uphill again to the trail juncture with the outbound leg of Trail 8 at 3.1 miles. Turn left (west) and go 0.4 mile back to the lookout tower parking lot.

41 Trail 5 at Ogle Hollow Nature Preserve

Type of hike:	Day hike, loop.
General description:	An interpretive trail down and up a steep slope of a nature preserve inside Brown County State Park.
General location:	Near Nashville in Brown County.
Total distance:	0.8 mile.
Difficulty:	Strenuous.
Elevation gain:	It is 240 feet from the rim of the ridgetop to the bottom of the ravine.
Jurisdiction:	Indiana Department of Natural Resources, Division of State Parks & Reservoirs.
Special attractions:	Yellowwood trees.
Maps:	Nashville USGS quad; Brown County State Park pamphlet; Ogle Hollow Nature Preserve pamphlet.
Permits/fees:	There is a $2 entry fee for vehicles with Indiana license plates; $5 for out-of-state vehicles. Season passes are available.
Camping:	Brown County State Park has 429 campsites modern or primitive, plus youth and rally tent areas.
Trailhead facilities:	A water fountain and restrooms are located on the south edge of the rally campground parking lot. The camp store is also located nearby.

Finding the trailhead: There are two entry gates to Brown County State Park. From Nashville, go 2.5 miles south on Indiana 46 to the West Gatehouse. Go 3.5 miles to a three-way intersection. Turn left (south) and go 1.5 miles to the rally campground parking lot. The trailhead is off the north side of the parking lot. The other entry option is through the North Gatehouse at the intersection of Indiana 135 and 46. Go 0.2 mile to a three-way intersection and turn right. Continue 2.2 miles to a second three-way intersection and go straight for 1.5 miles to the rally campground parking lot.

Key points:
- 0.0 Trailhead.
- 0.4 Reach the ravine bottom.
- 0.8 Arrive at the ridgetop.

The hike: In the early 1900s, what is now Brown County State Park had been stripped of trees and converted to pasture and farmland. Many areas were prone to erosion as a result. A few places escaped the hand of man, however, and Ogle Hollow is perhaps the best example. A small corner at the back end of the ravine was given state nature preserve status in 1970, making it the ninth nature preserve site in a system that now includes more than 160 sites across the state. Only 41 acres in size, the Ogle Hollow Nature Preserve is a mere fraction of the 16,000-acre state park that is the largest in Indiana.

Trail 5 at Ogle Hollow Nature Preserve

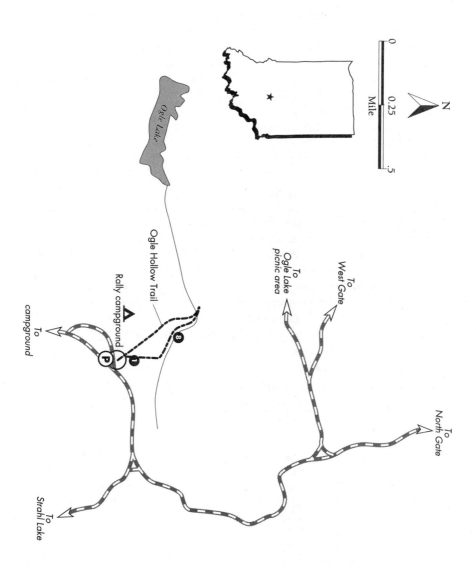

Trail 5 is short but demanding—almost vertical on the way down and the way back up. Because it is part of a state-protected nature preserve, it has been left undisturbed by human intervention other than the placement of signposts used to identify the 22 interpretive stations. The path is narrow but easy to follow, and it is not often a busy place.

The north-facing slope of the preserve, where Trail 5 is located, provides the moist environment necessary to the yellowwood, a tree found only in a few places in Indiana. Yellowwood is not a common tree anywhere, but is found more often in the cool forests of southern Appalachia and the Ozarks. With little indication of reproduction, it is listed as a threatened species in Indiana. Two of the 22 interpretive signposts on Trail 5 identify the rare tree, whose smooth, gray bark is similar in appearance to a beech tree. The yellowwood is smaller, however, and grows at an angle, producing clusters of pealike flowers every other year.

Wildflowers and ferns also cover the hillside, but the numbered markers primarily identify trees, beginning with a black oak at Station 1. Other trees along the route are black gum, American beech, sassafras, red elm, wild black cherry, pawpaw, sycamore, black walnut, bitternut hickory, shagbark hickory, basswood, sugar maple, pignut hickory, white ash, red oak, and chestnut oak. Station 8 marks the location of two trees—an American beech and black maple—that have grown so closely together that they appear to come from a single trunk.

Also present in the preserve are flowering dogwood, red bud, spicebush, ironweed, Christmas fern, maidenhair fern, and narrowleaf spleenwort. The first six stations are along the steep downhill leg, after which the trail follows a creek for six more stations before the grueling uphill stretch begins.

42 Twin Caves Trail

Type of hike:	Day hike, loop.
General description:	A trail through a nature preserve featuring virgin timber and several caves and sinkholes.
General location:	East of Mitchell in Lawrence County.
Total distance:	2.5 miles.
Difficulty:	Moderate.
Elevation gain:	Minimal.
Jurisdiction:	Indiana Department of Natural Resources, Division of State Parks & Reservoirs.
Special attractions:	Donaldson Woods State Nature Preserve, Twin Caves, and Bronson Cave.
Maps:	Mitchell USGS quad; Spring Mill State Park brochure.
Permits/fees:	There is a $2 entry fee for vehicles with Indiana license plates; $5 for out-of-state vehicles. Season passes are available.

Camping: Spring Mill State Park has a total of 223 campsites, both modern and primitive, plus a youth tent area.

Trailhead facilities: In addition to parking for two dozen vehicles, there are picnic shelters, pit toilets, and a water supply at the trailhead. Water and restrooms are also located elsewhere in the park.

Finding the trailhead: From its intersection with Indiana 37 on the southwest edge of Mitchell, go 3.3 miles east on Indiana 60 to Spring Mill State Park. Turn left (north) and go 0.4 mile to the gatehouse, then another 0.1 mile to a three-way intersection. Turn left (northwest) at the intersection and go 0.3 mile to a parking area on the right (northeast). The trail begins from the southeast edge of the parking lot.

Two boats are moored at a pier near one of the Twin Caves at Spring Mill State Park. Short boat trips are available into the cave.

Twin Caves Trail

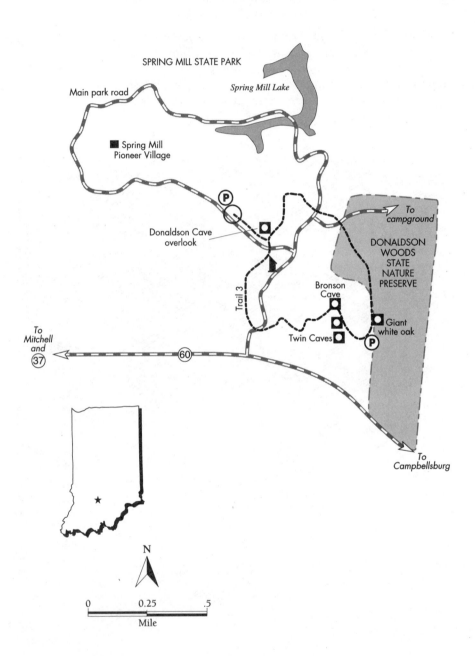

SPRING MILL STATE PARK

Spring Mill Lake

Main park road

Spring Mill
Pioneer Village

P

Donaldson Cave
overlook

Trail 3

To
campground

DONALDSON
WOODS
STATE
NATURE
PRESERVE

Bronson
Cave

Twin Caves

Giant
white oak

P

To
Mitchell
and
37

60

To
Campbellsburg

N

0   0.25   .5
Mile

Key points:

- 0.0 Trailhead.
- 0.2 At the trail juncture, turn left.
- 0.5 Cross the road.
- 0.7 At the road crossing, go straight into Donaldson Woods Nature Preserve.
- 1.2 Reach the Twin Caves parking lot.
- 1.3 At Bronson Cave, go straight.
- 2.1 Reach a road crossing.
- 2.3 At the trail juncture, turn left.

The hike: Karst topography is the geological name given to an area of limestone bedrock featuring caves, sinkholes, and underground streams. The Mitchell Plain, which stretches from the Ohio River north to central Indiana, is one of the best karst examples in the world. The area in which Spring Mill State Park is located has one of the highest concentrations of sinkholes in the United States, with an average of 100 per square mile. Just south on Indiana 37 near Orleans, an amazing 1,022 sinkholes were counted in one square mile.

The funnel-shaped sinkholes vary in size but play an integral role in the development of cave systems like the one at Spring Mill State Park. Groundwater mixed with vegetation creates a weak acid that dissolves the limestone. Over time, cracks become caves, and when caves collapse they form exposed openings known as karst windows. Three examples—Twin Caves and Bronson Cave—are found on the Twin Caves Trail (also known as Trail 3). The trail is well-marked and well-traveled, especially around Donaldson Cave and in the Spring Mill Pioneer Village.

Bronson Cave is one of several caves featured at Spring Mill State Park.

Trail 3 begins at the east end of the parking lot. Go east over a boardwalk, then follow a gravel trail along the rim above Donaldson Cave, which is connected to the other caves. At 0.2 mile, turn left (north) at a trail juncture that marks the start and end of the loop. Go past the overlook above the Donaldson Cave and continue north, then south, crossing the first of two paved roads at 0.5 mile.

At 0.7 mile, you will cross the second road and reach the Donaldson Woods State Nature Preserve. The 67-acre stand of virgin timber features several trees at least 300 years old, including one white oak protected by a split rail fence near the south end of the preserve that is believed to be between 400 and 500 years old. The preserve is named for George Donaldson, a wealthy Scotsman and nature lover who had a penchant for purchasing areas of unique beauty. Although he frequently hunted abroad, Donaldson zealously protected his property from disturbances of any kind.

Turn right (west) from the large oak tree to a paved parking lot at 1.2 miles. Cross the lot to a stone archway leading to Twin Caves, where boat trips are offered from April through October, depending on water levels in the cave. Backtrack from Twin Caves to the stone archway and turn left (north) to pick up Trail 3. Go 0.1 mile to a wooden viewing platform near the mouth of Bronson Cave at 1.3 miles.

Go west from the cave on a winding course through a forest dotted with sinkholes for 0.4 mile to the main park road. After crossing the road, head north for another 0.4 mile to the paved road leading to the trailhead parking area at 2.1 miles. Cross the road, go to the trail juncture at 2.3 miles, and turn left (west) for 0.25 mile to the parking area.

43 Spring Mill Village Trail

Type of hike:	Day hike, loop.
General description:	A trail to a cave, through a pioneer village, and to a pioneer cemetery.
General location:	East of Mitchell in Lawrence County.
Total distance:	2 miles, excluding optional tours of the village and cemetery.
Difficulty:	Moderate to strenuous.
Elevation gain:	150 feet from the parking lot to Spring Mill Village.
Jurisdiction:	Indiana Department of Natural Resources, Division of State Parks & Reservoirs.
Special attractions:	Donaldson Cave, Spring Mill Pioneer Village, and Hamer Pioneer Cemetery.
Maps:	Mitchell USGS quad; Spring Mill State Park brochure.
Permits/fees:	There is a $2 entry fee for vehicles with Indiana license plates; $5 for out-of-state vehicles. Season passes are available.

Camping: Spring Mill State Park has a total of 223 campsites, both modern and primitive, plus a youth tent area.

Trailhead facilities: In addition to parking for two dozen vehicles, there are picnic shelters, pit toilets, and a water supply at the trailhead. Water and restrooms are located elsewhere in the park. The trail is well-marked and well-traveled, especially around Donaldson Cave and in the pioneer village.

Finding the trailhead: From its intersection with Indiana 37 on the southwest edge of Mitchell, go 3.3 miles east on Indiana 60 to Spring Mill State Park. Turn left (north) and go 0.4 mile to the gatehouse, then another 0.1 mile to a three-way intersection. Turn left (west) at the intersection, and go 0.3 mile to a parking area on the right (northeast). The trail begins from the southeast edge of the parking lot.

Key points:
    0.0   Trailhead.
    0.1   Reach Donaldson Cave.
    1.2   Visit the pioneer village.
    1.4   Reach Hamer Cave.
    1.7   Arrive at the Hamer Pioneer Cemetery.

The hike: There are eight hiking trails in 1,319-acre Spring Mill State Park, including Trail 4, the Spring Mill Village Trail. History is the overriding theme of this trail, beginning with its most dynamic natural feature—Donaldson Cave. Known as Shawnee Cave until George Donaldson purchased the area in 1865, the cave is part of a network that includes two other exposed caves in the park. Professor Carl Eigenmann of Indiana Uni-

The mill at Spring Mill Pioneer Village was originally built in the early 1800s and is still in operation.

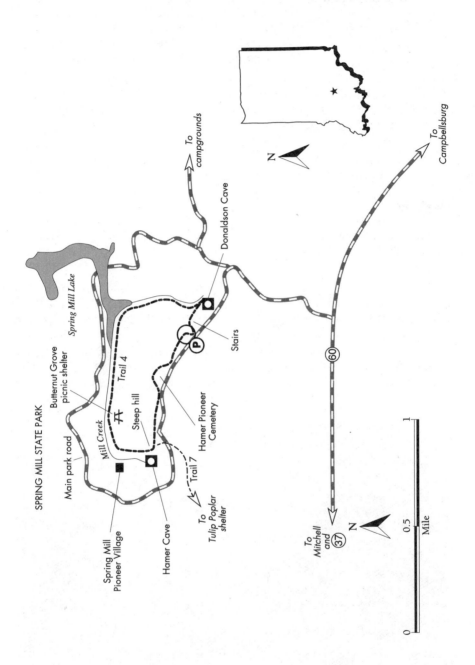

To campgrounds

Donaldson Cave

To Campbellsburg

Spring Mill Lake

Butternut Grove
picnic shelter

Trail 4

Stairs

P

SPRING MILL STATE PARK

Main park road

Mill Creek

Steep hill

Hamer Pioneer
Cemetery

Trail 7

To
Tulip Poplar
shelter

Spring Mill
Pioneer Village

Hamer Cave

60

To
Mitchell
and
37

N

N

0   0.5   1
Mile

versity began extensive studies of Donaldson Cave at the turn of the century and discovered the northern blind cavefish, which has been placed on the state endangered species list. The pinkish white fish with no eyes has adapted to the dark cave, as have other critters—the blind cave crayfish, the cave salamander, assorted spiders, and, of course, bats.

Other highlights along the trail are the Spring Mill Pioneer Village, Hamer Cave, and a pioneer cemetery. The history of the village dates to the early 1800s, when Samuel Jackson Jr. capitalized on a spring-fed stream to build a small grist mill. A Canadian naval officer who served the United States in the War of 1812, Jackson sold the property in 1817 to two brothers—Thomas and Cuthbert Bullitt of Kentucky. The Bullitts built a three-story grist mill, which is still in operation.

As a small village grew up around the prospering mill, ownership of the land changed hands several times. Hugh and Thomas Hamer purchased the mill and surrounding village in 1832, one year after its name was changed from Arcole Village to Spring Mill. The Hamer brothers had managed the mill for seven years for the previous owners. Under the brothers' ownership, the village thrived until the late 1850s. By 1898, it was abandoned.

Envisioning a restored village as the centerpiece of a park, the state of Indiana began acquiring the land in the 1920s, and Spring Mill State Park was established in 1927. Besides the grist mill, which produces cornmeal for sale, there are 19 other restored buildings in the village, including a post office, apothecary, blacksmith shop, tavern, distillery, and carpenter shop.

The mill at Spring Mill Pioneer Village.

Volunteers dressed in period costumes bring the village to life by performing routine daily chores.

Begin the hike at the east end of the parking lot by descending an elaborate wooden staircase to the stream running from Donaldson Cave. Turn right (southeast) to the mouth of the cave at 0.1 mile. The cave can be explored along its dry side; bring a flashlight and be prepared to get muddy.

From the cave, follow the left (west) side of the stream, crossing a long boardwalk before curling west past the Butternut Grove picnic area to the pioneer village at 1.2 miles. Explore the village; Trail 4 continues from the south side of the Munson House, and follows Mill Creek on a short spur to Hamer Cave at 1.4 miles.

Backtrack to the main trail, and turn right (east and south) to make a steep climb that will lead to Hamer Pioneer Cemetery. A trail splits to the right (south) near the top of the hill, but stay left (east) and go about 0.25 mile to the cemetery, which is at the 1.7-mile mark. The Hamer Pioneer Cemetery was established in 1832 and is typical of pioneer cemeteries—on high ground to avoid flooding and as a way of putting the deceased closer to Heaven. Hugh Hamer, who established the cemetery, was buried here after he died of smallpox in 1872.

Continue east from the cemetery for 0.25 mile to the trailhead parking area.

Southwest

The following hikes have been lumped into this region for lack of a better way to arrange them. They extend from Patoka Reservoir in south-central Indiana to Harmonie State Park on the Wabash River north of Evansville, and from Lincoln State Park near the Ohio River to McCormick's Creek State Park just west of Bloomington. They are listed in a clockwise sweep heading north from Evansville.

A few of the six trails—Patoka Lake and the two at McCormick's Creek, for instance—have interesting natural features. Others are singled out simply because they are nice hikes.

Patoka Lake is an 8,800-acre reservoir managed by the U.S. Army Corps of Engineers. The Indiana Department of Natural Resources manages the 25,800-acre recreational area surrounding the lake. The Main Trail passes by several unique sandstone formations, the most dynamic being Totem Rock. The trail skirts a peninsula that is a winter home for bald eagles.

McCormick's Creek is Indiana's first state park, and features a beautiful waterfall and canyon. Stone was quarried from the park to help build the first statehouse. North of the canyon and creek is Wolf Cave, which is open to the public. It is 57 yards from one end to the other, with the openings ranging from more than 5 feet to a narrow 18 inches at the east end.

Harmonie and Lincoln state parks have historical significance. Harmonie is located just south of New Harmony, the site of two utopian communities in the early 1800s. Lincoln State Park is situated near the pioneer farm where Abraham Lincoln spent his formative years, from age 7 to 21.

Shakamak State Park, south of Terre Haute, is a beehive on hot summer days as visitors take advantage of the popular park pool. The park and its three lakes are situated on abandoned coal mine property, which the citizens of Clay, Greene, and Sullivan counties donated to the state in the late 1920s. The park owes its name to the Kickapoo, a Native American tribe that resided in the area. The Kickapoo called nearby Eel River "Shakamak," meaning "river of long fish."

44 Harmonie State Park

Type of hike: Day hike, loop.
General description: A combination of loop trails through ravines and forest.
General location: About 25 miles northwest of Evansville in the southwest corner of the state.
Total distance: 3 miles.

Harmonie State Park

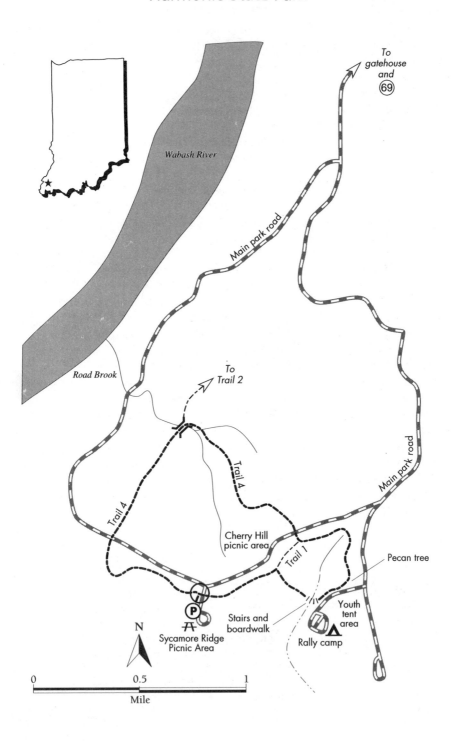

Wabash River

To
gatehouse
and
(69)

Main park road

Road Brook

To
Trail 2

Trail 4

Trail 4

Main park road

Cherry Hill
picnic area

Trail 1

Pecan tree

Stairs and
boardwalk

Youth
tent
area

N

P

Sycamore Ridge
Picnic Area

Rally camp

0   0.5   1
Mile

Difficulty:	Moderate.
Elevation gain:	About 70 feet.
Maps:	Solitude USGS quad; Harmonie State Park brochure.
Jurisdiction:	Indiana Department of Natural Resources, Division of State Parks & Reservoirs.
Permits/fees:	There is a $2 entry fee for vehicles with Indiana license plates; $5 for out-of-state vehicles. Season passes are available.
Camping:	Harmonie State Park has 200 modern campsites, plus a primitive youth tent area.
Trailhead facilities:	There is a picnic shelter and parking area at the trailhead. No water is available at the trailhead, but there are water sources at other park locations.

Finding the trailhead: From New Harmony, turn left (south) on Indiana 69 and go about 2.5 miles to Indiana 269. Turn right (west) and go 1 mile to the park gatehouse. From the gatehouse, follow the main park road for about 4 miles, pass the pool, and go left (south) at the turnoff for the Wabash River Picnic Area. Pass the property manager's residence before you turn left (south) at the entrance to Sycamore Ridge Picnic Area. The trailhead begins about 15 yards off the main park road.

Key points:
- 0.0   Trailhead.
- 0.4   Cross the main park road.
- 0.7   Cross the bridge and turn right.
- 1.5   Cross the main park road and connect with Trail 1.
- 2.0   Reach the youth camp area.
- 2.6   Connect with Trail 4 and turn left.
- 3.0   Reach the trail's end.

The hike: Established in 1966, this park draws its name from the nearby town of New Harmony, the site of two failed experiments at developing a utopian community in the early 1800s. The first was a religious experiment led by Father George Rapp, a German immigrant, who sold the town in 1824 to Robert Owen, a Scottish industrialist. Owen sought to establish a community in which everyone shared the work and the profit. During Owen's short, two-year leadership, New Harmony developed the first free public school and first kindergarten in America, as well as provided equal education for boys and girls and the first free public library. The town has been restored as a tourist attraction, but few of those elements are reflected in the park other than the name.

The hike is typical of state park hikes—an up-and-down venture over ridges and ravines with a couple of slow-moving streams. Well-marked and maintained, traffic on this trail is light compared to other routes in the park.

Take the hike in a clockwise direction by picking up Trail 4 where it crosses the Sycamore Ridge Picnic Area access road (there is a trail marker). The trail parallels the main park road for less than 0.25 mile before swinging left (southwest) on a slight downward slope. At 0.25 mile, it bends back to the right (north) and continues down and over an intermittent stream before rising to meet the main park road at the 0.4-mile mark.

Cross the main road and pick up the trail on the other side. Immediately, you will begin a long but gradual descent into another ravine. Walk up the opposite side of the ravine and drop down once more to where two streams converge near a small bridge at 0.7 mile. Cross the bridge and turn right (southeast) to climb out of the ravine, reaching the 1-mile mark near the top of a hill that in spring blossoms with Dutchman's breeches, violets, and other wildflowers.

Continue east and southeast along a ridgetop before dropping down slightly and then heading up to the main road near the Cherry Hill picnic area. Cross the road at 1.5 miles and pick up Trail 1, turning left (northeast). Trail 1 parallels the south edge of the park road for 100 yards before bending right (south) at a trail marker and crossing the back end of a ravine. As the trail reaches the back of the youth tent area at 2 miles, pass beneath one of the largest pecan trees in Indiana. Cross through the open area and follow the paved road, passing a latrine, before turning right (north) at a Trail 1 marker. Enter one final ravine, but this time on a wooden staircase designed to reduce erosion on the steep hillsides. After walking up the stairs on the other side, turn left (southwest) at a Trail 4 marker at 2.6 miles. Hike parallel to the main road for 0.4 mile west to the Sycamore Ridge access road and the trailhead.

45   Shakamak State Park

Type of hike:	Day hike, loop.
General description:	This trail loops around Lake Shakamak, the smallest of three lakes in the park.
General location:	South of Terre Haute in southwest-central Indiana.
Total distance:	3.5 miles.
Difficulty:	Moderate.
Elevation gain:	Minimal.
Jurisdiction:	Indiana Department of Natural Resources, Division of State Parks & Reservoirs.
Special attractions:	Backwater bays and boardwalks.
Maps:	Jasonville USGS quad; Shakamak State Park brochure.
Permits/fees:	There is a $2 entry fee for vehicles with Indiana license plates; $5 for out-of-state vehicles. Season passes are available.
Camping:	Shakamak State Park has 196 drive-in campsites, from modern to primitive, plus a youth tent area. The park also has 29 family cabins.
Trailhead facilities:	There are restrooms, a nature center, a swimming pool, and a picnic area at the trailhead.

Shakamak State Park

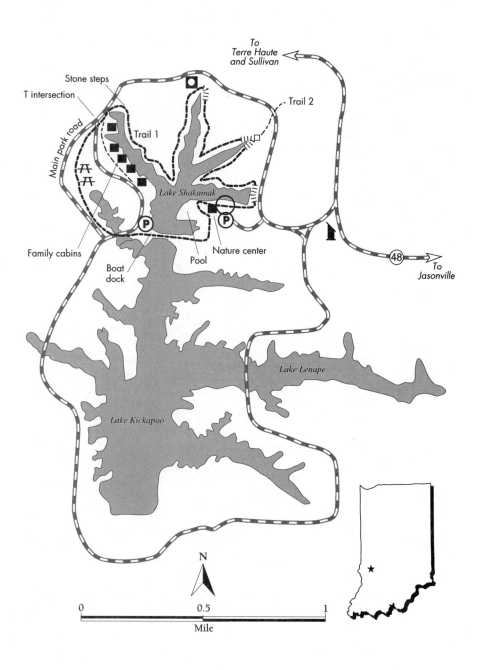

A footbridge across one of the bays at Shakamak Lake.

Finding the trailhead: Go 17 miles south on U.S. Highway 41 from Terre Haute to Indiana 48 and turn left (east). Go 9.5 miles to the park entrance on the west. After passing the gatehouse, turn right (west), go to the first intersection, and turn left (west) to the nature center and swimming pool. The park's Trail 1 can be hiked in either direction from the parking lot at the nature center. The best way is to begin at the nature center and head north of the parking lot, alongside the swimming pool, hiking in a counterclockwise direction.

Key points:
    0.0   Trailhead.
    0.3   Cross a floating boardwalk and turn left to follow lakeshore.
    2.4   Climb stone steps near the family cabins.
    2.7   Cross the main park road.
    3.0   Reach the boat ramp road; go left and cross the dam to the trailhead parking area.

The hike: Shakamak is the name Kickapoo Indians gave to nearby Eel River. The area is in the heart of Indiana's coal country, and the park is built on abandoned coal mines donated to the state in the late 1920s by Clay, Greene, and Sullivan counties. Shakamak was established as a state park in 1929, and much of its development was done during the 1930s by the Civilian Conservation Corps.

There are four hiking trails in the park totaling 6.5 miles. Trail 1 begins in an unnatural setting—a bustling area with a swimming pool, picnic area, and nature center—but it does not take long to escape the hubbub along the wooded lakeshore. For the most part, the trail is easy to follow because it hugs the lakeshore, although it is slightly confusing near the family cabin area. Trail use is modest, due in part to the popularity of the swimming pool.

From the north side of the nature center, facing the lake, walk down a set of stone steps and turn right to follow a path that skirts the shoreline for the majority of the hike. Footbridges, staircases, and boardwalks dominate the early portion of the hike, providing easy passage over areas prone to wetness or erosion.

At 0.3 mile, you will reach a floating boardwalk at the back of a bay that forms the first of the lake's four fingers. After crossing the boardwalk, turn left (west) and continue along the shore to complete the first finger at 0.6 mile. It is another 0.7 mile over more boardwalks and footbridges to walk around the second finger bay. At the back end of the second finger, Trail 2 cuts off to the right (north) and leads to the youth camp area. Stay left (west) instead, and continue on Trail 2 to the third finger of Lake Shakamak.

The back end of the lake's third finger is somewhat swampy, but a boardwalk, which includes a small viewing deck, zigzags through it. Exit the boardwalk at 1.8 miles, and turn left (south) along the shoreline to a point directly across the lake from the pool.

After bearing to the right (northwest) around that point, begin hiking the final finger. The family cabins are on the opposite (southwest) shore of this

In 1929, Shakamak was established as a state park .

bay. At the back end of the bay, leave the lakeshore by hiking uphill via stone steps at 2.4 miles. Take a right (southwest) turn when the trail meets a T intersection; a left (south) turn goes to the family cabins. Walk through a stand of pine trees to the main park road at 2.7 miles. The park road forks here; go directly across the left (east) fork, and follow the trail through more pine trees and over small footbridges. Pass a pair of picnic shelters. At 3 miles, reach a paved road that leads to the boat launch for Lake Shakamak. Turn left (east), pass the boat launch parking lot, and pick up the paved pathway that leads over the earthen dam that separates Shakamak from the much larger Lake Kickapoo. After crossing the dam, turn left (north) to the parking area for the pool and picnic area.

46 Falls Canyon Trail at McCormick's Creek State Park

Type of hike:	Day hike, loop.
General description:	A combination of park trails through McCormick's Creek Canyon that lead from the McCormick's Creek Falls to the White River and back.
General location:	West of Bloomington.
Total distance:	3 miles.
Difficulty:	Strenuous.
Elevation gain:	About a 150-foot drop from the falls to the White River.

Jurisdiction:	Indiana Department of Natural Resources, Division of State Parks & Reservoirs.
Special attractions:	McCormick's Creek Falls, the White River, and the old quarry.
Maps:	Gosport USGS quad; McCormick's Creek State Park brochure.
Permits/fees:	There is a $2 entry fee for vehicles with Indiana license plates; $5 for out-of-state vehicles. Season passes are available.
Camping:	McCormick's Creek State Park has 289 campsites, modern and primitive, plus a youth tent area.
Trailhead facilities:	There is ample parking at the trailhead for Trail 3, with restrooms, water, and other facilities spread throughout the 1,852-acre park.

Finding the trailhead: From its intersection with Indiana 37 near Bloomington, go 15 miles west on Indiana 46 to the McCormick's Creek State Park entrance. Turn right (north) to reach the gatehouse. From the gatehouse, follow the main park road just over 0.25 mile to the Canyon Inn entrance (the second left turn). Turn left (north) and go to the main parking lot. Begin the hike on Trail 3 at the east side of the parking lot.

Key points:
- 0.0   Trailhead.
- 0.3   Reach the falls overlook and stone steps.
- 0.8   Arrive at the junction with Trail 5.
- 1.0   Reach the junction with Trail 7.
- 1.6   Arrive at the Cedar Point Overlook.
- 2.3   At the junction of Trails 7 and 2, turn right (south) and cross the creek.
- 2.4   Reach the old quarry at the junction of Trails 2 and 3.
- 2.6   At the junction with Trail 7, go straight (southeast) on Trails 1, 2, and 3.
- 2.7   Reach the park road.

The hike: The Canyon Inn, near the starting point of this hike, has historic significance in that it rests on the original foundation of a sanitarium that became a turning point in the history of the area. The sanitarium was built more than a century ago by a physician, Frederick Denkewalter, who believed the tranquil canyon and cliffs provided an ideal setting as a resting place for the wealthy. The parklike surroundings also became a popular picnic and hiking spot for local residents. When Denkewalter died in 1914, the state and Owen County purchased the land, and established Indiana's first state park in 1916.

McCormick's Creek State Park has grown to more than five times its original size of 350 acres. Some sections of this loop are rough because the trail follows the rocky creekbed. Oher sections are steep climbs into and out of the canyon. The area near White River may be impassable during high water.

This hike combines parts of Trails 3, 7, 2, and 1. Begin northeast of the inn near the center of the parking lot, where a gravel trail leads to a Trail 3 marker. Signs along Trail 3 warn of hazardous areas along the cliffs overlooking the canyon. A stone stairway leads down to the canyon floor and the

Falls Canyon Trail at McCormick's Creek State Park

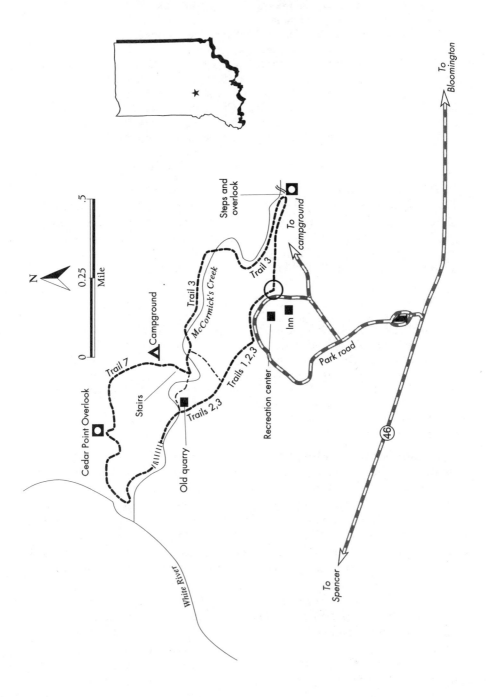

falls at 0.3 mile. McCormick's Creek is named for John McCormick, who, as the first settler in the area, homesteaded nearly 100 acres along the creek and canyon. It is not a very big creek—at times no more than 3 feet wide—which makes the high-walled canyon it carved from the limestone bedrock all the more impressive.

Turn left (northwest) at the creek and follow its rocky banks for about 0.5 mile before passing an elaborate wooden staircase (Trail 5) that leads up the left (south) side of the canyon to a campground at 0.8 mile. Cross over to the right (north) side of the creek, continue a little less than 0.25 mile to a bend in the creek, and cross back over to the left (south) side. Trail 7 joins from the left (south) at a steep wooden staircase at 1 mile. Cross once more to the right (north) side of the creek and turn right (north) to climb uphill on Trail 7 via another wooden staircase.

The trail passes over Trail 2, and continues north to a campground before curling left (west) along a gravel road that leads downhill to the White River. At 1.6 miles, stop at the Cedar Point Overlook, a wooden shelter on a bluff to the right (north) of the road that provides a nice spot from which to view the river. Gigantic sycamores punctuate the landscape near the river. Before you reach the river, you will pass a water filtration plant that services the park, and a pair of small stone buildings.

Turn away from the river and head southeast to an elevated boardwalk. Once off the boardwalk, continue east along the north bank of McCormick's Creek to Trail 2 at 2.3 miles. Turn right (southeast) on Trail 2, crossing the creek to an old limestone quarry at 2.4 miles. Blocks of stone are piled by the site, from which limestone was taken for use in construction of the statehouse in Indianapolis.

Go right (southeast) from the quarry as Trails 3 and 2 merge on a steep climb out of the canyon on a course to the southeast, joining with Trail 1 along the way. About halfway up the 100-foot ascent, at 2.6 miles, Trail 7 cuts off to the left (northeast) and downhill. Continue uphill on Trails 3, 2, and 1, pass the Trailside Shelter house, and reach the paved park road at 2.7 miles. Turn left (east) and follow the paved road about 0.25 mile back to the parking lot where Trail 3 began.

47 Wolf Cave Trail at McCormick's Creek State Park

Type of hike: Day hike, loop.
General description: A trail through a state nature preserve to an open cave.
General location: West of Bloomington.
Total distance: 3 miles.
Difficulty: Moderate.
Elevation gain: 110 feet.

Jurisdiction:	Indiana Department of Natural Resources, Division of State Parks & Reservoirs.
Special attractions:	Wolf Cave and Twin Bridges.
Maps:	Gosport USGS quad; McCormick's Creek State Park brochure.
Permits/fees:	There is a $2 entry fee for vehicles with Indiana license plates; $5 for out-of-state vehicles. Season passes are available.
Camping:	McCormick's Creek State Park has 289 campsites, modern and primitive, plus a youth tent area.
Trailhead facilities:	There are several places in the park to obtain water, including the stone restroom near the start of Trail 5.

Finding the trailhead: From its intersection with Indiana 37 near Bloomington, go west 15 miles on Indiana 46 to the McCormick's Creek State Park entrance. Turn right (north) to reach the gatehouse. From the gatehouse, follow the main park road just over 0.25 mile to the Canyon Inn entrance (the second left turn). Turn left (north) and go to the main parking lot. Start the hike on Trail 5, which begins north of the parking lot near a stone restroom facility on the right (north) side of the road.

Key points:
- 0.0   Trailhead.
- 0.1   Pass Camp Outpost.
- 0.2   Stairs lead down to McCormick's Creek.
- 0.4   Cross the campground road.
- 0.8   Enter Wolf Cave Nature Preserve at the Trail 8 juncture; go straight.
- 1.4   Reach Wolf Cave.
- 2.1   Turn right at the Trail 8 juncture; go 100 yards, and turn left.

Two young boys make their way through Wolf Cave at McCormick's Creek State Park.

Wolf Cave Trail at McCormick's Creek State Park

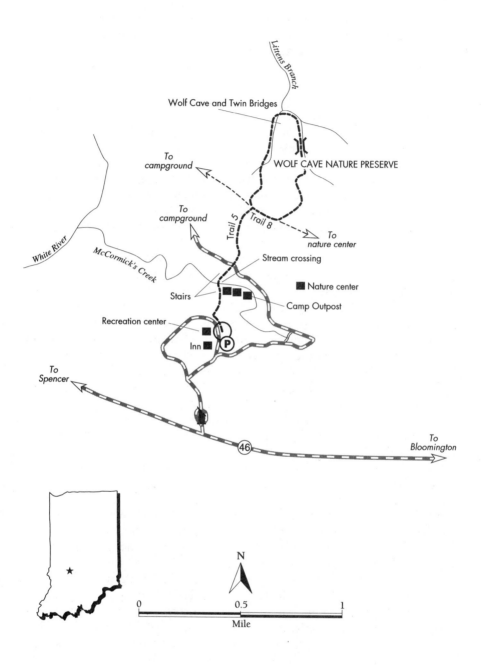

The hike: Wolf Cave, the focal point of this trail, has a storied past. But which story is true? One legend tells of a young pioneer woman who was walking home after selling goods to flatboat operators at the nearby White River. Passing the cave, she encountered a pack of wolves. She was able to elude them by throwing off her gloves and bonnet as decoys. Another tale has her washing clothes at nearby Littens Branch when the wolves attacked. Less romantic is a third story, in which the last wolf in Owen County was killed near the cave in 1845.

Regardless of how it got its name, Wolf Cave is an example of how caves are formed by groundwater erosion of the limestone bedrock. The popularity of Wolf Cave makes this one of the busier trails in the park, but many visitors hike only to the cave and then return the same way, skipping the eastern leg of the trail along Littens Branch.

To reach the cave, begin at the Trail 5 trailhead and walk northeast toward Camp Outpost, a collection of small, wood cabins at 0.1 mile. Turn left (northwest), and descend a 145-step wooden staircase to McCormick's Creek at 0.2 mile. Cross the creek and climb a 109-step wooden staircase on the north side of the canyon.

After reaching the canyon rim, cross to the north side of the campground road at 0.4 mile. The trail continues on a northerly course through a wooded area pockmarked with funnel-shaped sinkholes. At 0.8 mile, enter Wolf Cave Nature Preserve as Trail 5 intersects Trail 8, a paved path that leads from the campground (left and northwest) to the nature center and pool (right and southeast). Go straight, crossing over a footbridge at Littens Branch. You will cross the creek a couple of times before reaching Wolf Cave at 1.4 miles. Follow the trail around the cave to Twin Bridges, or go through the cave. The passageway is 57 yards long, with a narrow 18-inch opening at the far end. It is usually dry in summer, but can be wet after extended periods of rain. Wear long pants and bring a flashlight. It is dark in the cave, plus the light helps in spotting critters, such as the cave salamander.

The cave opens at Twin Bridges, which was created when a roof section of Wolf Cave collapsed. Follow the east fork of Littens Branch south from Twin Bridges, crossing the creek once on a footbridge and then by rock hopping several more times over the next 0.5 mile. Near the 1.9-mile mark, the trail turns right (southwest) for a gradual climb. Three benches are at scattered locations on the trail, providing pleasant places to pause and enjoy the solitude of the surrounding forest. The beech tree is the dominant species in the preserve, but maple, sycamore, walnut, tulip poplar, and elm trees are also present. Oak trees—red, white, and chinquapin—prevail on the high ground, along with hickory trees.

At 2.1 miles, join Trail 8, turn right (northwest), and go about 100 yards to the juncture of Trails 5 and 8. Turn left (south) and backtrack across the campground road, down to McCormick's Creek valley and up the other side of the ravine. Go past the Camp Outpost, and return to the trailhead.

Twin Bridges is a collapsed ceiling at the east end of Wolf Cave in McCormick's Creek State Park.

48 Patoka Lake Main Trail

Type of hike:	Day hike, loop.
General description:	This trail skirts the perimeter of a broad peninsula near the west end of Patoka Lake, the state's second-largest reservoir.
General location:	Southern Indiana, about 9 miles south of French Lick.
Total distance:	6.5 miles.
Difficulty:	Strenuous.
Elevation gain:	About 60 feet.
Jurisdiction:	Indiana Department of Natural Resources, Division of State Parks & Reservoirs.
Special attractions:	Totem Rock, Pilot Knob, and other sandstone cliffs.
Maps:	Cuzco and Birdseye USGS quads; Patoka Lake hiking area brochure.
Permits/fees:	There is a $2 entry fee for vehicles with Indiana license plates; $5 for out-of-state vehicles. Season passes are available.
Camping:	There are a total of 552 campsites at the Newton-Stewart State Recreation Area, some modern and some primitive, plus seven backpacking sites.
Trailhead facilities:	There is a large parking lot at the trailhead, with restrooms and a water supply available at the solar-heated nature center. Water is also available at the campgrounds.

Finding the trailhead: From French Lick, go 10 miles south on Indiana 145 to Indiana 164 and turn right (west). Go 1 mile to Crawford County 27 and turn right (north). Go just over 1 mile to the gatehouse, then another 1.7 miles before turning left (west) on Elon-Wickliffe Road and going 1 more mile to the nature center parking lot. The trailhead is off the northeast corner of the building.

Key points:

0.0	Trailhead.
0.1	Cross the Wildlife Management Demonstration Trail and turn right.
1.4	Reach Totem Rock.
2.5	Arrive at Pilot Knob.
3.8	Cross an abandoned road.
4.3	Go right at the trail sign that reads, "To Lake/Trail Continues."
5.7	The trail joins an abandoned road.
5.8	The trail leaves the abandoned road.

The hike: Archeological evidence indicates prehistoric man inhabited this area as long as 10,000 years ago. Stone tools, pottery shards, and flint points have been discovered here. Early white settlers found petroglyphs of three turtles carved into a rock and on nearby trees. No explanation was ever determined, but speculation was that the artwork represented some sort of totem or "family mark" to native peoples. Consequently, the site came to be

Patoka Lake Main Trail

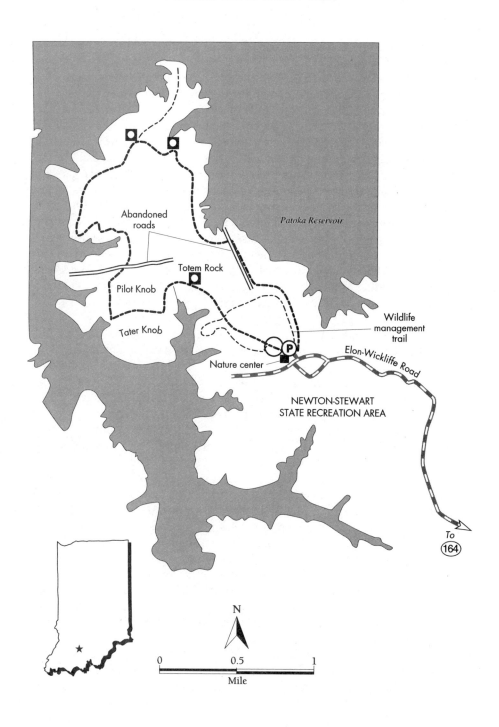

Abandoned roads

Patoka Reservoir

Totem Rock

Pilot Knob

Tater Knob

Wildlife management trail

Nature center

Elon-Wickliffe Road

NEWTON-STEWART STATE RECREATION AREA

To 164

N

0   0.5   1
Mile

known as Totem Rock. Although the carvings were destroyed more than 100 years ago, the name stuck.

Totem Rock remains one of the highlights on this trail. The rock is located in the beginning portion of a 6.5-mile trail loop that traces a clockwise path around the edge of 1,000-acre Newton-Stewart State Recreation Area, on the western end of Patoka Lake, an 8,800-acre reservoir. The lake was created by the U.S. Army Corps of Engineers in the 1970s as a flood-control project for the Patoka River and more than a half-dozen smaller creeks and rivers.

The Main Trail is one of three trails on the peninsula that makes up the Newton-Stewart area. There are various shortcuts and spurs that cross the trail, but the Main Trail is simple to follow because of the prominent trail markings. Orange and white circles are painted on trees and are visible from both directions. Occasional signs also point the way, and mileage markers are posted at 0.5-mile intervals beginning just beyond Totem Rock. Many hikers go no farther than Totem Rock before backtracking. Few hike the entire trail.

The outbound leg of the trail along the western side of the peninsula presents the most rugged aspects of the hike—a continuous series of gullies and rolling ridges decorated by sandstone outcroppings. The first evidence of the sandstone formations comes just past the 0.1-mile mark, when the Main Trail crosses the Wildlife Management Demonstration Trail. Turn right and take a short climb down to a rocky bluff that offers a prelude of the sandstone formations that lie ahead.

But it is Totem Rock that is the most impressive formation on the trail. Follow the Main Trail to the large rock overhang at 1.4 miles. The rock served as a gathering place for settlers for many years, either for church services or picnics. Local residents also called it Saltpeter Cave.

Head downhill away from Totem Rock, cross a creek, and head uphill toward a meadow at Tater Knob. Cross the meadow on an uphill course to the northwest, and reenter the woods before the 2-mile mark. Continue to pass through gullies and by rock ledges before coming to Pilot Knob at 2.5 miles. Go left (west) around the formation and head downhill. After passing another rock ledge on the right (east) side of the trail near the 3-mile mark, slip past one more gully and then hike a fairly flat stretch for more than 0.5 mile.

At about 3.8 miles, cross an abandoned road and pass through a small meadow. The trail reaches a juncture at 4.3 miles where a sign indicates the lake is to the left (north), but the Main Trail continues straight (east). Skirt the edge of two meadows, the second one being the largest, as the trail crosses the north end of the peninsula, then turn south for the final 2 miles.

Almost half that distance is over a series of gullies that carry seasonal runoff. Beech trees dominate this area, but it is in a pine plantation along this side of the peninsula where bald eagles regularly nest in winter. A watchful hiker might be able to spot one.

At 5.7 miles, the trail intersects with an abandoned road for 0.1 mile before dropping off left (east) into a broad ravine. After climbing out of the ravine, the final 0.5 mile is along a level grade above a stretch of sandstone bluffs to the left (east).

A hiker passes beneath the shadows of Totem Rock at Patoka Lake Main Trail. The sandstone formation has long been a drawing card for people.

49 Lincoln State Park

Type of hike:	Day hike, double loops.
General description:	This hike combines several park trails over ground walked by Abraham Lincoln during his boyhood years.
General location:	South of Dale in Spencer County.
Total distance:	5.5 miles.
Difficulty:	Easy.
Elevation gain:	Minimal.
Jurisdiction:	Indiana Department of Natural Resources, Division of State Parks & Reservoirs.
Special attractions:	Gravesite of Lincoln's only sister, Sarah; Sarah Lincoln's Woods Nature Preserve; Lincoln Lake; the Noah Gorden mill site.
Maps:	Chrisney and Santa Claus USGS quads; Lincoln State Park brochure.
Permits/fees:	There is a $2 entry fee for vehicles with Indiana license plates; $5 for out-of-state vehicles. Season passes are available.
Camping:	Lincoln State Park has a total of 270 campsites, some modern and some primitive, plus a youth tent area.
Trailhead facilities:	There is a parking lot, restrooms, and a water supply. Water and restrooms can also be found at other locations throughout the park.

Finding the trailhead: From Dale, go 5 miles south on U.S. Highway 231 to Indiana 162 in Gentryville. Turn left (east) and go 1.9 miles to the Lincoln State Park entrance, which is across from the Lincoln Boyhood National Memorial on the left (north) side of the highway. Turn right (south) to the park gatehouse and go 0.1 mile past the gatehouse to the Oak Grove Shelter parking lot. Turn left (east) into the parking area. The trailhead and Trail 4 markers are located on the east side of the shelter house.

Key points:
- 0.0 Trailhead.
- 0.1 Turn right (east) at the Trail 2 juncture.
- 1.0 Reach the abandoned strip mine pits.
- 1.4 Continue straight at an unmarked trail juncuture.
- 2.0 Cross the concrete bridge.
- 2.2 At the trail juncture, go left (west) along the lakeshore.
- 2.7 At the trail juncture, go left (south) on Trail 3.
- 4.0 Reach the Lincoln Lake dam and go left on a paved road.
- 4.3 Reach the gravel road and the Noah Gorden Trail.
- 4.4 Arrive at the Little Pigeon Primitive Baptist Church and cemetery.
- 5.0 At the gravel road and Noah Gorden Trail junction go right (east).

The hike: Born in Kentucky and elected from Illinois as the nation's 16th president, Abraham Lincoln spent his boyhood days here. The Lincolns

Lincoln State Park

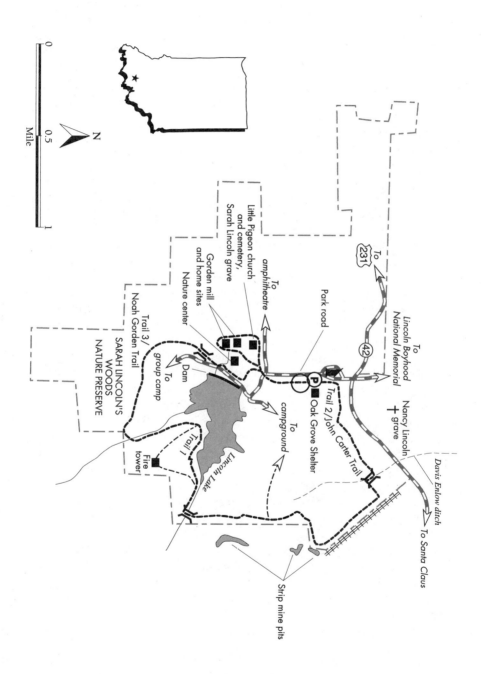

To 231

42

To Lincoln Boyhood National Memorial

Nancy Lincoln grave

Davis Enlow ditch

To Santa Claus

Trail 2/John Carter Trail

Oak Grove Shelter

Park road

To campground

To amphitheatre

Little Pigeon church and cemetery, Sarah Lincoln grave

Gordan mill and home sites

Nature center

To group camp

Dam

Trail 3/ Noah Gordon Trail

SARAH LINCOLN'S WOODS NATURE PRESERVE

Trail 1

Fire tower

Lincoln Lake

Strip mine pits

N

0

0.5

1

Mile

moved from Kentucky to this area in 1816, when Abraham was only seven years old and his sister, Sarah, was nine. Thomas Lincoln, their father, settled on 160 acres of dense forest.

Just a boy, Abe helped his father clear the land for a frontier farm that they worked for 14 years before moving on to Illinois. The actual farm site is across the highway from the state park at Lincoln Boyhood National Memorial, which is administered by the National Park Service. The gravesite of Lincoln's mother, Nancy Hanks Lincoln, who died in 1818 of "milksick" poisoning caused by white snakeroot, is also across the highway. The national memorial also has a visitor center, a cabin site memorial, a living historical farm, and several short hiking trails.

Although farming occupied much of young Abe's life, he no doubt explored some areas of the state park that now bears his name. It is known that he frequented the Noah Gorden mill.

Park management has been in the process of revising the trail system, and park brochures may not reflect the changes made to the trails. The following hike combines elements of Trails 1, 2, 3, 4, and 5. Trail 5 is a new trail that passes the Gorden mill site and Sarah Lincoln Grigsby's grave. Most traffic is confined to the area around Lincoln Lake and the Sarah Lincoln Grigsby gravesite. The eastern leg of the trail bears very little traffic, and neither does the southern leg through Sarah Lincoln's Woods Nature Preserve.

From the Oak Grove picnic shelter, begin the hike by heading north on Trail 4, parallel to the main park road. Go about 0.1 mile before joining Trail 2, and turn right (east) into a stand of pine trees. Trail 2 is also known as the John Carter Trail, named for a Lincoln family neighbor.

At 0.4 mile, the trail angles to the northeast and makes the first of several crossings over Davis Enlow Ditch, a creek that trickles off to the southeast. There are several footbridges along the way. Part of the trail is an old roadbed that runs parallel to railroad tracks that lie just outside the park's east boundary. At 1 mile, pass a couple of abandoned coal strip mine pits, after which the trail turns to the west to go uphill slightly.

Turn south at the hilltop, following the park's east boundary for more than 0.5 mile over a couple of ridges. At 1.4 miles, an unmarked trail joins from the right. Keep going straight (south), crossing more footbridges before reaching a concrete bridge at 2 miles. Cross the bridge and turn right (northwest), walking parallel to the creek that feeds Lincoln Lake. Trail 2 ends at the lakeshore, where it links with Trail 1 at 2.2 miles.

Turn left (west) on Trail 1, passing a spur trail to a fire tower at 2.2 miles, and continue to where Trail 1 joins Trail 3 at 2.7 miles. Turn left (south) onto Trail 3, also referred to as the Noah Gorden Trail, and head up through a ravine, crossing several times over a creekbed that frequently is either dry or has a very shallow stream.

Trail 3, marked in places by red numerals, leads through Sarah Lincoln's Woods Nature Preserve, a 95-acre area extending from the creek west over a ridgetop. The preserve has a variety of oak species—red, white, black, post, blackjack, and scarlet—plus many other common hardwoods like pignut hickory, sugar maple, white ash, and shagbark hickory trees.

Leave the west end of the preserve as the trail descends off the ridgetop to curl clockwise through a low spot. Cross a footbridge before exiting the woods just below the lake dam near the group camp area. Walk along the paved road below the dam at 4 miles, past the nature center, and take the first left (northwest) on the paved road. Before joining the main park road, turn left (west) at 4.3 miles on a gravel path that leads to the Little Pigeon Primitive Baptist Church, the church the Lincolns joined when Abe was 14. His sister is buried in the graveyard behind the church.

Continue west on the gravel road past the church, and turn left (south) to pass the site of Noah Gorden's mill and home at 4.5 miles. Turn left (east) at the home site and hike back through the woods to complete the loop just east of the church at 5 miles. Turn right (east), cross the paved road, and turn left (north) to cross the main park road and go up a set of stone steps. Follow Trail 2, which runs parallel to the main park road to return to the Oak Grove Shelter.

The gravesite of Sarah Lincoln, sister of Abraham Lincoln. The cemetery and Little Pigeon Primitive Church are located in the park.

Hoosier National Forest

From just south of Bloomington to Tell City on the Ohio River, the Hoosier National Forest forms a patchwork quilt covering almost 200,000 acres. But despite its size, the Hoosier represents a mere 1 percent of the massive hardwood forest that blanketed Indiana before settlement by pioneers.

Lumber was a major commodity by the late 1800s, and Indiana led the nation in timber production in 1899 by harvesting more than 1 billion board feet, most of it prime hardwoods like white oak, black walnut, and tulip poplar. It is estimated that an average of 800 million board feet of timber was cut annually from 1869 to 1903.

Trees documented as being 6 to 12 feet in diameter were chopped down and sold off. Most of the virgin forest was gone within 50 years. In addition, wildlife species that once roamed Indiana were gone, including white-tailed deer and wild turkeys.

The demolition of forest land happened everywhere across the state, but the consequences seemed most wasteful in southern Indiana, where settlers learned a hard lesson. Land was cheap at $1 per acre, but the steep, rocky ground, now devoid of trees and depleted of nutrients, was prone to erosion and unsuitable for agriculture.

Small farms were failing, and the Great Depression only made matters worse. As farms were abandoned, the tax delinquent land created a mounting fiscal problem for state and local governments. In 1934, Governor Paul McNutt sought help from the U.S. Forest Service, asking the agency to purchase land with the intent to establish a national forest.

The first parcels were acquired in 1935, and in 1951 the Hoosier National Forest was established. In the meantime, the Civilian Conservation Corps played a hand in reforestation efforts on the land. Although it does not match its presettlement glory, the forest

Wilderness boundary marker at the Charles C. Deam Wilderness in the Hoosier National Forest.

has returned to a healthy condition. The end result is the largest landholding in the state, and within its scattered boundaries are some noteworthy sites.

The Charles C. Deam Wilderness, a 12,900-acre tract just south of Bloomington, is named in honor of Indiana's first state forester. Granted wilderness protection by Congress in 1982, the Deam Wilderness borders Lake Monroe and contains forested ridgetops and ravines typical of southern Indiana.

Hemlock Cliffs is a box canyon carved out of sandstone by seasonal waterfalls. Eastern hemlock, an uncommon tree in Indiana, grows along the high cliffs of this canyon.

Pioneer Mothers Memorial Forest features the largest known stand of virgin timber in the state. The 88-acre property has been preserved since 1816.

There are countless other treasures in the Hoosier National Forest, including an abundance of wildlife. The deer and turkeys that were once absent have been restored, making the Hoosier a popular area for hunters, who can also pursue ruffed grouse, squirrels, and other game.

The Forest Service maintains a 236-mile trail system in the Hoosier National Forest, most of which are multiple-use trails for hikers, mountain bikers, and horseback riders. There are countless additional miles of abandoned trails, primitive roads, and forest service roads for the more adventuresome explorer.

The trails in this chapter are presented south and southwest from Bloomington.

50 Cope Hollow Loop

Type of hike:	Day hike or backpack, loop.
General description:	This trail leads through the Charles C. Deam Wilderness of the Hoosier National Forest.
General location:	South of Bloomington in south-central Indiana.
Total distance:	9.5 miles.
Difficulty:	Moderate to strenuous.
Elevation gain:	A drop of 270 feet from the trailhead to the low point at Tanyard Branch, with several other drops and rises along the way.
Jurisdiction:	Hoosier National Forest, Brownstown District.
Special attractions:	Todd Cemetery, Tanyard Branch of Salt Creek, and Dennis Murphy Hollow.
Maps:	Elkinsville, Allens Creek, and Norman USGS quads; Trails Illustrated/National Geographic map of Hoosier National Forest; Hoosier National Forest's Charles C Deam Wilderness map.
Permits/fees:	None required.

Camping: Walk-in camping is permitted anywhere in the wilderness area, except within 100 yards of Tower Ridge Road, and is restricted to designated sites when within 100 feet of ponds, lakes, trails, or streams. Other wilderness rules on food and beverage containers also apply, and group size is limited to ten persons or less.

Trailhead facilities: There is a small, gravel parking lot for about six vehicles, but no restrooms and no potable water source.

Finding the trailhead: From the intersection of Indiana 46 and Indiana 446 on the east side of Bloomington, go about 12 miles south on Indiana 446 to Tower Ridge Road. Turn left (east) and go 5.5 miles to the Grubb Ridge parking area. The trail begins on the north edge of the small parking area.

Key points:
- 0.0   Trailhead.
- 0.1   Turn left at the trail junction.
- 0.2   Cross to the south side of Tower Ridge Road.
- 0.6   At the trail intersection, go right.
- 1.1   Cross to north side of Tower Ridge Road.
- 3.5   Cross to south side of Tower Ridge Road.
- 4.0   Reach the Tanyard Branch of Little Salt Creek.
- 4.7   Reach Little Salt Creek.
- 5.0   Turn left (northeast) from the creek and climb uphill.
- 6.5   Descend to Dennis Murphy Hollow.
- 7.1   Reach the creek in the bottom of the hollow.
- 7.8   Arrive at the Hunter Creek Trail juncture.
- 9.0   At the trail juncture, turn left (west).
- 9.3   Return to Tower Ridge Road and cross over to the north side.

The hike: It takes a degree of tolerance for horses to appreciate this hike, because the trail is a multi-use venue, and it is hard to avoid horse traffic in the Hoosier National Forest (HNF). About 10 percent of the more than 200 miles of trails in the HNF are for foot traffic only, so if hikers want to see the area they must share.

There is plenty to see on this hike, but it takes some effort to get to the highlights—Tanyard Branch and Dennis Murphy Hollow. Foot traffic is light, probably because horseback riders make heavy use of the trail. That makes for pretty rough trail conditions in certain spots, where the horses turn the soil into a sloppy mess that retains water. When dried out, the stiffened mud can be hard on your ankles. The horse impact is less on the section south of Tower Ridge Road. Be alert to abandoned trails that occasionally join the main trail. Look for standard U.S. Forest Service trail markers—thin, plastic markers about 3 feet tall—when uncertain.

Begin the hike at the Grubb Ridge Trailhead by walking past the metal gate on the north side of the parking lot. It is the same start as for the Peninsula Trail (Hike 51). At 0.1 mile, turn left off the Peninsula/Grubb Ridge Trail to pick up the westbound leg of the Cope Hollow Trail. Pass

Cope Hollow Loop

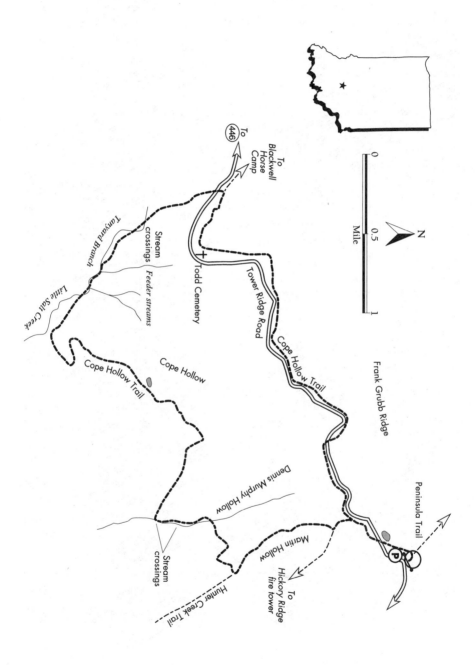

The Tanyard Branch of Salt Creek on the south loop of the Cope Hollow Loop.

a small pond, then cross over to the south side of Tower Ridge Road at 0.2 mile.

The trail does not wander far from the lightly traveled road over the next few miles. At 0.6 mile, the trail splits. The left (south) path is the inbound leg of the Cope Hollow Trail. Go right (west) and continue, with Tower Ridge Road to the right (north) and the back end of Dennis Murphy Hollow to the left (south). Pass an abandoned trail that joins from the left (south). At 1.1 miles, cross to the north side of Tower Ridge Road.

Pass through a stretch of clearings in the forest as the trail curves toward the southwest. A series of deep ravines drops off to the right (north) over the next mile, but the trail keeps a relatively level course. The last of the ravines forms the east edge of Frog Pond Ridge, a 1.5-mile finger pointing almost directly north to Saddle Creek, which flows into Lake Monroe. Continue left (south), hugging the Tower Ridge Road to Todd Cemetery at the 3-mile mark. Pass along the west edge of the cemetery and make a fishhook turn to the northwest. Go another 0.5 mile to a trail split. Stay left, crossing Tower Ridge Road to the southeast at 3.5 miles.

Pass through a meadow and head downhill to connect at 4 miles with one of several feeder streams that form Tanyard Branch. The trail crisscrosses the trickling, geode-filled stream several times over the next 0.75-mile stretch of trail. The downward trend is so gradual that you will hardly notice the 150-foot drop from Tower Ridge Road. Along the way, three seasonal streams feed Tanyard Branch from the left (east) before Tanyard Branch spills into Little Salt Creek at 4.7 miles. At the third stream, the trail turns left (northeast) into Cope Hollow.

After walking up the unnamed stream in Cope Hollow, begin a sharp uphill climb of more than 100 feet to a ridge forming the eastern boundary of the hollow. The next stretch of trail rises 100 feet over a span of about 1.25 miles, alternating between woods and meadows. Take a 0.25-mile trek uphill to a ridgetop, turn right (southeast) for 0.1 mile, then angle left (southeast) and drop into Dennis Murphy Hollow at 6.5 miles. After reaching the creek at the floor of the hollow at 7.1 miles, turn left (north). Follow the small stream through a fern-laden valley for 0.4 mile before turning right (northeast). Cross the creek and climb to a ridge that separates Dennis Murphy Hollow from Martin Hollow.

The ridge flattens out noticeably at the top as the trail passes through a couple of stands of pine trees before it intersects with the Hunter Creek Trail at 7.8 miles. Turn left (northwest) at the intersection and drop just below the ridgetop to meander around a series of gullies that tumble into Martin Hollow. Move back up to the ridgetop and follow a northward course before reaching a trail intersection at 9 miles. Turn left (west), passing a small pond on the left before reconnecting with the outbound leg of the Cope Hollow Trail near Tower Ridge Road at 9.3 miles. Turn right (northeast) and follow the trail back to the Grubb Ridge Trailhead.

51 Peninsula Trail

Type of hike:	Day hike or backpack, out-and-back.
General description:	This hike through the Charles C. Deam Wilderness leads to a peninsula jutting into Lake Monroe, the state's largest lake.
General location:	Hoosier National Forest, 16 miles southeast of Bloomington in south-central Indiana.
Total distance:	9 miles.
Difficulty:	Moderate.
Elevation gain:	300 feet from the trailhead to the lakeshore.
Jurisdiction:	Hoosier National Forest, Brownstown District.
Special attractions:	The peninsula campsite.
Maps:	Elkinsville USGS quad; National Geographic/Trails Illustrated map of Hoosier National Forest.
Permits/fees:	None required.
Camping:	Walk-in camping is permitted anywhere in the wilderness area, except within 100 yards of Tower Ridge Road, and is restricted to designated sites when within 100 feet of ponds, lakes, trails, or streams. Other wilderness rules on food and beverage containers also apply, and group size is limited to ten persons or less.
Trailhead facilities:	There is a small, gravel parking lot for about 6 vehicles. No potable water source or restroom is available.

Finding the trailhead: From the intersection of Indiana 46 and Indiana 446 on the east side of Bloomington, go about 12 miles south on Indiana 446 to Tower Ridge Road. Turn left (east) and go 5.5 miles to the Grubb Ridge parking area. The trail begins on the north edge of the small parking area.

Key points:
- 0.0 Trailhead.
- 2.5 Go right at the trail junction.
- 3.0 Reach the Lake Monroe overlook.
- 4.5 Arrive at the peninsula campsite.
- 9.0 Reach the trail's end.

The hike: Although this trail is shared with horseback riders, it is a worthy stretch because of the destination—a backcountry campsite at the edge of a peninsula that overlooks a sizable portion of Lake Monroe, the perfect setting from which to view spectacular sunsets. The area features two ridges—Frank Grubb Ridge and John Grubb Ridge. The majority of the Peninsula Trail lies along the latter.

Established by Congress in 1982, the wilderness area covers 13,000 acres. It is a well-used and well-marked area despite the wilderness designation, largely because lengthy portions of the trail follow abandoned roadbeds. Unlike other multi-use trails in the Hoosier National Forest, this one has minimal damage from horse traffic.

Peninsula Trail

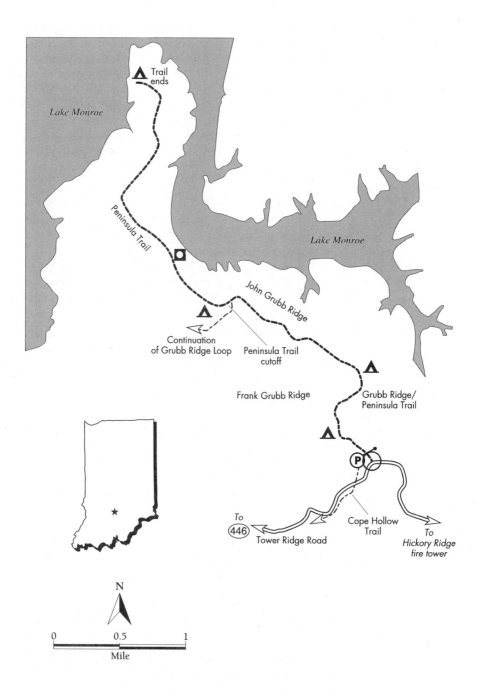

Trail
ends

Lake Monroe

Peninsula Trail

Lake Monroe

John Grubb Ridge

Continuation
of Grubb Ridge Loop

Peninsula Trail
cutoff

Frank Grubb Ridge

Grubb Ridge/
Peninsula Trail

P

To
446
Tower Ridge Road

Cope Hollow
Trail

To
Hickory Ridge
fire tower

N

0   0.5   1
Mile

From the trailhead, hike 100 yards before reaching a trail split—the left (southwest) fork begins the Cope Hollow Loop (Hike 50). The right (northwest) fork is the beginning of the Grubb Ridge Loop and the Peninsula Trail; take this fork.

The trail, on an abandoned roadbed, curves through a forest of mixed hardwoods punctuated by occasional stands of pine trees. Backcountry campsites can be located along the trail. Eventually, the route straightens out on a northwesterly course along John Grubb Ridge. The ridgetop provides a reasonably level path, with occasional uphill stretches, but most of the topographic changes occur on either side of the trail—gradual slopes to the left, sharper drops on the right toward Lake Monroe.

At 2.5 miles, the trail splits and the Grubb Ridge Loop (Peninsula Trail cutoff) breaks to the left (southwest). Turn right (northwest) to continue toward the peninsula, passing through an area dotted with older hardwoods and little undergrowth. After 0.5 mile, begin a descent of about 100 feet in elevation. It is here, at 3 miles, that the trail overlooks a very steep dropoff to the lake nearly 200 feet below to the right (northeast). The remainder of the hike is a gradual descent in which the scenery alternates through pine and hardwood stands, clearings, cedar thickets, and patches of scrub brush.

Near the end of the trail, look for signs of old farmsteads—fence posts, rusted barbed wire strands, perhaps an old pot or two, or remnants of an abandoned vehicle. Walk right to the rocky shores of Lake Monroe at 4.5 miles; this 10,750-acre reservoir was created when the U.S. Army Corps of Engineers dammed up Salt Creek and several smaller tributaries—Clear, Sugar, Allens, Moore, and Saddle. The east side of the peninsula borders the Middle Fork State Wildlife Refuge, a haven for waterfowl.

To complete the hike, retrace the outbound path to the Grubb Ridge parking area at 9 miles.

Option: Hikers have the option of heading southwest on the continuation of the Grubb Ridge Loop (the Peninsula Trail cutoff), which offers a counterclockwise trek through the heart of the Deam Wilderness. The Grubb Ridge Loop begins at the trail intersection at 2.2 miles. Hikers attempting the Grubb Ridge Loop option should note that the Saddle Creek Area below Frog Pond Ridge can be impassable during high-water periods, and an extremely messy, muddy stretch at other times.

52 Sycamore Loop

Type of hike:	Day hike or backpack, loop.
General description:	A trail that leads along a creek and to ravine overlooks of the Charles C. Deam Wilderness.
General location:	Southeast of Bloomington.
Total distance:	6.3 miles.

Difficulty:	Moderate.
Elevation gain:	Gains and losses of 250 feet.
Jurisdiction:	Hoosier National Forest, Brownstown District.
Special attractions:	Sycamore Branch valley, a pioneer cemetery, and the Hickory Ridge fire tower.
Maps:	Elkinsville USGS quad; National Geographic/Trails Illustrated map of Hoosier National Forest.
Permits/fees:	None required.
Camping:	Walk-in camping is permitted anywhere in the wilderness area, except within 100 yards of Tower Ridge Road, and is restricted to designated sites when within 100 feet of ponds, lakes, trails, or streams. Other wilderness rules on food and beverage containers also apply, and group size is limited to ten persons or less.
Trailhead facilities:	There is a gravel parking area, but no restrooms and no potable water source at the trailhead.

Finding the trailhead: From the intersection of Indiana 46 and Indiana 446 on the east side of Bloomington, go about 12 miles south on Indiana 446 to Tower Ridge Road. Turn left (east) and go 8 miles to the Hickory Ridge fire tower parking area. The trail begins on the north edge of the parking area on the other side of the gate.

Key points:
    0.0   Trailhead.
    0.25   At the marked campsite, turn right (east) off the gravel road.

One of the few hiking-only trails in the Hoosier National Forest passes through a stand of pine trees along Sycamore Branch.

1.0	Cross the Sycamore Branch.
2.4	Turn left (northwest) and leave the valley on the climb to Terril Ridge.
3.2	At the old roadbed, turn right (northeast).
3.5	At the trail juncture, turn left.
4.3	At the gravel road, turn right (north).
4.6	Take the turnoff to Terril Cemetery.
4.8	Return to the gravel road and turn right (south).
6.3	Reach the trail's end.

The hike: The Forest Service maintains very few hiker-only trails in the Hoosier National Forest, and this ranks near the top of that limited number. Difficulty is minimal, and the chance for solitude is superb.

The trail gets its name from the Sycamore Branch of Salt Creek, and about a third of the hike follows the meandering rocky stream on an easterly course through a thick stand of towering white pine trees. But it is the tall sycamore trees near the headwaters that make it obvious how settlers came to name the stream that trickles east and then northeast into the South Fork of Salt Creek, which feeds nearby Lake Monroe, the state's largest lake.

The secluded stretch is popular for overnight campers at marked and unmarked campsites. The beginning and ending legs of this trail receive the heaviest traffic because of campsite locations and the cemetery.

Begin by hiking down the gravel road that leads to Terril Cemetery and will later serve as the inbound leg of this hike. At 0.25 mile, turn right (east) off the roadway at a marked campsite, and begin a gradual downhill walk along a ridgetop for another 0.25 mile. At the east tip of the ridge, the path becomes a little steeper, and a series of switchbacks leads into a valley near the headwaters of Sycamore Branch.

While crossing the stream for the first time at the 1-mile mark, it is possible to hear traffic along Tower Ridge Road on the high bluff to the right (south). Continue to hop back and forth across the stream several times over the next mile while hiking through a valley dominated by white pine trees and some tulip poplar trees.

At 2.4 miles, take an abrupt left (northwest) turn to begin an uphill stretch of trail that is almost leisurely in that it takes a full mile to climb 250 feet from the valley floor to the top of Terril Ridge. Along the way the forest switches from the thickly clustered pine trees of the valley floor to a mixture of hardwoods—oak, hickory, beech—and occasional pine trees.

At 3.2 miles, turn right (northeast) on an old roadbed and head downhill for 0.1 mile, then back uphill to where the roadbed turns right (southeast) at 3.3 miles. Go straight (north) and continue uphill. At 3.5 miles, turn left (west) and begin a walk that winds to the west and south along a ledge that overlooks the Jones Branch ravine on the right (northwest) side of the trail.

At 4.3 miles, reconnect with the gravel road and turn right (north). At 4.6 miles, turn left (west) to the Terril Cemetery, which can be seen from the roadway, or continue straight (north) for 0.25 mile to a remote pond that offers camping possibilities.

Grave markers in the small cemetery mark the final resting places for members of the Terril, Axsom, and Grubb families, whose legacies survive

Sycamore Loop

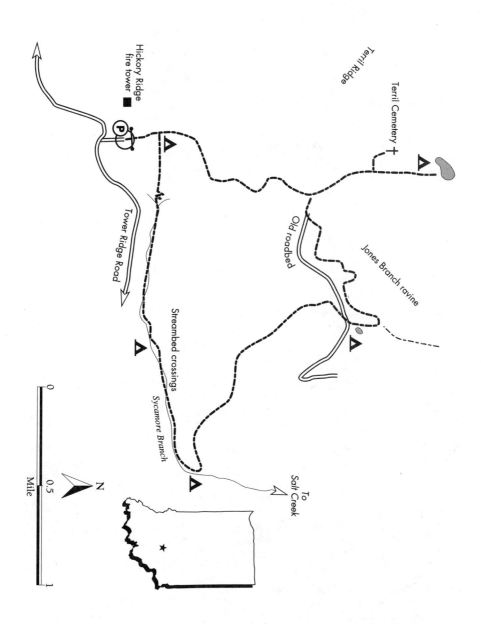

Hickory Ridge
fire tower

Terril Ridge

Terril Cemetery

Tower Ridge Road

Old roadbed

Jones Branch ravine

Streambed crossings

Sycamore Branch

To
Salt Creek

N

0   0.5   1
Mile

The Hickory Ridge fire tower at the trailhead parking lot for the Sycamore Loop.

as place names in the Deam Wilderness—Terril and Grubb ridges and the Axsom Branch of Salt Creek. The fading headstones give a clue to the harsh times the families endured while attempting to scratch out a living during the late 1800s and early 1900s. With rare exception, dates indicate that few lived beyond 60 years. Hezekiah and Alice Axsom have five children under the age of 13 buried here, including four who died in one year—1931. The Whites lost a son who lived but two days.

Upon returning from the cemetery to the gravel road at 4.8 miles, turn right (south) and follow its winding path for about 1.5 miles back to the Hickory Ridge parking area at 6.3 miles. Before leaving, get an impressive view of the Hoosier National Forest and surrounding areas from the Hickory Ridge fire tower.

53 Pioneer Mothers Memorial Forest

Type of hike:	Day hike, out-and-back.
General description:	This linear trail passes through the largest known section of old-growth forest in the state.
General location:	Just outside Paoli in south-central Indiana.
Total distance:	1.2 miles.
Difficulty:	Easy.
Elevation gain:	180 feet from the parking lot to the memorial wall.
Jurisdiction:	Hoosier National Forest, Tell City District.
Special attractions:	A white oak tree estimated to be 600 years old and the Pioneer Mothers Memorial Wall.
Maps:	Paoli USGS quad; National Geographic/Trails Illustrated map of Hoosier National Forest.
Permits/fees:	None.
Camping:	None.
Trailhead facilities:	There is a trailhead parking lot, but no restrooms and no potable water source.

Finding the trailhead: From the Paoli town square, go west on Indiana 56 for one block to the first stoplight. Turn left (south) on Indiana 37 and go 2 miles to a parking area on the left (east) side of the highway. The trail begins at the north end of the parking lot. There is an east entrance as well. To reach it from the Paoli town square, go west on U.S. Highway 150 to the first stoplight, and turn right (south). A gate blocks the access road, leaving very limited parking. Follow the paved road 0.4 mile to the Pioneer Mothers Memorial Wall.

Key points:
   0.0   Trailhead.
   0.6   Reach the Pioneer Mothers Memorial Wall.

Pioneer Mothers Memorial Forest

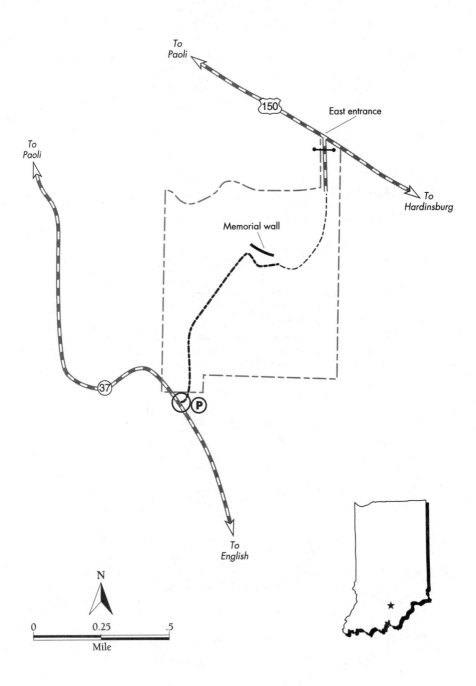

To
Paoli

150

East entrance

To
Hardinsburg

To
Paoli

Memorial wall

37

P

To
English

N

0   0.25   .5
Mile

The hike: Joseph Cox was the original owner of this property, and it was his decision in the early 1800s that preserved the ancient trees gracing an 88-acre section of this 250-acre property. It is the last virgin forest of this size known to exist in Indiana. When gazing at the massive oak and walnut trees in this small preserve, imagine what it must have been like when the state had over 19 million acres of forest like this.

Cox and his family managed to keep the woods untouched, despite numerous bids from timber companies. A community-wide effort to purchase the property from the Cox estate gained national exposure through the *Saturday Evening Post,* and the citizens were able to carry on Cox's pledge by raising the necessary $24,300 to purchase the property. The U.S. Forest Service acquired the property in 1944 and designated it a "natural area," which gave it federal protection while providing the Forest Service an area in which to study plant succession, tree growth, and forest conditions. The area was made a national landmark in 1974.

The trail is unmarked other than at the entrance, but it is easy to follow for the short distance to the memorial wall and back. The area is not heavily visited.

From the west-end parking lot, locate the trail near an information marker. Enter the woods and begin a gradual downhill walk through a cathedral of enormous hardwoods.

Just before reaching the Pioneer Mothers Memorial Wall at 0.6 mile, look for the remains of a white oak tree estimated to be more than 600 years old. The top of the tree has broken off, but the base remains standing. From the memorial wall, backtrack along the trail to return to the west-end parking lot.

54 Hemlock Cliffs National Scenic Trail

Type of hike:	Day hike, loop.
General description:	This trail leads through a box canyon draped with hemlock trees and featuring seasonal waterfalls and high sandstone cliffs.
General location:	Seven miles south of English in south-central Indiana.
Total distance:	1.4 miles.
Difficulty:	Moderate.
Elevation gain:	About 70 to 80 feet.
Jurisdiction:	Contact the Hoosier National Forest, Tell City District.
Special attractions:	Two waterfalls.
Maps:	Taswell USGS quad; National Geographic/Trails Illustrated map of Hoosier National Forest; Hoosier National Forest map.

Permits/fees: None.
Camping: None.
Trailhead facilities: There is only a gravel parking lot at the trailhead. There is no potable water source.

Finding the trailhead: From the intersection of Indiana 37 and Interstate 64, go north 2.7 miles to Crawford County 8 and turn left (west). Go 2.5 miles to an unnamed gravel road. Take the gravel road 1.7 miles west and then north to a marked entrance for Hemlock Cliffs National Scenic Trail. Turn right (north) at the sign, take the gravel road (Forest Service 1134) to the loop at its end, and park. The trailhead is east of the parking lot.

Key points:
- 0.0 Trailhead.
- 0.3 Descend into the box canyon to the waterfall via a narrow gap in the cliff.
- 0.7 Reach the second waterfall.
- 1.1 Go uphill to exit the ravine.
- 1.4 Return to the parking lot.

The entrance sign for Hemlock Cliffs National Scenic Trail.

Hemlock Cliffs National Scenic Trail

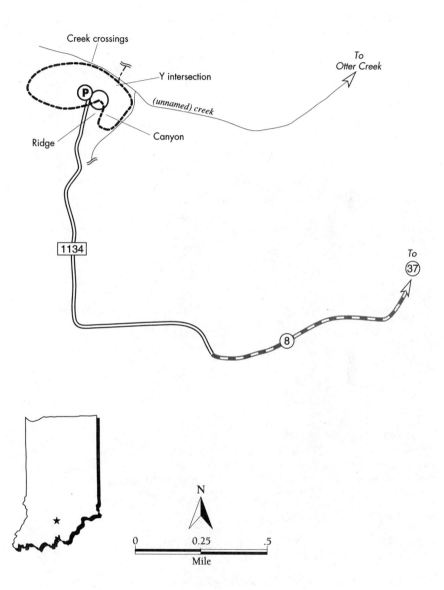

Creek crossings

To
Otter Creek

Y intersection

(unnamed) creek

Canyon

Ridge

1134

To
37

8

N

0   0.25   .5
Mile

Hemlock trees hang from the cliffs along Hemlock Cliffs National Scenic Trail.

The hike: This trail has more dynamic scenery packed into its short distance than many longer hikes. There are two waterfalls that flow on a seasonal basis, steep-walled box canyons, a meandering creek, and hemlock trees dotting the sandstone cliffs.

The trail's remote location serves as a limiting factor on the area. The box canyons were popular with rock climbers, but visitation was reduced beginning in 1996 when a Forest Service ban on rock climbing was imposed.

The trailhead marker is easily visible east of the parking area. Follow the crushed stone walkway downhill to the trailhead and turn right (south). At 0.2 mile, the trail turns left (east) and descends through a gap in the ledge. Wiggle through the opening to the left and descend a set of natural stone steps into the canyon. Its closed, bowl-shaped end to the right (south) is wet with a trickle of water even in the middle of summer.

The trail heads left (northeast) from the waterfall and crosses the small creek before reaching a Y intersection at the 0.6-mile mark. The right fork leads to another box canyon and small waterfall at 0.7 mile, which can be viewed from below or from a higher vantage point, depending on which side path is taken. Climbing or rappelling on the rock face of the box canyon and waterfall is prohibited by order of the Forest Service.

Return to the Y intersection and take the left (west) fork to resume the hike. Sheer cliffs and gradual slopes shadow the passage as it crosses a meandering creek four or five times before heading out of the ravine at 1.1 miles on an uphill walk through woodlands. The trail gradually levels off before reaching the parking lot at 1.4 miles.

55 Two Lakes Loop

Type of hike:	Day hike or backpack, loop.
General description:	A double-loop trail around Celina and Indian lakes.
General location:	Northeast of Tell City in southern Indiana.
Total distance:	13.5 miles.
Difficulty:	Moderate to strenuous.
Elevation gain:	About 340 feet from high point to low point, with variations in between.
Jurisdiction:	Hoosier National Forest, Tell City District.
Special attractions:	Sandstone bluffs along the northeast shores of both lakes, the historic Rickenbaugh House, and two river crossings.
Maps:	Branchville and Bristow USGS quads; National Geographic/Trails Illustrated map of Hoosier National Forest.
Permits/fees:	There is a $2 per vehicle parking fee, plus fees for camping ($5 for walk-in sites, $8 to $18 for non-electric and electric sites).

Camping: There are 63 campsites at two adjacent locations near the east side of the property.

Trailhead facilities: There is a small gravel parking lot for six vehicles, but no restrooms or potable water source. There are drinking water sources in the two campgrounds, as well as pit toilets and seasonal shower facilities.

Finding the trailhead: From Tell City, go about 18 miles northeast on Indiana 37, passing intersections with Indiana 145 and Indiana 70, to the marked entrance to Indian-Celina Lakes of Hoosier National Forest. Turn left (west). From the gatehouse, go about 2.5 miles to the trailhead parking lot on the left (south) side of the main road.

Key points:
- 0.0   Trailhead.
- 0.7   At the trail juncture, go right (west) to travel the loop in a clockwise direction.
- 1.8   Leave the woods to cross Indian Lake Dam.
- 2.6   Cross a seasonal stream.
- 3.1   Reach a trail juncture at a logging road.
- 3.5   At the trail juncture, turn right.
- 4.3   The trail changes direction; go left (northwest) and uphill.
- 5.1   Wade across the Anderson River.
- 5.5   Ford Tige Creek.
- 6.3   At the trail juncture, go left (east) to continue Two Lakes Loop.
- 7.6   Reach the Winding Branch and turn right (south).
- 7.8   Cross over the main road, turn left (east) to the gravel road, then turn right (south).
- 8.3   Turn left (east) and go uphill.
- 8.7   Cross over the boat ramp road and turn onto the Celina Lake Interpretive Loop.
- 9.0   Visit the Rickenbaugh House.
- 11.7 Reach the Celina Lake Dam.
- 12.4 Turn right (north) on the abandoned road.
- 12.8 Reach the trail juncture; turn right (north) to the trailhead parking lot.

The hike: Restricted to hikers only, this trail is as easy to follow as those in state parks, but without the traffic. There are several stream crossings, including the two over the Anderson River and Tige Creek, that can be knee-deep or deeper; take along a pair of thick-soled beach booties or water socks for these two short water crossings. Although there is an elevation difference of nearly 350 feet between the high and low points on the trail, there are few elevation changes of more than 100 feet at one time.

Begin at the designated main trailhead. There are other entry points, but the main trailhead provides the option of taking the hike as a whole or in two halves by using a connector trail that bisects the overall hike into almost equal parts, which can each be handled without difficulty in a few hours.

From the parking lot, go southwest on the connector trail, and look for markers that designate the path as part of the American Discovery Trail (ADT). Markers are varied on the trail—white paint blazes on trees, white

Two Lakes Loop

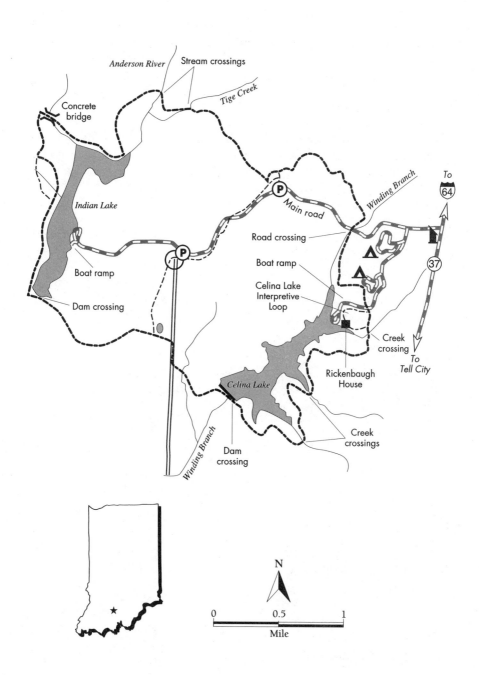

plastic Forest Service tags, tin tags, ADT tags, and brown plastic Forest Service posts. Confused? Actually, the blend of markers all follow the same course. The only differences worth noting are the orange markings on the Forest Service brown posts that designate the connector trail.

The connector trail moves quickly into a stand of pine trees; look for a pond downhill to the left (east). After reaching the pond at 0.5 mile, join the main trail at a T intersection at 0.7 mile. A right (west) turn leads to Indian Lake, a left (east) turn to Celina Lake. Take the right option, and head uphill towards a noticeable knob. Upon passing the knob, veer to the left (southwest) and continue toward another knob—the high spot of the Indian Lake loop at 775 feet elevation, or about 275 feet above the lake.

A saddle leads to another knob, but the trail bends before reaching the peak and takes a counterclockwise path around the knob while beginning a gradual descent toward Indian Lake. The north-facing slopes are a good location in spring to see toothwort, trillium, and dogtooth violets. Round a stand of white pine trees, and catch a glimpse of Indian Lake through the trees.

At 1.8 miles, exit the woods into a stretch through ankle-deep grass that goes over Indian Lake Dam. The dam forms the 150-acre Indian Lake by controlling the flow from Anderson River and Tige Creek. At the west edge of the dam, turn right (north) and walk the west shore of Indian Lake, aptly named because it parallels an old Indian treaty boundary. The terrain is noticeably different here as the trail rolls over small ridges and through shallow gullies for about 1 mile. The landscape is punctuated by the presence of large, rocky outcroppings above and to the left (west) of the trail.

Celina Lake, one of the two lakes on the trail in the Hoosier National Forest.

After crossing a seasonal stream at 2.6 miles, begin climbing as the trail bends toward the northwest and away from the lake. Reach a clearing near the top of the hill, and connect with an abandoned roadway at a T intersection at 3.1 miles. Turn right (north) and follow the gravel road downhill to another T intersection, crossing a small concrete bridge over a stream. The gravel road turns left (northwest), but the trail turns right (southeast). Go 0.1 mile to cross another creek by hop-scotching over the rocks. The trail is not well-marked in this area, but the path can be located without much trouble on the other side of the creek.

Pass a stand of pine trees near the northeast corner of the lake—a stretch that can be muddy at times or littered with wind-blown trash at other times. In contrast to the mess, however, are some beautiful sandstone cliffs about 50 yards inland from the lakeshore. At 4.3 miles, before you reach the northeast corner where the Anderson River and Tige Creek flow into the lake, turn left (north) and head uphill. Daffodils bloom in abundance on this hillside in springtime. Near the top of the hill, pass through another pine plantation before sliding down off the ridge to Anderson River at 5.1 miles.

There is no bridge here, and no shallow patch of rocks over which to hop, but the water is shallow enough under most circumstances to wade the 20-foot distance from bank to bank without getting wet above the calf. It is a good idea to remove your hiking boots—no need to get them wet with another creek to cross and miles to go before completing the hike. The river bottom is gravel and rock, so take care to avoid cutting or injuring your feet if you did not bring the recommended beach booties or water socks.

Once on the other side, walk along a flat stretch that bends around the point of a ridge that separates Anderson River from Tige Creek. After rounding the point, link up with Tige Creek and walk its bank for less than 0.25 mile before having to cross the creek at 5.5 miles. Again, this may require removal of hiking boots, depending on the depth of the water. It is shallow enough at times to cross without having to change footwear.

After crossing the creek, enter a stand of tall pine trees. At the other end of the pines, turn right and head uphill for 0.75 mile to intersect with the orange-marked connector trail at 6.3 miles. With almost 7 miles behind you, you can take a 1-mile shortcut from here back to the main trailhead parking lot. Turn left (east) to add the remaining mileage around Celina Lake, a loop that begins by descending part of the way into a broad ravine, and then climbing the other side to a pine plantation. A marked crossroad provides another chance to head back to the trailhead parking lot. Turn left, instead, to continue toward Celina Lake, heading northeast around the base of a knob that peaks at 815 feet in elevation.

The trail itself levels off around 700 feet, and then heads down to Winding Branch at 7.6 miles; this is the main tributary that feeds Celina Lake. Before you reach the creek, however, you will pick up an old roadbed and follow it on a southwest course to the main road. Turn left (southeast) at the road, and walk about 100 yards before crossing the road at 7.8 miles to pick up another old roadbed. This goes south along Winding Branch for about 0.5 mile before the trail makes a sharp left (east) turn at 8.3 miles, and heads uphill just as Celina Lake comes into view.

Go uphill away from the lake, passing the campgrounds and crossing the paved road leading to the boat ramp at 8.7 miles. Turn right (west), and follow the Celina Lake Interpretive Loop, which leads to the historic Rickenbaugh House at 9 miles. Jacob Rickenbaugh and his family settled on the shore of Celina Lake in the 1870s, largely because bark from the abundant oak trees provided tannin for his trade as a master hide tanner. He paid three Belgian stone masons $3 a day to build the sandstone block house. It took one year to complete. It served as the local post office and church meeting house until a church was constructed at Winding Branch, a small town now beneath the waters of Celina Lake. The interpretive loop also passes sandstone cliffs that provided shelter for Native Americans.

When the interpretive loop rejoins the main trail, turn right (south) and head downhill to cross a small stream. There is no need to change footwear here, or at the next stream crossing. After crossing the second stream, go up over a ridge, and drop into another ravine. Go up the other side of the ravine, and the trail closes in on Celina Lake. Continue along the east shore of the lake with minor elevation changes, hiking in and out of a series of fingerlike coves that become increasingly larger, except for the last one. The first two coves require dropping down off the ridges to cross over small streams before going back uphill.

After rounding the final, smaller cove, exit the woods at the southeast corner of the earthen dam at 11.7 miles. After crossing the dam, the trail turns slightly to the left (southwest) below a ridge and crosses one last stream. This one is filled with larger rocks and is easy to get over. Head uphill from the stream to where the trail turns right (north) along an abandoned road at 12.4 miles. Go about 300 yards before turning left (north) off the road. Go another 300 yards to intersect with the orange-marked connector trail at 12.8 miles. Turn right (north) and it is about 0.75 mile back to the main trailhead parking lot.

56 Tipsaw Lake Trail

Type of hike:	Day hike, loop.
General description:	A trail around Tipsaw Lake.
General location:	Northeast of Tell City in southern Indiana.
Total distance:	6 miles.
Difficulty:	Moderate.
Elevation gain:	About 80 feet.
Jurisdiction:	Hoosier National Forest, Tell City District.
Special attractions:	The Tipsaw Lake shoreline.
Maps:	Bristow, Gatchel, and Branchville USGS quads; National Geographic/Trails Illustrated map of Hoosier National Forest; Hoosier National Forest map.

Permits/fees: None are required for trail access. There is a $3 entry fee for the campgrounds or boat ramp.

Camping: Tipsaw Lake has 41 campsites, modern or primitive, plus a group camp area. Campgrounds are open from mid-April to mid-October.

Trailhead facilities: There is only a parking lot at the trailhead, although water and restrooms are available at the Tipsaw Lake Recreation Area campgrounds. A gate fee is charged to enter.

Finding the trailhead: Go north from Tell City for 17 miles on Indiana 37 to the Tipsaw Lake Recreation Area sign. Turn left (west) and go 2 miles to the trailhead parking lot on the left (south) side of the road.

Key points:
- 0.0   Trailhead.
- 0.7   Cross the main road.
- 1.8   Cross the unnamed creek.
- 2.4   Cross the dam.
- 3.5   Reach the metal barricade and gravel road.
- 3.6   Cross the Snake Branch.
- 3.7   Reach the T intersection and turn left (northwest).
- 3.9   Turn left off the road.
- 5.9   Cross Sulphur Fork Creek.

The hike: Tipsaw Lake, formed primarily by Sulphur Fork Creek, Massey Creek, Snake Branch, and one other unnamed stream, is one of four small reservoirs within this area of the Hoosier National Forest, all of which are circled by a trail. This may be the easiest of the four trails—a flat course except for a series of modest climbs at the outset that traverse the hillside between the boat ramp, picnic area, and the campground. Otherwise, this trail is hardly a challenge, but nevertheless it is a pleasant hike.

Although the trail is also open to mountain bikes, it does not suffer from overuse. Hikers have the right of way over bikers. The trail is clearly marked with yellow diamond tags on trees, plus brown plastic marker posts. The yellow tags have black directional arrows. The trail has been rerouted recently to avoid the boat ramp and picnic area. Ticks can be troublesome along the meadow and dam portions of the trail.

To begin, head southwest from the small trailhead parking lot on a crushed stone pathway with stands of pine trees on one side and tulip poplar trees on the other. The trail continues on a southwest course between the main road on the right (north) and Sulphur Fork Creek on the left (south). At 0.7 mile, turn right (north) to cross the main road, and hike up the wooded hillside, turning left (northwest) on a meandering stretch that works up and down the hill while crossing a footbridge and a couple of small streams.

Return to the lake at 1.4 miles, and hug the shoreline around a fingerlike bay pointing to the northwest. At the back end of the bay, cross an unnamed creek at 1.8 miles and continue south, then southwest, crossing several more small seasonal creeks. Exit the woods at 2 miles to enter a shoreline meadow

Tipsaw Lake Trail

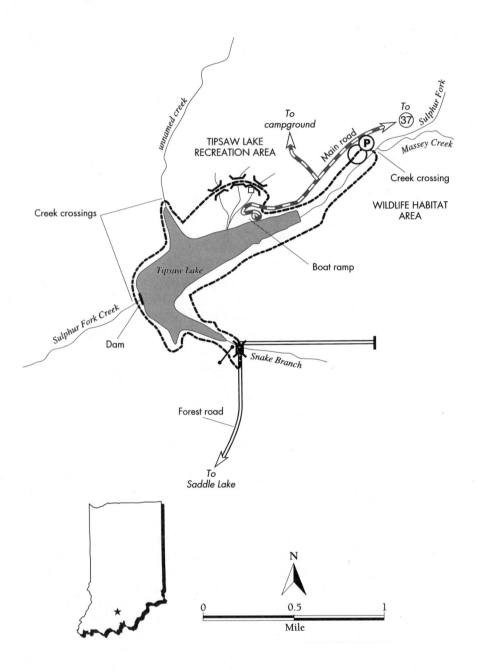

that lead to the earthen dam at 2.4 miles. Hike across the dam to enter a stand of pine trees whose fallen needles help cushion the trail.

Cross a small creek at 3 miles. The trail then hugs the shoreline of another fingerlike bay, following an old roadbed for 0.5 mile. Pass a metal barricade at 3.5 miles, cross another small stream, and briefly follow a gravel road that serves as a back entrance to the property. Turn left (north), cross Snake Branch at 3.6 miles, and come to a T intersection at 3.7 miles. Go left (west) for 0.2 mile before leaving the road and heading north at 3.9 miles.

The trail again follows the shoreline, first along the bay formed by Snake Branch, and then turning northeast along the southeast shore of the main lake. Move up and down over small gullies and ridges for about 0.5 mile before coming to a large meadow that is managed as a wildlife clearing through a cooperative program of the Forest Service and the Indiana Department of Natural Resources. The clearing is a good place to see deer or other woodland wildlife, so approach quietly.

At 5.9 miles, the trail makes a hairpin turn to the left (northwest) and crosses Sulphur Fork Creek before returning to the trailhead parking lot.

57 Saddle Lake Loop

Type of hike: Day hike, loop.
General description: A short, scenic walk along the shores of Saddle Lake.
General location: North of Tell City.
Total distance: 2 miles.
Difficulty: Moderate.
Elevation gain: Minimal.
Jurisdiction: Hoosier National Forest, Tell City District.
Special attractions: Lake views.
Maps: Gatchel USGS quad; National Geographic/Trails Illustrated map of Hoosier National Forest; Hoosier National Forest map.
Permits/fees: None.
Camping: Limited to ten sites, but no fees.
Trailhead facilities: There are pit toilets, a parking area, a boat ramp, and a beach at the trailhead. No potable water source is available.

Finding the trailhead: From Tell City, go 10 miles northeast on Indiana 37 to the marked Gatchel exit. Turn left (northwest) and go 0.2 mile to a T intersection with Old Indiana 37. Turn right (northeast) and go 0.5 mile through Gatchel to a gravel entry road (Forest Service 443) to Saddle Lake. Turn left (north) and go about 1 mile to a paved parking lot near the lake's boat ramp. Trail markers are located on the north side of the parking lot at the boat ramp.

Saddle Lake Loop

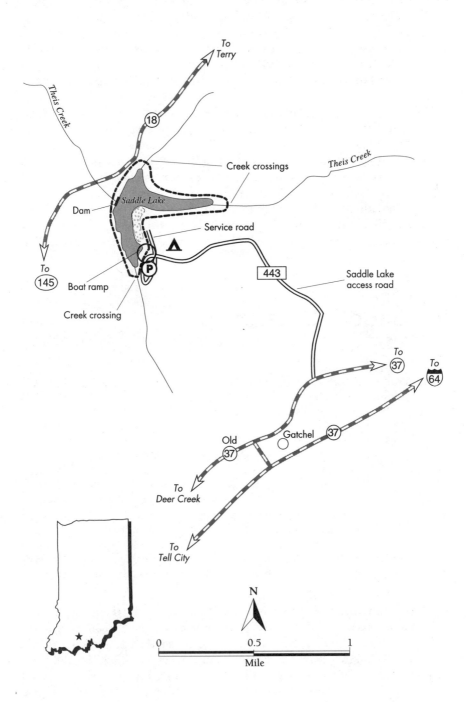

To Terry

Theis Creek

18

Creek crossings

Theis Creek

Saddle Lake

Dam

Service road

To 145

Boat ramp

443

Saddle Lake access road

Creek crossing

To 37

To 64

Old 37

Gatchel

37

To Deer Creek

To Tell City

N

0   0.5   1
Mile

Key points:

- 0.0   Trailhead.
- 0.7   Reach a creek crossing.
- 1.0   Cross a culvert.
- 1.4   Cross the Saddle Lake Dam.
- 1.9   Make the last creek crossing.
- 2.0   Reach the trail's end.

The hike: This trail can be hiked in either direction—clockwise or counter-clockwise—but is described here via the latter. The trail is well-maintained but appears to get little use.

Begin at the boat ramp and walk through a wooded area to a service road at 0.1 mile. Turn left (north) and head up a slight incline past a service shed to an amphitheater-like structure overlooking the beach. After passing this area, enter the woods and continue along the southeastern lakeshore. Rocky

Butterfly and wildflower.

outcrops punctuate the hillside to the right (east), and wildflowers dot the pathway.

Make the first creek crossing at 0.7 mile and enter a stand of large pine trees whose trunks are 2.5 feet in diameter. Make a slight climb out of the pines and back into hardwood forest, and begin an up-and-down stretch over a series of moderate humps.

Cross a culvert at 1 mile and walk back uphill again to a section of beech trees. Descend from this hump into a gully and the second creek crossing. Once more, go uphill and come close to a county road (Perry County 18) before dropping back downhill to cross the lake's earthen dam at 1.4 miles. In spring and summer, wildflowers and plants along the dam—bergamot, milkweed, butterfly weed, Queen Anne's lace, black-eyed Susan—attract an array of butterflies.

At the other end of the dam, follow a stretch of trail along the southwest shore of the lake that slips across two gullies. After the second gully, the trail is a straight shot on flat terrain about 30 feet above the lakeshore to another stand of pine trees. Drop off the flat at about 1.8 miles to make another creek crossing. The boat ramp is visible from here. Cross one last creek at 1.9 miles, go uphill, and follow the gravel path back to the parking area.

58 Mogan Ridge East

Type of hike:	Day hike, loop.
General description:	A trail through an abandoned farm field, over a narrow ridge, and across a shallow creek.
General location:	Northeast of Tell City, near Derby.
Total distance:	5.5 miles.
Difficulty:	Strenuous.
Elevation gain:	390 feet from Kuntz Ridge to Clover Lick Creek.
Jurisdiction:	Hoosier National Forest, Tell City District.
Special attractions:	Kuntz Ridge and Clover Lick Creek.
Maps:	Derby USGS quad; National Geographic/Trails Illustrated map of Hoosier National Forest; Hoosier National Forest map.
Permits/fees:	None required.
Camping:	None available.
Trailhead facilities:	There is a parking area for about a half-dozen vehicles. No water or restroom facilities are available.

Finding the trailhead: Go 1 mile north on Indiana 66 from its intersection with Indiana 70 in Derby. Turn left (north) on Perry County 370/Utopia Road and pass the private boat ramp as you head uphill. The trailhead parking lot is on the right (east) side of the road 0.7 mile from Indiana 66. Because high water on the nearby Ohio River can flood access to the east trailhead, there is an alternate entry point. Go 2.9 miles west on Indiana 70 from the

Mogan Ridge East

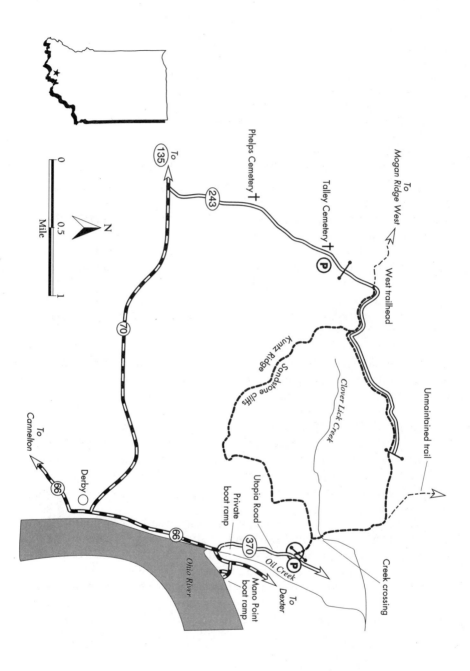

intersection with Indiana 66 in Derby to Perry County 243/Ultima Road. Turn right (north) and go 1.3 miles to a small gravel parking lot on the right (east) across from the Talley Cemetery. It is a 0.5-mile walk up the dirt road to a connector spur that joins the Mogan Ridge East and Mogan Ridge West trails.

Key points:
- 0.0   Trailhead.
- 0.2   Reach a trail juncture and turn left (southwest).
- 0.5   The trail turns left (south).
- 1.2   Arrive at Kuntz Ridge and the sandstone cliffs.
- 3.0   Reach a trail juncture at a gravel road and turn right.
- 4.7   Turn right at a T intersection.
- 5.2   Cross Clover Lick Creek.
- 5.3   Reach the trail juncture and turn left (southeast) to the trailhead.

The hike: It requires a little geography lesson to understand how Mogan Ridge East got its name, considering the fact that no part of the trail is within a mile of Mogan Ridge. Once part of a larger multi-use trail, Mogan Ridge East has been set aside exclusively for hikers. Mogan Ridge West, which in part traverses Mogan Ridge, is an 11-mile trail that is open to hikers, bikers, and horseback riders. The two trails are connected by a 0.5-mile spur. Although half as long, Mogan Ridge East is just as challenging as its counterpart.

Although the trail has few directional markings, it is an easy one to follow. Traffic typically is light.

Both the Mogan Ridge East and West trails are part of the American Discovery Trail. Mogan Ridge East is a prime spot for wildflowers, especially in spring when the path is festooned with splashes of sweet William, self-heal, daisy fleabaine, wild geranium, Jacob's ladder, Virginia bluebell, and Virginia waterleaf.

To hike the Mogan Ridge East Trail from its east end, begin in the parking area off Utopia Road, cross the gravel road, pass the metal gate, and slip through a gap between a pair of knob-like hills. Go downhill to a trail juncture at 0.2 mile. Turn left (southwest), and go through a meadow to the 0.5-mile mark, where the trail turns left (south) and goes uphill to the eastern tip of Kuntz Ridge.

At 1.2 miles, swing clockwise around the base of a triangular-shaped ridgetop. Curl to the right (west) and pass a very narrow backbone with sandstone cliffs dropping steeply off to the right (north) side of the trail. Continue along Kuntz Ridge, gradually turning northwest.

At 2.5 miles, go downhill briefly before climbing again to a gravel road at 3 miles. This is the connector spur to Mogan Ridge West. Turn right (east), and continue along the Mogan Ridge East Trail as it follows the gravel road for about 0.5 mile. The surface of the road changes to dirt at a metal gate. Go straight (east), heading uphill briefly before descending to the edge of a meadow. Continue downhill, passing a stand of pine trees, to a T intersection at 4.7 miles. Turn right (south) on a downhill course to Clover Lick Creek, which is at 5.2 miles.

The cross-country American Discovery Trail (ADT) winds its way through southern Indiana.

The rocky stream has an intermittent flow and is easy to cross most of the time. Go uphill for 0.1 mile from the creek to complete the loop at the trail junction at 5.3 miles. Turn left (southeast) and go 0.2 mile to the parking lot.

59 German Ridge Lake Trail

Type of hike: Day hike, loop.
General description: A short trail past sandstone cliffs overlooking a lake.
General location: Perry County in southern Indiana, east of Tell City.
Total distance: 1 mile.
Difficulty: Easy.
Elevation gain: Minimal.
Jurisdiction: Hoosier National Forest, Tell City District.
Special attractions: Moss-covered sandstone cliffs.
Maps: Rome USGS quad; National Geographic/Trails Illustrated map of Hoosier National Forest; German Ridge/Hoosier National Forest map.
Permits/fees: None required.
Camping: There are 23 campsites at German Ridge Lake.
Trailhead facilities: There is a shelter house with pit toilets.

Finding the trailhead: From Tell City, go east on Indiana 66 through Cannelton to Rocky Point. Go 6.4 miles east on Indiana 66 from Rocky Point to Perry County 3 and turn left (north). Go 0.75 mile to a gated entrance to German Ridge. After passing the gate, take the right fork to the picnic area. Locate the shelter house on the left (north) side of the parking lot. The trailhead is on the opposite, or north side, of the picnic shelter.

Key points:
    0.0   Trailhead.
    0.1   Cross a footbridge.
    0.3   Reach the sandstone cliffs.
    0.6   At the trail juncture, stay right.

The hike: The German Ridge area of the Hoosier National Forest is primarily devoted to horseback riding, but hikers get to see a slice of it with this loop trail, which is described here in a clockwise direction. The trailhead behind the picnic shelter can be a little tricky to find, but the trail itself is a wide path and easy to follow. German Ridge was developed nearly 50 years ago by the Civilian Conservation Corps.

It doesn't take long to get to the focal point of this brief hike. After crossing a footbridge at 0.1 mile, the striking sandstone cliffs are almost immediately visible. Even on the hottest of summer days, the tree-shaded cliffs can be a cool setting. At 0.3 mile, a feeder trail to the horseman's camp connects from the left (southeast). Be sure to take the path to the right (south) that leads

German Ridge Lake Trail

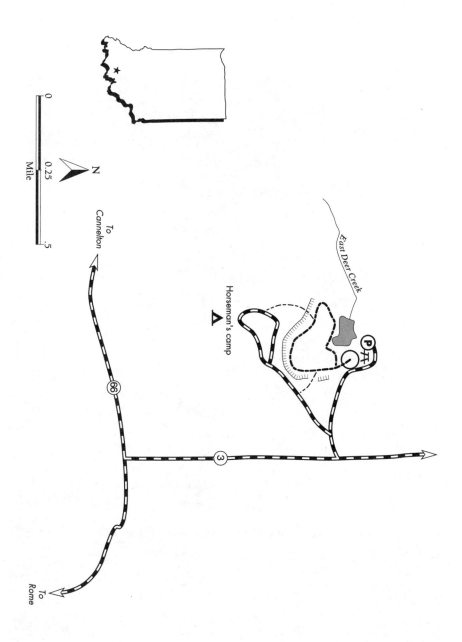

in a clockwise direction. The cliffs rise on the left (south), while glimpses of the lake can be seen through the trees below and to the right (north).

At 0.6 mile, reach another feeder trail that connects to the horseman's camp to the south. Stay right (west and north) and walk downhill away from the cliffs to a T intersection near the lake's edge. Circle the lake to the beach near the parking lot and trailhead.

Exposed sandstone cliffs guard the trail at German Ridge.

Knobstone Trail

Hikers do not have to leave Indiana to get a taste of the Appalachian Trail.

An adequate sample can be found in southeast Indiana along the state's most distinctive geographic feature—the Knobstone Escarpment. The escarpment appears like a fortress rising 300 to 400 feet above the Scottsburg lowlands to the east. It meanders for more than 100 miles from the Ohio River northwest toward Martinsville.

The Knobstone Trail (KT) follows the spiny ridges and deep ravines for 58 miles, beginning at Deam Lake State Recreation Area and ending at Delaney Park. It passes through 40,000 acres of public forest land. The area is richly diverse, with abundant fauna and flora.

The KT is relatively new. It was first opened in 1980, and at the time measured only 32 miles. The Indiana Department of Natural Resources is exploring ways to extend the trail farther through the Jackson-Washington State Forest, the Hoosier National Forest, the Morgan-Monroe State Forest, and along private-land corridors. By the time it is finished, the KT may be double its present length. It already is the longest trail in the state.

Trailhead locations along the route shorten the legs of the trail to between 6 and 12 miles, making it a popular trail not only for long-distance hikers, but for day hikers as well.

Backcountry camping is permitted along the KT, as long as campsites are on public land and are at least 1 mile by trail away from all roads, recreation areas, and trailheads.

The KT is well-marked with white blazes. Most locations where the various trail legs intersect are further marked with signs. All trailheads are marked with 4-inch by 4-inch KT posts on the access roads, and large trailhead signs. As the premier hiking trail in Indiana, the KT is well cared for by the Indiana Department of Natural Resources and volunteer groups.

Water supplies along the trail are limited, so many hikers stash supplies at the trailheads. Many of the streams and creeks that the KT crosses are seasonal, so do not count on them for water.

Whether in pieces or as a whole, the KT has earned its nickname as "the little Appalachian Trail."

The trail is described in linear sections on a northwest course from about 20 miles north of Louisville, Kentucky, toward Salem.

---

60 Deam Lake to Jackson Road

Type of hike: Shuttle, backpack, or day hike.
General description: This is the shortest leg of the Knobstone Trail, and is a good warm-up for more challenging legs of the trail.

General location:	Between Borden/New Providence and Sellersburg in Clark County.
Total distance:	5 miles.
Difficulty:	Strenuous.
Elevation gain:	Two climbs of more than 150 feet.
Jurisdiction:	Indiana Department of Natural Resources, Division of Outdoor Recreation.
Special attractions:	Bowery Creek and Bartle Knobs.
Maps:	Speed and Henryville USGS quads; Indiana Department of Natural Resources Knobstone Trail brochure.
Permits/fees:	None required unless you park at Deam Lake State Recreation Area, which has a $2 entry fee per vehicle with Indiana license plates. The fee for nonresidents is $5. Season passes are available.
Camping:	Camping is permitted on public land along the Knobstone Trail as long as the camp is at least 1 mile by trail from all roads, recreation areas, and trailheads, and as long as it is not visible from the trail and all lakes. Also, Deam Lake State Recreation Area has 286 campsites.
Trailhead facilities:	There are only parking areas at the Deam Lake and Jackson Road trailheads, although water and restrooms are located at Deam Lake State Recreation Area.

Finding the trailhead: From the Interstate 65 exit at Sellersburg, go south 0.8 mile on Indiana 311 to Indiana 60. Turn right (west) on Indiana 60, and go 8 miles to the Deam Lake State Recreation Area sign at Waggoner Knob Road. Turn right (north) and go 0.8 mile to Wilson Switch Road near Miller Cemetery. Turn right (east) and go 1.4 miles to the Deam Lake Trailhead on the left (north) side of the road. A 4-inch by 4-inch wooden post with a KT on the right (south) side of the road marks the location.

Key points:
- 0.0   Trailhead.
- 1.9   Cross over the gravel road.
- 2.4   Cross Bowery Creek.
- 4.5   Hike over the Bartle Knobs.
- 5.0   Cross Bartle Knobs Road and turn left (west) to the Jackson Road Trailhead.

The hike: Deception is the best way to describe the opening leg of the Knobstone Trail because it might not seem all that difficult at first. Once you hike a few miles in, however, you will know firsthand the kinds of challenges you will encounter along the remainder of the trail. Trail traffic may be high near the Deam Lake Trailhead because of its proximity to the state recreation area.

The trail, marked by white blazes, begins east of Deam Lake with a gradual climb of about 120 feet over the first mile, then drops into a ravine before intersecting with a gravel road at 1.9 miles. Cross over the road, turn right

226

Deam Lake to Jackson Road

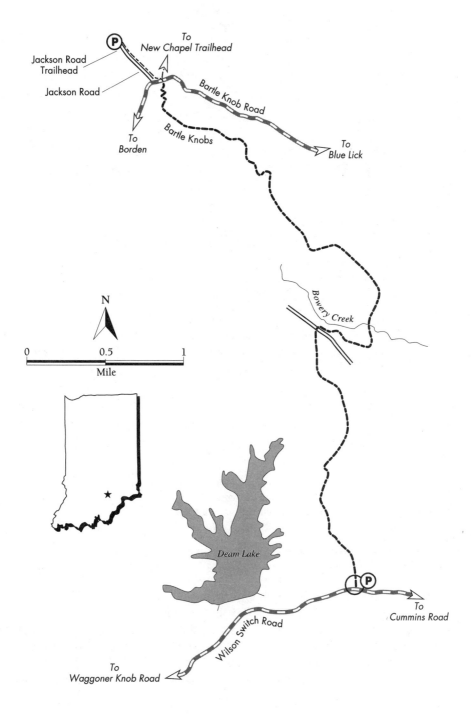

(southeast), and continue downward to Bowery Creek at 2.4 miles.

From here, the Knobstone is anything but easy. Over the next 1.5 miles, go uphill along a series of round hilltops named Bartle Knobs. From the creek to the highest knob, there is an elevation change of 400 feet, which is typical of what the next 50-plus miles are like.

After peaking out at Bartle Knobs at about the 4.5-mile mark, slide down the back end of the Berry Run ravine and climb to Bartle Knob Road at 5 miles. Cross the road to continue on the trail, or turn left (west), then right (north), and follow the gravel Jackson Road for 0.4 mile to the Jackson Road Trailhead.

61 Jackson Road to New Chapel

Type of hike:	Shuttle, backpack, or day hike.
General description:	A demanding stretch of the Knobstone Trail along ridgetops and through ravines.
General location:	Clark State Forest.
Total distance:	12 miles.
Difficulty:	Strenuous.
Elevation gain:	Multiple climbs of more than 250 feet.
Jurisdiction:	Indiana Department of Natural Resources, Division of Outdoor Recreation.
Special attractions:	Round Knob and the Virginia Pine-Chestnut Oak Nature Preserve.
Maps:	Henryville USGS quad; Indiana Department of Natural Resources Knobstone Trail brochure.
Permits/fees:	None required.
Camping:	Camping is permitted on public land along the Knobstone Trail as long as the camp is at least 1 mile by trail from all roads, recreation areas, and trailheads, and as long as it is not visible from the trail and all lakes. Also, Deam Lake State Recreation Area has 286 campsites.
Trailhead facilities:	Only parking is available at the Jackson Road and New Chapel trailheads.

Finding the trailhead: To reach the Jackson Road Trailhead from the Deam Lake Trailhead, go left (east) from the Deam Lake Trailhead on Wilson Switch Road for 0.5 mile to the intersection of Flower Gap Road and Wilson Switch Road. Turn right (south) and go 0.2 mile to Cummins Road. Turn left (east) and go 1.3 miles to Crone Road. Turn left (northeast) and go 1.1 miles to Beyl Road. Turn left (northwest) and go 1 mile to Bolling Road. Turn right (northeast) and go 1 mile to the intersection of Mayfield Road. Go straight (northwest) onto Bartle Knob Road and continue for 3.9 miles to Jackson Road, a gravel road on the right. Turn right (northwest) onto Jackson Road,

Jackson Road to New Chapel

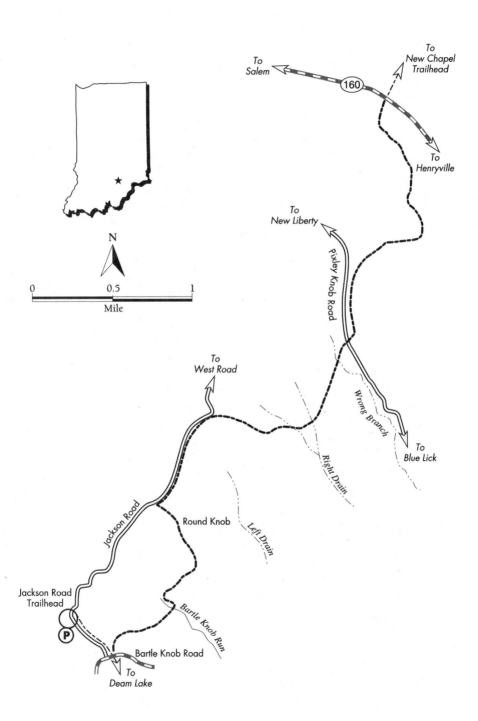

To Salem

To New Chapel Trailhead

160

To Henryville

To New Liberty

Pixley Knob Road

N

0   0.5   1
Mile

To West Road

Wrong Branch

To Blue Lick

Right Drain

Round Knob

Left Drain

Jackson Road

Jackson Road Trailhead

P

Bartle Knob Run

Bartle Knob Road

To Deam Lake

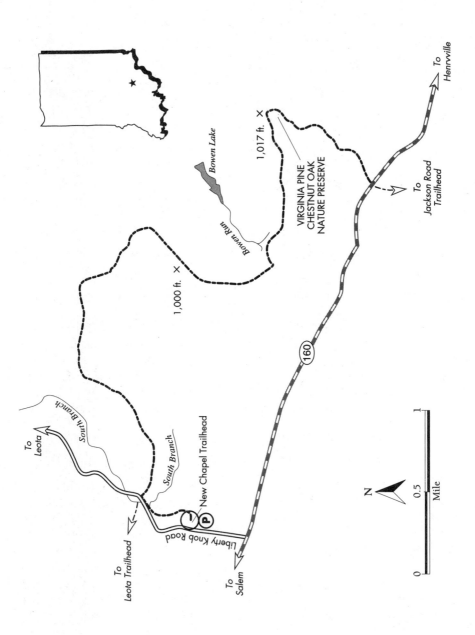

and go 0.3 mile to the Jackson Road Trailhead on the left (west).

Key points:
- 0.0   Trailhead.
- 1.2   Reach Round Knob.
- 1.6   At Jackson Road, go right (northeast).
- 2.5   The trail turns right (east) off Jackson Road.
- 4.0   Cross over Pixley Knob Road and turn left (north).
- 6.3   Cross Indiana 160.
- 7.3   Reach the Virginia Pine-Chestnut Oak Nature Preserve.
- 8.8   Arrive at Bowen Run.
- 12.0   Reach the New Chapel Trailhead; go left (south) to parking lot.

The hike: Bartle Knobs, Bartle Knob Road, Bartle Knob Run—in short order, the trail touches all three before coming to one of the toughest challenges in the full 58-mile hike—a steep, 360-foot climb up Round Knob. Traffic generally is not significant along the middle legs of the trail. The area is open to hunting during regulated seasons.

It all starts after crossing Bartle Knob Road and angling down the north-facing side of a ravine to Bartle Knob Run and the creek that wanders through the ravine. Turn left (northwest) along the creek before heading uphill to Round Knob at 1.2 miles. The climb starts as somewhat gradual, but the final 150-foot rise is covered in less than 0.25 mile. The view from Round Knob is spectacular, however, especially to the southeast. On a clear day, it is possible to see downtown Louisville, Kentucky, more than 20 miles away.

After leaving Round Knob, cross a saddleback that leads to Jackson Road at 1.6 miles. Turn right (north) and walk along the gravel road for nearly a mile before turning right (southeast) at 2.5 miles to hike through the Right Drain ravine. Yes, there is a nearby ravine named Left Drain, and the trail soon crosses Wrong Branch, which later joins Right Branch. Cross the Wrong Branch and Pixley Knob Road at 4 miles and turn left (north) to parallel the road while going up a narrow ridge point. You have made a 350-foot climb by the time you reach the top.

Go from one knob to another before making a sharp downhill maneuver to the crossing of Indiana 160 at 6.3 miles. Cross the road, and go uphill on an old logging road to the Virginia Pine-Chestnut Oak Nature Preserve at 7.3 miles. The 24-acre hilltop site is dominated by a native stand of Virginia pine, an uncommon tree in Indiana except in the Knobstone region. Chestnut oak trees control the lower slopes.

After leaving the preserve, come to the highest point on the Knobstone Trail—a knob at 1,017 feet above sea level. Turn left (west) from here and follow a long narrow ridge descending about 200 feet to Bowen Run at 8.8 miles. This stream feeds Bowen Lake, which is about 0.5 mile to the northeast. Cross the creek a couple of times before heading uphill to another 1,000-foot knob. Swing northeast, then northwest along a string of knobs before descending to the South Branch ravine and New Chapel Trailhead at 12 miles. The trailhead parking lot is about 0.25 mile southwest and uphill from the trail.

62 New Chapel to Leota

Type of hike:	Shuttle, backpack, or day hike.
General description:	This part of the trail features long stretches along ridgetops, with occasional drops into ravines, including the scenic North Branch Valley.
General location:	Clark State Forest in Scott County.
Total distance:	9 miles.
Difficulty:	Strenuous.
Elevation gain:	Multiple changes of 250 feet or more.
Jurisdiction:	Indiana Department of Natural Resources, Division of Outdoor Recreation.
Special attractions:	North Branch Valley.
Maps:	Henryville, South Boston, and Little York USGS quads; Indiana Department of Natural Resources Knobstone Trail brochure.
Permits/fees:	None required.
Camping:	Camping is permitted on public land along the Knobstone Trail as long as the camp is at least 1 mile by trail from all roads, recreation areas, and trailheads, and as long as it is not visible from the trail and all lakes.
Trailhead facilities:	Only parking is available at the New Chapel and Leota trailheads.

Finding the trailhead: To locate the New Chapel Trailhead, go left (east) from the Jackson Road Trailhead for 3.9 miles to Mayfield Road. Turn left (northeast) and go 1.3 miles to Blue Lick Road. Turn left (northwest) and go 0.5 mile and continue right (northeast) on Blue Lick Road. Go 1.5 miles to Beers Road. Turn left (northwest) on Beers Road and go 1.8 miles to a T intersection with Indiana 160. Turn left (west) and go 4.7 miles to Liberty Knob Road. Turn right (north) and go 0.4 mile to the New Chapel Trailhead parking lot on the right (east) side of the road.

Key points:
- 0.0 Trailhead.
- 4.5 Reach the North Branch Valley.
- 8.9 Cross Leota Road.
- 9.0 Reach the Leota Trailhead.

The hike: Unlike the earlier segments of the Knobstone Trail (KT), where the high point were knobs, the highlight of this 9-mile stretch is the North Branch Valley, a narrow, high-sided ravine rich with wildflowers, ferns, and some of the biggest trees on the KT. Generally, traffic is not significant along the middle legs of the trail. The area is open to hunting during regulated seasons.

The first half of the New Chapel-to-Leota leg wanders along the edge of the forest and rolls along ridgetops, occasionally dipping across the back

New Chapel to Leota

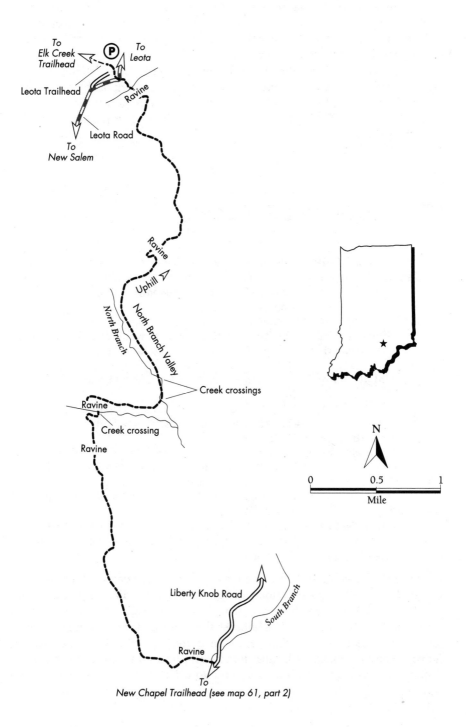

To
Elk Creek
Trailhead

P

To
Leota

Leota Trailhead

Ravine

Leota Road

To
New Salem

Ravine

Uphill

North Branch

North Branch Valley

Creek crossings

Ravine

Creek crossing

Ravine

Liberty Knob Road

South Branch

Ravine

To
New Chapel Trailhead (see map 61, part 2)

N

0   0.5   1
Mile

end of ravines. Near the 3-mile mark, drop into a ravine and cross the creek, then climb the other side, cross over a narrow ridge, and make a steep descent into a side ravine of North Branch Valley at 4.5 miles. Turn right (east) to round a point, and turn left (north) for a 1-mile walk through the lush ravine. Climb the right (east) side of the ravine, crossing the ridgetop and descending into another ravine.

Go uphill again, and follow the ridgeline north for 1.5 miles before turning northwest to traverse one last ravine. Cross the creek at the ravine bottom and head uphill to cross Leota Road at 8.9 miles. Continue up for 0.1 mile to the Leota Trailhead parking lot at 9 miles. The parking area lies along a utility corridor.

63 Leota to Elk Creek

Type of hike:	Shuttle, backpack, or day hike.
General description:	Three hills and several ravines lead to a scenic lake.
General location:	Between Salem and Scottsburg.
Total distance:	7 miles.
Difficulty:	Strenuous.
Elevation gain:	Climbs of 250 to 350 feet, descents of 150 to 250 feet.
Jurisdiction:	Indiana Department of Natural Resources, Division of Outdoor Recreation.
Special attractions:	Vic Swain Hill and the Elk Creek Fish and Game Area.
Maps:	Little York USGS quad; Indiana Department of Natural Resources Knobstone Trail brochure.
Permits/fees:	None required.
Camping:	Camping is permitted on public land along the Knobstone Trail as long as the camp is at least 1 mile by trail from all roads, recreation areas, and trailheads, and as long as it is not visible from the trail and all lakes.
Trailhead facilities:	Only parking is available at the Leota Trailhead. Parking and latrines are available at the Elk Creek Trailhead.

Finding the trailhead: From the New Chapel Trailhead parking lot, turn left (south) on Liberty Knob Road and go 0.4 mile to Indiana 160. Turn right (west) and go 1.8 miles to New Salem Road. Turn right (north) and go 3.4 miles, passing through New Salem. At the 3.4-mile mark, turn right (east) onto Leota Road and go 1.7 miles to an unmarked gravel road on the left (north) side of Leota Road. Turn left (north) and go 0.1 mile to the Leota Trailhead entrance. Turn left (east) and go 0.1 mile to the parking lot and trailhead.

Leota to Elk Creek

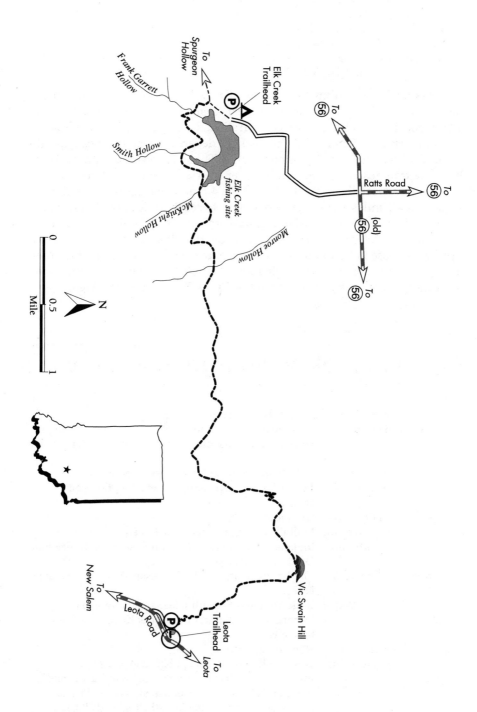

Key points:

0.0 Trailhead.
1.5 Climb Vic Swain Hill.
4.7 Arrive at Monroe Hollow.
5.7 Cross McKnight Hollow.
6.2 Reach Smith Hollow.
6.7 Cross Frank Garrett Hollow.
7.0 Reach the Elk Creek Trailhead.

The hike: The trail from Leota to Elk Creek begins at an opening on the north side of the Leota parking lot near a small pond. Descend from the 1,000-foot elevation level of the Leota Trailhead along a ridgeline that leads to Vic Swain Hill at 1.5 miles. The hill marks a departure from the mostly northward direction that the Knobstone Trail (KT) has followed until now. From here, the trail heads west for 6 miles over a series of ridges and ravines.

After an especially steep climb near the 4.5-mile mark, drop into Monroe Hollow at 4.7 miles. Cross the next "knob" to reach McKnight Hollow at 5.7 miles, and close in on Elk Lake. The trail crosses Smith Hollow at 6.2 miles, and makes a 200-foot climb to a knob overlooking the lake. Turn south briefly and descend into Frank Garrett Hollow at 6.7 miles. Cross the creek and turn right (north) at the trail spur to reach the trailhead at Elk Lake. Trail traffic may be higher near the Elk Creek Fish and Game Area.

64 Elk Creek to Spurgeon Hollow

Type of hike:	Shuttle, backpack, or day hike.
General description:	This section of the Knobstone Trail crosses ridgetops, ravines, and roads, plus offers optional segments at its north end.
General location:	Jackson-Washington State Forest east of Salem.
Total distance:	12 to 15 miles, depending on which option you choose.
Difficulty:	Strenuous.
Elevation gain:	Multiple changes of between 150 and 250 feet.
Jurisdiction:	Indiana Department of Natural Resources, Division of Outdoor Recreation.
Special attractions:	The Back Country Area of Jackson-Washington State Forest.
Maps:	Little York and Kossuth USGS quads; Indiana Department of Natural Resources Knobstone Trail brochure.
Permits/fees:	None required.
Camping:	Camping is permitted on public land along the Knobstone Trail as long as the camp is at least 1 mile by trail from all roads, recreation areas, and trailheads, and as long as it is not visible from the trail and all lakes.

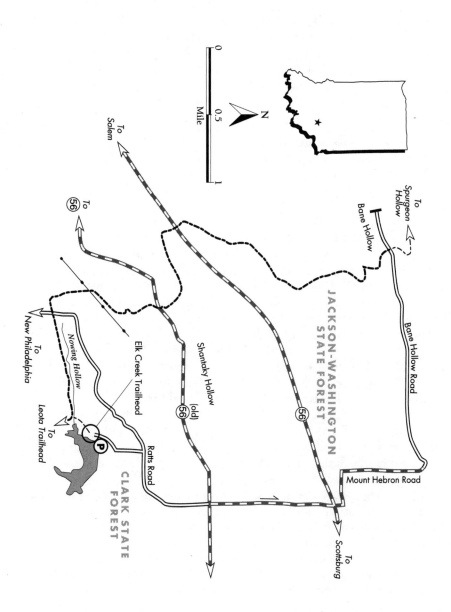

Trailhead facilities: There is parking and latrines at the Elk Creek Trailhead; parking only at Spurgeon Hollow.

Finding the trailhead: To reach the Elk Creek Trailhead from the Leota Trailhead parking lot, turn left (south) and go 0.1 mile to the paved Leota Road. Turn left (east) on Leota Road and go 1.1 miles to the first paved road (an unmarked county road) on the left. Turn left (north) and go 1.2 miles to a T intersection with Bloomington Trail Road. Turn left (northwest) on Bloomington Trail Road and go 1.8 miles to U.S. Highway 56. Turn left (west) and go 2.8 miles to the sign for Elk Creek Public Fishing Area. Turn left (south) on Ratts Road and go 1.8 miles to the fishing area entrance. At the KT post, turn left (west) to the Elk Creek Trailhead.

Key points:
0.0   Trailhead.
1.1   Cross the gravel road.
1.7   Reach the powerline corridor
2.5   Cross Old State Road 56.
3.5   Cross Indiana 56.
6.0   Cross Bane Hollow Road.
7.5   Reach and cross Pull Tight Road.
8.5   Cross West Point Road to a trail fork.

The hike: From one of its most remote stretches (Leota to Elk Creek), the Knobstone Trail (KT) switches to its longest and perhaps least spectacular section between Elk Creek and Spurgeon Hollow to the northwest. A half-dozen road crossings, a powerline corridor, and occasional logging operations interrupt the natural setting.

This part of the trail is not without challenges, however. There are several steep knobs to be climbed, although the severity of the elevation change is only 150 to 250 feet, unlike the 250- to 400-footers on the KT's southern sections. Traffic generally is not significant along the middle legs of the trail. The area is open to hunting during regulated seasons.

Beginning at the Elk Creek Trailhead, go south down the connecting trail to the main trail. Turn right (west) and walk through Nowing Hollow for about 0.5 mile before climbing a ridge. Make the first road crossing at 1.1 miles, beyond which the trail drops into a ravine and climbs on a northeast slant along the south-facing slope.

Atop the ridge at 1.7 miles, connect with a powerline corridor for about 0.25 mile before dropping off the left (north) side into a ravine. Climb the other side and cross Old State Road 56 at 2.5 miles. Cut across the back end of Shantaky Hollow and work uphill to a knob that at 974 feet is the high point of this section. Descend more than 200 feet to cross Indiana 56 at 3.5 miles, then head back uphill to follow a ridgeline for about a mile as the KT enters the Jackson-Washington State Forest.

On a northward course for the next 2 miles, the KT crosses two roads and traverses a half-dozen ravines, including Bane Hollow and Bane Hollow Road at 6 miles, and then Herron Hollow.

From Herron Hollow, go uphill for 0.5 mile to cross Pull Tight Road at 7.5

Elk Creek to Spurgeon Hollow (part 2)

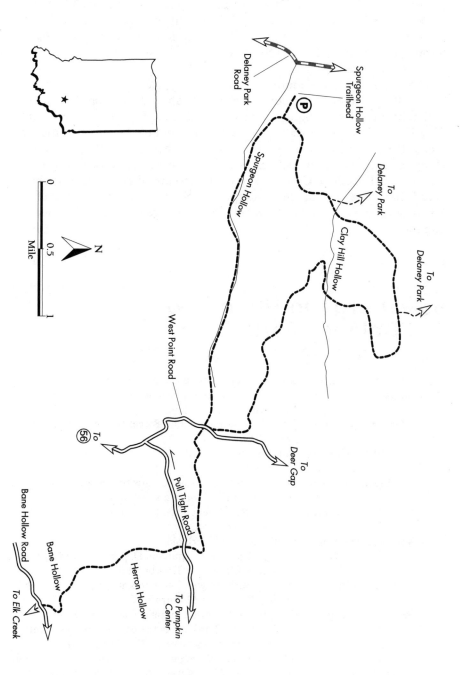

miles. Continue uphill about 0.25 mile, and the KT turns left (west). Hike up and down along a ridgeline to the final road crossing—West Point Road at 8.5 miles.

Just across the road, the KT splits—the left (west) route leads 3.5 miles to the Spurgeon Hollow Trailhead, the right (north) option also takes you to the trailhead, but is 6.5 miles long. The shorter option is fairly easy as it passes through Spurgeon Hollow, with more than half the distance squeezed between a steep-walled ravine.

The longer option is more rugged, and in places is marked with blue blazes. It also intersects twice with the Delaney Park Loop. The longer option begins with a lengthy trek along a ridgeline before descending into Clay Hill Hollow. Turn right (east) at the bottom of the ravine, cross the creek, then start a 250-foot climb on a very steep grade. Follow the trail along the ridge for about 1.5 miles before turning south for a return trip into Clay Hill Hollow. Cross the creek and go uphill 200 feet, pass over a broad, flat ridge, and descend sharply to rejoin the shorter option of the KT. Turn right (west) and go 0.25 mile to the Spurgeon Hollow Trailhead at 15 miles.

65 Spurgeon Hollow to Delaney Park

Type of hike:	Shuttle or loop, backpack, or day hike.
General description:	This section of the Knobstone Trail features ridgetops and ravines.
General location:	Jackson-Washington State Forest between Salem and Brownstown.
Total distance:	6 or 2 miles.
Difficulty:	Strenuous.
Elevation gain:	There are three 200-foot climbs on the long option; one 200-foot climb on the short option.
Jurisdiction:	Indiana Department of Natural Resources, Division of Outdoor Recreation.
Special attractions:	Scenic ridgetop overlooks.
Maps:	Kossuth USGS quad; Indiana Department of Natural Resources Knobstone Trail brochure.
Permits/fees:	Delaney Park is owned and operated by Washington County. There is a $2 entry fee.
Camping:	Camping is permitted on public land along the Knobstone Trail as long as the camp is at least 1 mile by trail from all roads, recreation areas, and trailheads, and as long as it is not visible from the trail and all lakes. Also, county-owned Delaney Park has overnight camping.

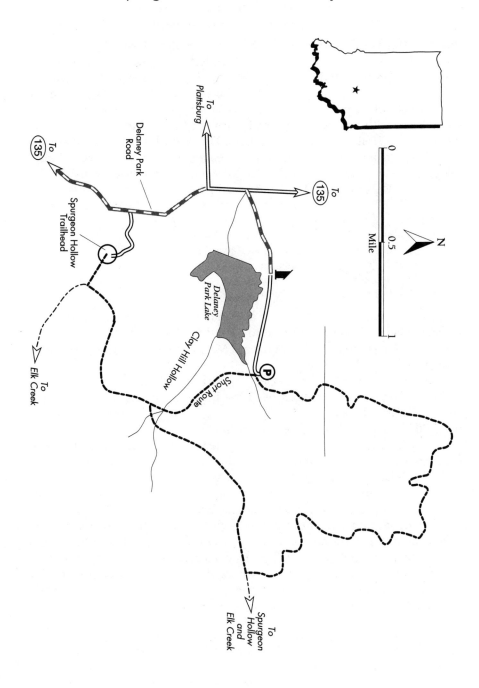

Trailhead facilities: Only parking is available at both the Spurgeon Hollow and Delaney Park trailheads, although water and restrooms are available at other locations in Delaney Park, which is open year-round.

Finding the trailhead: To reach Spurgeon Hollow from the Elk Creek Trailhead turnoff at U.S. Highway 56, turn left (west) and go 10.2 miles to its intersection with Indiana 135 in Salem. Turn right (north) and go 8.4 miles to Plattsburg. Turn right (east) on Rooster Hill Road and go 1.7 miles to a T intersection with Winslow Road. Turn right and go 0.6 mile to a T intersection with Delaney Park Road. Turn right (south) and go 0.5 mile to the Spurgeon Hollow Trailhead. To reach Delaney Park from the Spurgeon Hollow Trailhead, turn right (north) on Delaney Park Road and go 0.7 mile to the Delaney Park entrance. Go 0.5 miles to the gatehouse, then 0.5 mile more to the Delaney Park Trailhead parking lot.

Key points:
0.0   Trailhead.
1.2   Reach the trail intersection. Go left (west) for the short leg to Delaney Park or right (north) for the long leg.
2.4   Turn left at a trail intersection.
6.0   Reach the Delaney Park Trailhead.

The hike: Delaney Park is the north terminus of the Knobstone Trail (KT) . . . for now. Plans are being evaluated to extend the KT another 40 to 50 miles along the Knobstone Escarpment toward Martinsville. Traffic may be higher near the Delaney Park Trailhead.

There are two ways to get to Delaney Park from Spurgeon Hollow—one short and the other long. Both begin by heading east from the Spurgeon Hollow Trailhead for 0.25 mile to an intersection with the two KT segments from Elk Creek Trailhead (Hike 64). Turn left (north) and go up and over a ridge into Clay Hill Hollow. At 1.2 miles, the trail splits. The left (north) fork is the shorter route to Delaney Park, leading along the pine-forested eastern shore of Delaney Lake. The right (northeast) fork retraces a portion of the Elk Creek-to-Spurgeon Hollow route before turning left (north) at 2.4 miles to wander over flat ridgetops and into a couple of ravines.

After traveling north through two ravines, turn left (west) for 1 mile, curling along the back end of a ravine. The trail bends left (south) for the stretch run to the Delaney Park Trailhead. Descend one steep hill to a creek that runs through Mandy Hollow, then climb over a ridge to another creek.

At the second creek, turn right (west) and go 0.25 mile to the Delaney Park Trailhead.

Appendix A: Further Reading

Allen, Durward. *Our Wildlife Legacy.* New York: Funk and Wagnalls, 1962.

Baker, Ronald L. and Marvin Carmony. *Indiana Place Names.* Bloomington, Ind.: Indiana University Press, 1975.

Deam, Charles C. and Thomas E. Shaw. *Trees of Indiana.* Indianapolis, Ind.: Indiana Department of Conservation, 1953.

Goll, John. *Indiana State Parks.* Saginaw, Mich.: Glovebox Guidebooks, 1995.

Jackson, Marion T. *The Natural Heritage of Indiana.* Bloomington/Indianapolis, Ind.: Indiana University Press, 1997.

Lindsey, Alton A. *Natural Features of Indiana.* Indianapolis, Ind.: Indiana Academy of Science, 1966.

McPherson, Alan. *Nature Walks in Northern Indiana.* Indianapolis, Ind.: Hoosier Chapter Sierra Club. 1996.

McPherson, Alan. *Nature Walks in Southern Indiana.* Indianapolis, Ind.: Hoosier Chapter Sierra Club. 1991.

Nature Preserves, Indiana Division of Natural Resources. *Directory of Indiana's Dedicated Nature Preserves.* 1991.

Runkel, Sylvan T. and Bull, Alvin F. *Wildflowers of Indiana Woodlands.* Ames, Iowa: Iowa State University Press, 1994.

Seng, Phil T. and Case, David J. *Indiana Wildlife Viewing Guide.* Helena, Mont.: Falcon Publishing, 1992.

Thomas, Phyllis. *Indiana: Off The Beaten Path.* Saybrook, Conn.: Globe Pequot Press, 1998.

Appendix B: For More Information

Public Agencies—State

Indiana Department of Natural
  Resources
Executive Office
402 West Washington Street,
  Room W256
Indianapolis, IN 46204
(317) 232-4020
http://wwwstate.in.us/dnr/

Division of Fish & Wildlife
402 West Washington Street,
  Room W273
Indianapolis, IN 46204
(317) 232-4080

Division of Forestry
402 West Washington Street,
  Room W296
Indianapolis, IN 46204
(317) 232-4105

Division of Maps
402 West Washington Street,
  Room W160
Indianapolis, IN 46204
(317) 232-4180

Division of Nature Preserves
402 West Washington Street,
  Room W267
Indianapolis, IN 46204
(317) 232-4052

Division of Outdoor Recreation
402 West Washington Street,
  Room W271
Indianapolis, IN 46204
(317) 232-4070

Division of State Parks & Reservoirs
402 West Washington Street,
  Room W298
Indianapolis, IN 46204
(317) 232-4124

Public Agencies—Federal

Indiana Dunes National Lakeshore
1100 North Mineral Springs Road
Porter, IN 46304
(219) 926-7561

Muscatatuck National Wildlife
  Refuge
12985 East U.S. Highway 50
Seymour, IN 47274
(812) 522-4352

Patoka National Wildlife Refuge
510 $^1/_2$ West Morton Street
Oakland City, IN 47660
(812) 749-3199

U.S. Fish & Wildlife Service
Ecological Services Field Office
620 South Walker Street
Bloomington, IN 47403
(812) 334-4261

Ecological Services Field Office
120 South Lake Street
Warsaw, IN 46580
(219) 269-7640

USDA Forest Service
Hoosier National Forest
Supervisor's Office and
  Brownstown Ranger District
811 Constitution Avenue
Bedford, IN 47421
(812) 279-5987; TTY (812) 279-3423

Tell City Ranger District
248 15th Street
Tell City, IN 47586
(812) 547-7051; TDD (812)547-6144

Public Agencies—Local

Allen County Parks & Recreation
  Department
7324 Yohne Road
Fort Wayne, IN 46809
(219) 449-3180

Tippecanoe County Parks &
  Recreation Department
4449 State Road 43 North
West Lafayette, IN 47906

Conservation and Hiking Organizations

ACRES Land Trust, Inc.
2000 North Wells Street
Fort Wayne, IN 46808
(219) 422-1004;
http://wwwacres-land-trust.org/

Carroll County Wabash &
  Erie Canal Association
P.O. Box 277
Delphi, IN 46923

Hoosier Hikers Council
P.O. Box 82
Indianapolis, IN 46202-0822
(317) 349-0204

Merry Lea Environmental
  Learning Center
P.O. Box 263
Wolf Lake, IN 46796
(219) 799-5869
http://wwwgoshen.edu/merrylea

The Nature Conservancy
Indiana Chapter
1330 West 38th Street
Indianapolis, IN 46208-4103
(317) 923-7547

Pokagon-Kekionga Trails Inc.
P.O. Box 192
Angola, IN 46703
(219) 833-1550

About the Author

Phil Bloom is a native Hoosier and lifelong resident of Indiana. He is an award-winning outdoors editor for the Fort Wayne Journal Gazette, which has twice been honored for the best outdoors page in the nation by the Outdoor Writers Association of America.

American Hiking Society

American Hiking Society is the only national nonprofit organization dedicated to establishing, protecting and maintaining foot trails in America.

Establishing...

American Hiking Society establishes hiking trails with the AHS National Trails Endowment, providing grants for grassroots organizations to purchase trail lands, construct and maintain trails, and preserve hiking trails' scenic values. The AHS affiliate club program, called the Congress of Hiking Organizations, brings trail clubs together to share information, collaborate on public policy, and advocate legislation and policies that protect hiking trails.

Protecting...

American Hiking Society protects hiking trails through highly focused public policy efforts in the nation's capital. AHS affects federal legislation, shapes public lands policy, collaborates with grassroots trail organizations, and partners with federal land managers to protect the hiking experience. Members become active with letter-writing campaigns and by attending the annual AHS Trails Advocacy Week.

Maintaining...

American Hiking Society maintains hiking trails by sending volunteers to national parks, forests and recreation lands; organizing volunteer teams to help affiliated hiking clubs; and publishing national volunteer directories. AHS members get involved, get dirty and get inspired by participating in AHS programs like National Trails Day, America's largest celebration of the outdoors; and Volunteer Vacations—week-long work trips to beautiful, wild places.

Join American Hiking Society...

Be a part of the organization dedicated to protecting and preserving the nation's footpaths, our footpaths, the ones in our backyards and our backcountry. Visit American Hiking Society's website or call to find out more about membership. When you join, Falcon Publishing will send you a FREE guide as a special thank you for contributing to the efforts of American Hiking Society.

American Hiking Society
1422 Fenwick Lane
Silver Spring, MD 20910
OR CALL: (888) 766-HIKE ext. 1
OR VISIT: www.americanhiking.org